The Foundations of Democracy

Deliberative democracy is now an influential approach to the study of democracy and political behavior. Its key proposition is that, in politics, it is not only power that counts, but good discussions and arguments too. This book examines the interplay between the normative and empirical aspects of the deliberative model of democracy. Jürg Steiner presents the main normative controversies in the literature on deliberation, including self-interest, civility, and truthfulness. He then summarizes the empirical literature on deliberation and proposes methods by which the level of deliberation can be measured rather than just assumed. Steiner's empirical research is based in the work of various research groups, including experiments with ordinary citizens in the deeply divided societies of Colombia, Bosnia–Herzegovina, and Belgium, as well as Finland and the European Union. Steiner draws normative implications from a combination of both normative controversies and empirical findings.

JÜRG STEINER is Professor Emeritus in the Department of Political Science at both the University of Bern and the University of North Carolina at Chapel Hill. He is the author of *Deliberative Politics in Action* (Cambridge, 2005, with André Bächtiger, Markus Spörndli, and Marco R. Steenbergen) and the textbook *European Democracies* (8th edition 2012, with Markus Crepaz).

The Foundations of Deliberative Democracy

Empirical Research and Normative Implications

JÜRG STEINER

CAMBRIDGE
UNIVERSITY PRESS

CAMBRIDGE UNIVERSITY PRESS
Cambridge, New York, Melbourne, Madrid, Cape Town,
Singapore, São Paulo, Delhi, Mexico City

Cambridge University Press
The Edinburgh Building, Cambridge CB2 8RU, UK

Published in the United States of America by Cambridge University Press, New York

www.cambridge.org
Information on this title: www.cambridge.org/9781107625013

First published 2012

Printed in the United Kingdom at the University Press, Cambridge

A catalogue record for this publication is available from the British Library

Library of Congress Cataloging in Publication data
Steiner, Jürg.
   The foundations of deliberative democracy : empirical research and
   normative implications / Jürg Steiner.
      pages   cm
   Includes bibliographical references and index.
   ISBN 978-1-107-01503-6 (hardback) – ISBN 978-1-107-62501-3 (paperback)
   1. Deliberative democracy.   I. Title.
   JC423.S8485 2012
   321.8–dc23
   2012011693

ISBN 978-1-107-01503-6 Hardback
ISBN 978-1-107-62501-3 Paperback

To our grandchildren
Alex, Elsa, Stefan, Sophie, Leah, Annabel
May you always be curious about what others say

Contents

Figures

Acknowledgments

On the long way to this book I got advice from many friends and colleagues, in particular Rudy Andeweg, Lucio Baccaro, André Bächtiger, Mauro Barisione, Stefano Bianchini, Lyn Carson, Simone Chambers, Markus Crepaz, Andreas Diekmann, John Dryzek, Bob Goodin, Kimmo Grönlund, Damir Grubisa, Clodagh Harris, Evelyne Huber, Blaž Komac, Bill Keech, Raphaël Kies, Hanspeter Kriesi, Claudia Landwehr, Giovan Francesco Lanzara, Christiane Lemke, Rudy Lewanski, Arend Lijphart, David Lowery, Franc Mali, Jenny Mansbridge, Gary Marks, Sverre Midthjell, Patrizia Nanz, Michael Neblo, Simon Niemeyer, Tony Oberschall, Ian O'Flynn, Seamus O'Tuama, Luigi Pellizzoni, Bernard Reber, Gwen Sasse, Philippe Schmitter, Erik Schneiderhan, Donald Searing, Maija Setälä, Kazimierz Sowa, Marco Steenbergen, Julien Talpin, Rupert Taylor, Dennis Thompson, Kivanc Ulusoy, and Mark Warren. Within the family, I talked often about the project and got advice from my wife Ruth and our three sons Beat, Markus, and Niklaus. Part of the research was supported by the Swiss National Science Foundation.

Introduction

The deliberative model of democracy was initially developed at a normative philosophical level.[1] Many claims were made about favorable antecedents and the beneficial consequences of a high level of deliberation. In recent years, some of these claims have been subjected to empirical tests. In this book, I look at the interplay between normative and empirical aspects of deliberation. Empirical data, of course, cannot solve normative questions, but they can throw new light on such questions. I come from the empirical side, so I do not claim to write as a professional philosopher; I will instead take the perspective of an engaged citizen in the sense of the French *citoyen engagé*. I will begin my normative stance not with ultimate philosophical premises but will proceed with pragmatic reflections on what empirical findings may mean for the role of deliberation in a viable democracy. Let me make clear at the outset that it is not my view that a viable democracy should consist only of deliberation. Thus, the concept of *deliberative democracy* in the title of this book does not mean that this form of democracy consists only of deliberation: it only means that deliberation has an important role. Besides deliberation, a viable democracy must have space, in particular, for competitive elections, strategic bargaining, aggregative votes, and street protests. The trick is to find the right mix among all these elements, and this will depend on the context. I will argue that in this mix the role of deliberation is often not strong enough and must be strengthened.

More specifically, empirical analyses should allow answering questions such as the following: To what extent and under what circumstances can the norms and values favored by deliberative theorists be

---

[1] According to some readings, Aristotle has already made a normative deliberative argument; see, for example, James Lindley Wilson, "Deliberation, Democracy, and the Rule of Reason in Aristotle's Politics," *American Political Science Review* 105 (2011), 259–74.

put into praxis? Are there trade-offs among the various elements of deliberation in the sense that, once put in praxis, some elements may be in tension with each other? How might the feasibility of deliberation be improved? Is deliberation compatible with other valuable goals? What are the opportunity costs of deliberation? Does increased deliberation have diminishing returns? How does deliberation causally relate to policy outcomes? What are the alternative democratic models to deliberation? If we have good answers to such questions, it is easier to arrive at a judgment of how moral principles favored by deliberative theorists should be applied in the real world of politics. In this sense, this book should show how empirical research can provoke reflection on normative values. Such reflection is postulated in a concise way by Thomas Saretzki, who writes: "What we can and should try to achieve is critical reflection and cooperative conceptualization of empirical and normative aspects of deliberative democracy."[2] In the same vein, Michael A. Neblo *et al.* expect that "many of the big advances in our understanding of deliberation are likely to come by carefully aligning normative and empirical inquiries in a way that allows the two to speak to each other in mutually interpretable terms."[3] Maija Setälä postulates that thought experiments of deliberative philosophers "should be experimentally testable because they abstract from the real world like experiments."[4] Simon Niemeyer claims that "the 'coming of age' of deliberative democracy requires the interplay of theoretical insight and empirical investigation."[5]

If the empirical world does not correspond to the normative ideals, one may argue that the empirical world has to be changed. One may

---

[2] Thomas Saretzki, "From Bargaining to Arguing, from Strategic to Communicative Action? Theoretical Perspectives, Analytical Distinctions and Methodological Problems in Empirical Studies of Deliberative Processes," paper presented at the Center for European Studies, University of Oslo, December 4, 2008, p. 38.

[3] Michael A. Neblo, Kevin M. Esterling, Ryan P. Kennedy, David M.J. Lazer, and Anand E. Sokhey, "Who Wants to Deliberate: And Why?," *American Political Science Review* 104 (2010), 566.

[4] Maija Setälä and Kaisa Herne, "Normative Theory and Experimental Research in the Study of Deliberative Mini-Publics," paper presented at the Workshop on the Frontiers of Deliberation, ECPR Joint Sessions, St. Gallen, April 12–17, 2011.

[5] Simon Niemeyer, "Deliberation and the Public Sphere: Minipublics and Democratization," paper presented at the Workshop on Unity and Diversity in Deliberative Democracy, University of Bern, October 4, 2008, p. 2.

also argue, however, that the normative ideals need to be adjusted to the world as it is. I will show that there is always tension between deliberative ideals and the praxis of deliberation. It is exactly this tension that is at the core of this book. In order to render the interplay of normative and empirical questions most visible, each chapter has three sections. The first sections deal with the normative philosophical literature on deliberation; the aim is not to give an introductory overview of the literature but rather to present the most important controversies among deliberative theorists. Having initially been trained as a historian, I will stick as much as possible to the texts, letting the theorists speak in their own words. In the second sections, I discuss the relevant empirical research for these controversies, including our own research. In the third sections, I discuss possible normative implications, relating the empirical data to the philosophical controversies.

(a) The theoretical model of deliberation

In the philosophical literature, the deliberative model of democracy is usually constructed as a "regulative" ideal, which, according to Jane Mansbridge, "is unachievable in its full state but remains an ideal to which, all else equal, a practice should be judged as approaching more or less closely."[6] This follows Immanuel Kant, who defines a "regulative principle" as a standard "with which we can compare ourselves, judging ourselves and thereby improving ourselves, even though we can never reach the standard."[7] Jürgen Habermas writes in this context of "pragmatic presuppositions of discourse."[8] The ideal type of deliberation can best be understood in contrast to the ideal type of strategic bargaining. The real world of politics is most often a mixture of the two ideal types. Before I address mixed types, it is conceptually helpful to present first the two ideal types. In the ideal type of strategic bargaining, political actors have fixed preferences. They know what

[6] Jane Mansbridge with James Bohman, Simone Chambers, David Estlund, Andreas Follesdal, Archon Fung, Christina Lafont, Bernard Manin, and José Luis Marti, "The Place of Self-Interest and the Role of Power in Deliberative Democracy," *Journal of Political Philosophy* 18 (2010), 65, footnote 3.

[7] Immanuel Kant, *Critique of Pure Reason*, ed. Paul Guyer and Allen W. Wood (New York: Cambridge University Press, 1998 [1781]), p. 552.

[8] Jürgen Habermas, *On the Pragmatics of Communication* (Cambridge: Polity Press, 1998).

they want when entering a political process. They maneuver to arrive at an outcome that is as close as possible to their preferences. They engage in deal-making with the motto, "if you give me this, I give you that." In order to strengthen their bargaining position, they may work with promises and threats. Ideally, strategic bargaining results in an equilibrium win–win situation where, thanks to mutually beneficial trading, everyone is better off than before. In sophisticated models of strategic bargaining, actors are not necessarily always egotistical; they may also, for example, care for the well-being of future generations as personal preference. If new information becomes available, actors may also change their preferences; new research on the hazards of driving a car, for example, may change the preference of actors to give up the car and use public transportation instead. In such sophisticated models of strategic bargaining, the basic point remains that actors are driven by their individual preferences, whatever these preferences may be.

By contrast, in the ideal type of deliberation preferences are not fixed but open, and actors are willing to yield to the force of the better argument. What counts in a political debate is how convincing are the arguments of the various actors. Actors attempt to convince others by good arguments, but they are also open to being convinced by the arguments of others. Thus, a learning process takes place in the sense that actors learn in common debate what the best arguments are. It is not clear from the outset what the best arguments are, but it is rather through mutual dialogue that the best arguments are expected to emerge. In this sense, actors learn to think and act in new ways. Deliberation may bring a rupture with the past. Mansbridge summarizes the essence of the deliberative model in a succinct way: "We conclude by pointing out that 'deliberation' is not just any talk. In the ideal, democratic deliberation eschews coercive power in the process of coming to decision. Its central task is mutual justification. Ideally, participants in deliberation are engaged, with mutual respect, as free and equal citizens in a search for fair terms of cooperation."[9] This definition comes close to the initial meaning of *deliberare* in Latin, where it means to weigh, to ponder, to consider, and to reflect. As Robert E. Goodin points out, such deliberation can also take place individually in the sense of inward reflection. Such individual deliberation Goodin

---

[9] Mansbridge *et al.*, "The Place of Self-Interest," 94.

considers to be particularly fruitful before and after group deliberation.[10] In the same vein, Thomas Flynn and John Parkinson argue from the perspective of social psychology that inward deliberation may be helped if it confronts imagined *ideal* deliberators.[11] Bernard Reber insists in a particularly strong way that individual deliberation should come before group deliberation, since otherwise argumentation risks lacking coherence. First, actors have to become clear about their ethical standards before they can engage with others in fruitful deliberation.[12]

For a long time, scholarly interest was predominantly in the model of strategic bargaining. In recent years, however, the deliberative model has attracted more attention. As Alain Noël puts it:

Predominantly, the study of politics has been a study of interests, institutions and force, focused on bargaining and power, with some attention being occasionally paid to ideas, considered as intervening variables. In recent years, the study of democratic deliberation has brought back a more traditional understanding of politics as a forum, where ideas and arguments are exchanged, evolve over time, and matter in their own right.[13]

There are still many political scientists who insist that politics is nothing but strategic bargaining. How can a case be made that deliberation is not simply an ideal philosophical concept but is actually present in the real world of politics? Let me illustrate this question with the conflict in Northern Ireland, specifically with the 1998 Belfast Agreement and its implementation. Ian O'Flynn offers the following interpretation:

At bottom, Irish nationalists endorsed it because it held out the promise of achieving a united Ireland, whereas British unionists endorsed it because it held out the best opportunity of reconciling nationalists to the union. The important point about the agreement, however, is that both sets

---

[10] Robert E. Goodin, *Reflective Democracy* (Oxford University Press, 2003), p. 38.

[11] John Parkinson and Thomas Flynn, "Deliberation, Team Reasoning, and the Idealized Interlocutor: Why It May Be Better to Debate with Imagined Others," paper presented at the Workshop on the Frontiers of Deliberation, ECPR Joint Sessions, St. Gallen, April 12–17, 2011.

[12] Bernard Reber, "Les risques de l'exposition à la deliberation des autres," *Archives de philosophie du droit* 54 (2011), 261–81.

[13] Alain Noël, "Democratic Deliberation in a Multinational Federation," *Critical Review of International Social and Political Philosophy* 9 (2006), 432.

of aspirations are underpinned by a shared commitment to principles of self-determination, democratic equality, tolerance and mutual respect. It is those principles that give the agreement legitimacy, in the eyes of both ordinary citizens and the international community, and that sustain the hope for enduring peace and stability.[14]

How does O'Flynn know that not only interests and power but also deliberation with tolerance and mutual respect played a role? He immersed himself in the decision process, studying documents and doing interviews. Other scholars, however, based on similar sources, see only interests and power at play.[15] Who is right? It is my view that neither side can prove its argument in any definitive way. One's analysis always depends on one's world-view, and how one sees the world depends to a large extent on how one was socialized. Some have cognitive schemata making them see politics as a pure power game. For others, their cognitive schemata are such that they also see some deliberation at play. I do not claim that the axiom of politics as a pure power game is not plausible. I only claim that the axiom that politics is not exclusively about power has plausibility. It just happened that while writing this book, I read the autobiography of Nelson Mandela; I was struck that in his concluding chapter he offers his world-view that the human heart is open for others:

I always knew that deep down in every human heart, there is mercy and generosity. No one is born hating another person because of the color of his skin, or his background, or his religion. People must learn to hate, and if they can learn to hate, they can be taught to love, for love comes more naturally to the human heart than its opposite. Even in the grimmest times in prison, when my comrades and I were pushed to our limits, I would see a glimmer of humanity in one of the guards, perhaps just for a second, but it was enough to reassure me and keep me going. Man's goodness is a flame that can be hidden but never extinguished.[16]

---

[14] Ian O'Flynn, "Divided Societies and Deliberative Democracy," *British Journal of Political Science* 37 (2007), 741. See also Ian O'Flynn, *Deliberative Democracy and Divided Societies* (Edinburgh University Press, 2006).

[15] See, for example, some of the papers in Rupert Taylor (ed.), *Consociational Theory: McGarry and O'Leary and the Northern Ireland Conflict* (London: Routledge, 2009).

[16] Nelson Mandela, *Long Walk to Freedom* (New York: Little, Brown and Company, 1995), p. 622.

This world-view of Mandela is precisely the type on which the deliberative research agenda is built. Even when Mandela was treated cruelly by the white guards in prison, he was able to see sometimes a glimmer of humanity in these guards. He never completely gave up on the flame of humanity's goodness. I acknowledge with Mandela that quite often this flame is hidden, although it will never be fully extinguished. A hope in this flame is the basis for a rewarding research program, at least for me and many of my deliberative colleagues.

As Mauro Barisione has pointed out to me,[17] it is at the very basis of the deliberative model that all assumptions must be open to being challenged. Therefore, the assumption of human goodness cannot be taken as an unchallenged meta-assumption. In this way, however, the logic of deliberation puts in danger its very basis. Barisione is certainly correct to make this point because it is indeed a basic assumption of deliberation that everything must be open to challenge. My response is that every research agenda must start from some basic assumption about human nature, and the assumption of my research agenda is that despite all the evil in the world, at least some humans have, some of the time, a sense of goodness in truly caring for the well-being of others. It is fine for me if other researchers do not accept this assumption and create their own research agenda. After all, good research benefits from competition, including competition on basic assumptions about human nature.

Having established why working with the deliberative model makes sense, I now look more closely at the model. First I address a question on terminology. Some theorists like Dennis F. Thompson,[18] Joshua Cohen,[19] and Claudia Landwehr and Katharina Holzinger[20] use the term "deliberation" only for forums where a decision has to be made, such as parliamentary committees, but not, for example, for discussions on television

---

[17] Personal communication, July 30, 2011.
[18] Deliberation for Thompson means "decision-oriented discussion." Dennis F. Thompson, "Deliberative Democratic Theory and Empirical Political Science," *Annual Review of Political Science* 11 (2008), 503–4.
[19] Deliberation for Cohen means "weighing the reasons relevant to a decision with a view to making a decision on the basis of that weighing." Joshua Cohen, "Deliberative Democracy," in Shawn W. Rosenberg (ed.), *Participation and Democracy: Can the People Govern?* (New York: Palgrave Macmillan, 2007), p. 219.
[20] Claudia Landwehr and Katharina Holzinger, "Institutional Determinants of Deliberative Interaction," *European Political Science Review* 2 (2010), 373–400.

or among neighbors. Mansbridge proposes "to use adjectives to make the important distinction between deliberation in forums empowered to make a binding decision and other forms of discussion."[21] For situations in which a binding decision has to be made, she coins the term "empowered deliberation." If no binding decision has to be made, Mansbridge uses other distinctions with the help of further adjectives such as "consultative deliberation" for "a forum empowered only to advise an authoritative decision-maker," or "public deliberation" for "a forum that is open to the public but makes no binding decisions, such as a public hearing."[22] Mansbridge uses still other adjectives to make further distinctions of deliberation. I agree that Thompson, Cohen, Landwehr, Holzinger, and Mansbridge make important distinctions. I prefer, however, to use the term deliberation in a generic form and then to verbally characterize the forums in which deliberation occurs. When I write, for example, in Chapter 8 about deliberation in the media, I do not use a term such as "media deliberation," but I rather characterize the specific media in which I am interested, for example, deliberation in elite newspapers, deliberation in boulevard newspapers, deliberation on the Internet.

Having settled this terminological issue, I take a closer look at the model of deliberation in its various expressions. Although there is consensus among deliberative theorists on the general principle that arguments should matter in a political discussion, there are quite strong disagreements on how this principle should be implemented. Mansbridge points out that these disagreements have become greater in the last few years.[23] Today, deliberation has become quite a fluid concept. Jensen Sass and John S. Dryzek see deliberation as a cultural practice "with a meaning and significance which varies substantially between contexts and over time ... Thus, the forms of deliberation seen in North America or Western Europe look quite different to those appearing in Botswana, Madagascar, or Yemen."[24] Given such

---

[21] Jane Mansbridge, "Everyday Talk Goes Viral," paper presented at the annual meeting of the American Political Science Association, Washington, DC, September 2–5, 2010.

[22] Mansbridge, "Everyday Talk Goes Viral."

[23] Jane Mansbridge, "Recent Advances in Deliberative Theory," paper presented at the Max Weber Workshop on Deliberation in Politics at New York University, October 29, 2010.

[24] Jensen Sass and John S. Dryzek, "Deliberative Cultures," paper presented at the Workshop on the Frontiers of Deliberation, ECPR Joint Sessions, St. Gallen, April 12–17, 2011, p. 4.

variation, it is appropriate for Sass and Dryzek that we do not use a one-size-fits-all definition of deliberation but adapt the definition to the respective historical and cultural context.[25] Given this broad orientation of research, it is not surprising that increasingly there are disagreements on the exact definition of deliberation. I give a first overview of these definitional disagreements, which I will discuss in greater detail in the respective chapters.

One disagreement concerns the question of how strongly ordinary citizens should be involved in the deliberative process. On one hand, you have the position that ordinary citizens should participate as much as possible in the deliberative processes. In their everyday life, they should discuss political matters in their families, with friends and neighbors, in the workplace, and in their clubs and associations. In this sense, they are also political actors, and for them, too, the principle should apply that they are willing to be convinced by the force of the better argument. Thus, at the citizen level, opinion-formation takes place in a reflective way. These reflected opinions are communicated to the political leaders through a variety of channels like personal encounters, public meetings, the media, and the Internet. On the other hand, some theorists consider this position of deliberative participation of all ordinary citizens as utterly unrealistic. In their view, it would be more realistic to expect that all citizens have the *opportunity* to participate, while in praxis only a small number would participate on a regular basis in political deliberations, for example in randomly chosen mini-publics.

One further disagreement on what is meant by deliberation concerns the justification of arguments, whether they all need to be justified in a rational, logical, and elaborate way or whether narratives of life stories can also serve as deliberative justifications. When actors present their arguments in a rational, logical, and elaborate way, their arguments can be evaluated on the basis of formal logic. To allow only rational, logical, and elaborate arguments raises the critique from some theorists that such a definition discriminates against persons with little rationalistic skill. Given the inclusionary spirit of the deliberative model, such persons should also be allowed to participate in the political process. If there is, for example, a public school board meeting in a local community, it should also count as a deliberative justification if

---

[25] Sass and Dryzek, "Deliberative Cultures," p. 11.

parents tell the stories of how their children have severe drug problems. Telling such personal stories will involve much emotion and empathy not allowed in a purely rational approach to deliberation.

There is also disagreement on whether in deliberation all arguments must refer to the public interest or whether arguments referring to self-interest or group interests also count. Clean air is an example of a public interest, since everyone profits from this good. Some theorists argue that only such public interest belongs to a deliberative discourse. Other theorists, however, would also allow self and group interests, for example that tighter clean air standards would cause unemployment and suffering for workers in the automobile industry. Generally speaking, it is not easy to make the distinction between the public interest and group interests. Group interests like those of workers in the automobile industry may cut across national borders, for example between the US and Canada. For some issues, several countries or the entire world share a common public interest. Therefore, the concepts of public interest and group interests cannot be seen only within the narrow borders of nation states.

Do all arguments have a place in deliberation? Here again there is disagreement. Some theorists take the position that all arguments, however offensive, should be listened to with respect and taken seriously. A criticism of this position is that if an argument violates core human rights, its merits should not be considered at all. If someone argues, for example, a racist position, this should not be substantively discussed because racism violates a core human right. Although the position should not be discussed, one would still have the obligation to justify why the position is racist and therefore should not be discussed.

A further disagreement concerns the question of whether deliberation does necessarily have to end with a consensus. On the one hand, there is the expectation that reasonable people will ultimately agree on the strength of the various arguments so that consensus will naturally result. This view is based on the assumption that behind all individual preferences there is a basic core of rationality that is self-evident if people use only their reasoning skills. Therefore, consensus would be built on the same reasons. A weaker form of the consensus argument is that actors may have different reasons to arrive at consensus. On the other hand, there is the view that some deep-seated values may turn out to be so irreconcilable that, despite all references to rationality, consensus is not possible nor even desirable. There is also the pragmatic argument against consensus that time constraints often preclude talking until everyone agrees; sometimes a vote must be taken, putting some participants into a minority. The key for deliberation is that the opinions of losing minorities are treated with respect and duly considered. It is also important that majority decisions are considered as fallible and can be taken up again at a later stage if new information and new arguments arise.

For some theorists, good deliberation means transparency and openness to the public eye, while other theorists point out that under certain conditions deliberation is helped if a discussion takes place behind closed doors, so that there is less grand-standing and more serious discussion. These theorists also point out that deliberation behind closed doors may help later deliberation in the public eye.

There is also disagreement among theorists concerning the importance of truthfulness for deliberation. Some theorists are not much interested in knowing why someone engages in deliberation. What counts, according to this view, is whether participants show respect for the arguments of others, regardless of whether this respect is meant in a truthful way or not. By contrast, other theorists see truthfulness as a key element of deliberation. Untruthful deliberation would be nothing but clever strategic rhetoric. Demonstrating respect for the arguments of others would merely be to further one's own interests. This would take the essence out of deliberation, which also has an important intrinsic value for self-actualization, and this value would be negated by a lack of truthfulness.

I hope that this book will shed some light on these controversies in the theoretical deliberative literature. The empirical data to be presented can certainly not solve the controversies. How one defines a concept depends on one's research agenda, and this, in turn, depends on one's norms and values. Whether one counts, for example, storytelling as deliberative depends, among other things, on one's notion of rationality. Although empirical data cannot solve such controversies, data can help to clarify the empirical relations and causalities among the various deliberative elements. Does, for example, a logical, rational, and elaborate justification of one's arguments lead to more or less respect for the arguments of others than when one's arguments are justified with a personal story? Empirical data can also show how the antecedents and consequences of deliberation vary depending on the definition of deliberation.

(b) Empirical research on deliberation

So what are the empirical data that I will use to shed light on the normative controversies about the deliberative model of democracy? In
the literature, one finds both observational and experimental data. In
our research group, we use both methods. We began with observational data of parliamentary debates in Germany, Switzerland, the UK,
and the US. These analyses have been discussed in an earlier book,
published by Cambridge University Press in 2004.[26] To measure the
level of deliberation in both plenary sessions and committee meetings,
we developed an index that we call *Discourse Quality Index* (DQI),
which initially covered the following aspects of deliberation (how the
DQI is used in practice we will show elsewhere[27]):

1. participation in the debate;
2. level of justification of arguments;
3. content of justification of arguments;
4. respect shown toward other groups;
5. respect shown toward demands of other participants;
6. respect shown toward counter-arguments of other participants;
7. change of positions during debate.

Critical theorists and postmodernists are usually uneasy about any
attempt to measure the quality of deliberation.[28] They argue that
measurements of deliberation are never objective but always subjective
interpretations. I do not deny that our coding is subject to interpretation; in our book-length presentation of the DQI we explicitly state
that "assessing the quality of discourse requires interpretation. One
needs to know the culture of the political institution, the context of the
debate, and the nature of the issue under debate."[29] Interpretation, to

---

[26] Jürg Steiner, André Bächtiger, Markus Spörndli, and Marco R. Steenbergen,
Deliberative Politics in Action: Analysing Parliamentary Discourse (Cambridge
University Press, 2005).

[27] André Bächtiger, Jürg Steiner, and John Gastil, "The Discourse Quality Index
Approach to Measuring Deliberation," in Lyn Carson, John Gastil, Ron
Lubenski, and Janette Hartz-Karp (eds.), *The Australian Citizens' Parliament
and the Future of Deliberative Democracy* (College Park: Penn State University
Press, forthcoming).

[28] See, for example, Martin King, "A Critical Assessment of Steenbergen *et al.*'s
Discourse Quality Index," *Roundhouse: A Journal of Critical Theory and
Practice* 1 (2009), online: www.essl.leeds.ac.uk/roundhouse, pp. 6–7.

[29] Steiner *et al.*, *Deliberative Politics in Action*, p. 60.

be sure, can never obtain absolute objectivity. The choice is not between objectivity and subjectivity. No serious social science researcher ever claims to reach objective truth. All interpretations have a subjective element, but not all interpretations are equal. Not everything goes. The criterion for a scholarly, fruitful interpretation is whether one succeeds in attaining some level of inter-subjectivity, resulting in a sufficient degree of inter-coder reliability. This is what we attain in our research with the DQI. It was always considered as a flexible measurement instrument that needs to be adapted to specific research projects. I applaud such pluralism in research methods, which corresponds to an application of a deliberative discourse on how to do deliberative research. It is precisely the point of good deliberation that nobody claims to look at the world with absolute objectivity. This must also hold for scholarly research on deliberation.

Having attempted to measure the level of deliberation of parliamentary debates, we looked at causalities for both the antecedents and the consequences of variation in the level of deliberation. With regard to the antecedents, we were mainly interested in institutional aspects and looked at the following dimensions:

1. institutions favoring consensus versus institutions favoring competition;
2. strong versus weak veto players;
3. parliamentary versus presidential systems;
4. first versus second chambers of parliament;
5. public versus non-public arenas.

We also looked at the substantive issues under debate, focusing on the dimension of polarized versus non-polarized issues. With regard to the consequences of variation in the level of deliberation, we looked at both the formal and the substantive aspects of decision outcomes. For the formal aspect, our focus was on whether decisions were made unanimously or by majority vote; for the substantive aspect, how far the decision outcomes correspond to criteria of social justice.

Let me now describe how I will organize the empirical sections in each chapter. At the beginning of most empirical sections, I will come back to our earlier study on parliamentary debates, but only to the extent that the results shed light on the philosophical controversies and help me support my normative conclusions. I then continue with an extensive review of the empirical literature on deliberation.

Thereby, I consider all studies that I could get hold of where the level of deliberation is actually measured and not merely assumed. I attempt to give as far as possible a full review of the research where the level of deliberation is measured in a sufficiently reliable and valid way. By necessity, some countries are covered more than others, and some conflict dimensions more than others. As the final part of each empirical section, I present results of the recent experiments on deliberation that our research group has undertaken in Colombia, Bosnia–Herzegovina, Belgium, the EU, and Finland.

Why the choice of these particular countries? Most of the existing empirical literature on deliberation comes from stable democracies such as Germany, the Netherlands, France, and Canada. Such empirical data are useful for thinking in a general way about deliberative democracy. Where deliberation is most needed, however, is in deeply divided countries with internal military strife. Of course, it is in such countries that deliberation is most difficult to achieve. The most that one can probably expect is that people are willing to acknowledge that positions at the other side of the deep divide also have a legitimate point, although one does not agree. If such acknowledgment is obtained, the other side is humanized, which should make it less likely that one shoots and kills across the deep divide. If we look at the current world, the real trouble spots are deeply divided countries involved in internal military strife. My hope is that the deliberative approach can offer something to these countries so that they learn to deal peacefully with their conflicts. Thereby, my hope is more with ordinary citizens than with political leaders, who are often only interested in maintaining the deep divisions in order to stay in power. Therefore, the focus of our experiments is at the citizen level.

Colombia corresponds exactly to my research interest, with military combat still going on between leftist guerrillas and rightist paramilitaries. In Bosnia–Herzegovina, with deep divisions among Serbs, Croats, and Bosnjaks, the civil war has stopped but its consequences are still very much felt. We also include Belgium, where the linguistic divide between Flemish and Walloons grows wider and wider, although up to now without resulting in political violence. Belgium is a borderline case for my primary research interest, and it will be interesting to see how far the level of deliberation differs in Belgium from Colombia and Bosnia–Herzegovina. Finland we have included as a real contrast case, with little divide between Finnish and Swedish speakers. The

EU, finally, is an interesting case per se, with many wars among its members in past centuries and still-uneasy relations among some of its members today.

I will not present a full-fledged analysis of our experiments in these four countries and the EU, limiting myself to what is useful for this normatively oriented book. An analytically oriented, co-authored book entitled *Potential for Deliberation Across Deep Divisions* is in preparation. The collaborators for the individual parts of the experimental investigations are:

- Maria Clara Jaramillo (Colombia);
- Juan Ugarriza (Colombia);
- Simona Mameli (Bosnia–Herzegovina);
- Didier Caluwaerts (Belgium);
- Marlène Gerber (Europolis);
- Staffan Himmelroos (Finland).

Why did we choose the experimental method? One possible research method would have been to use surveys asking people how deliberative they are when they talk about politics in their families, with friends and neighbors, and in the workplace. Such surveys run the risk that respondents say what is socially desirable, namely that they are deliberative when they talk about politics, showing, for example, respect for the opinion of others and a willingness to yield to the force of the better argument. Given this problem of surveys for the present research question, we chose experiments as the appropriate method. This meant concretely that we brought ordinary citizens together to discuss a specific topic. Participants had to fill out questionnaires before and after the experiments. The discussions were taped and then coded with an expanded DQI that the reader will find in the Appendix. I now present the research designs for the five test cases.

Research design for Colombia

Maria Clara Jaramillo and *Juan Ugarriza* are responsible for the Colombian part of our research. Initially, they planned to do the research with university students, which from an organizational perspective would have been relatively easy to do. But they looked for a greater challenge where deliberation is particularly difficult to achieve and thus all the more needed. They found this challenge with ex-combatants of the internal armed conflict. It just happened that, when Jaramillo and Ugarriza began their research, the Colombian government had a program of decommissioning under way. This program applied to combatants of both leftist guerillas (in particular FARC, Fuerzas Armadas Revolucionarias de Colombia, and some smaller guerrilla groups) and the paramilitary forces on the extreme right. Would ex-combatants who, a short while ago, were still shooting at each other be willing to participate in common deliberative experiments? This was the challenge at the beginning of the research, and it took much patience, enthusiasm, and skill on the part of Jaramillo and Ugarriza to ultimately organize 28 experiments with altogether 342 participants.

In order to get a financial stipend, the ex-combatants were required to participate in a program of the Office of the High Commissioner for Reintegration. Psychologists and social workers acted as tutors, and ex-combatants had to attend twice a month small-group sessions with these tutors. We focused our research on the greater Bogotá area, where there were about 3,000 ex-combatants participating in the reintegration program. They were mostly men, young and of little education. Initially, we attempted to select a random sample to participate in the experiments. But tutors warned us of security problems since many of the ex-combatants were severely traumatized and therefore violent or otherwise troubled. There was also a motivation problem; in the first research phase many ex-combatants invited to the experiments simply did not show up. The tutors helped us then with a solution that gave the ex-combatants the necessary incentives to come to the experiments. They could replace the bi-monthly tutorial sessions with participation in a single experiment and still get the full stipend. It also helped that the experiments could take place in the offices of the tutors. The tutors stood close by should some violence occur. Thanks to the Office of the High Commissioner for Reintegration, we have approximate data about the total population of the 3,000 ex-combatants in the Bogotá area with regard to gender, age, and education. For these criteria, the 342 ex-combatants participating in the experiments correspond roughly to the total population of ex-combatants in the Bogotá area.[30] This is comforting, although

---

[30] Of the ex-combatants in our experiments, 15 percent were women, compared with 16 percent among all ex-combatants in the Bogotá area. Some 30 percent in the experiments were 18 to 25 years old, compared with 37 percent in

we cannot claim that the ex-combatants we studied are a random sample of the total population of ex-combatants.

How large were the differences between the ex-guerrillas and ex-paramilitaries who volunteered to participate in the experiments? As a null hypothesis, we assume that there were no differences. This hypothesis has a certain plausibility because it could be that the ex-combatants were not ideologically driven but were simply looking for a paying job and did not care which side they joined. This would be fatal for the purpose of our experiments since we are interested in investigating political discussions across deep divisions. The null hypothesis can be rejected. The ex-guerrillas were over-represented in the youngest age group, and they also had more women in their ranks than the ex-paramilitaries. With regard to education and social class, the ex-guerrillas had less formal schooling and were poorer than the ex-paramilitaries.[31] Of particular importance for the interpretation of the experiments is that politically there were strong differences between the two groups. The ex-guerrillas come much more often from a leftist family background; the ex-paramilitaries from a rightist background. Therefore, it was not due to random chance on which side the ex-combatants were involved in the internal armed conflict. The clearest indicator for the still-deep divisions between the two groups came to light in response to the question about their attitudes toward the combatants still fighting in the jungles. Although the participants in the experiments had left their former comrades, they expressed a more positive attitude toward their own side than to the other side. This was not necessarily to be expected, because one could imagine that the ex-combatants left the fighting because they no longer agreed with the cause of their side. Although there were some who left the fighting for this reason, most still had more sympathy for their side than for the other side. They probably came out of the jungles because they had had enough of the fighting and were attracted by the benefits of the government program of reconciliation. The conclusion of all

---

the Bogotá area. For education we must differentiate between ex-guerrillas and ex-paramilitaries. Of the ex-guerrillas in the experiments, 60 percent had schooling of 11 years or less, 64 percent of all the ex-guerrillas in the Bogotá area. For the ex-paramilitaries, the corresponding figures are 41 and 36 percent.

[31] It has to be considered, however, that ex-guerrillas had some informal education during the time they were in the field.

these data is that the participants in the experiments formed two distinct groups, not only with regard to demographic characteristics but also in a political sense.

As an ideal research design, each experiment would have had the same number of participants with an equal distribution between ex-guerillas and ex-paramilitaries. But given all the difficulties with attendance, we were far from reaching this ideal. This was not a laboratory situation where everything can be held under control. To learn something about ex-combatants, this was the best that we could do. In the social sciences the really interesting questions often cannot be studied in a fully controlled situation, so that one has to use a less-than-perfect research design. Before and after the experiments, participants had to fill out questionnaires about demographic characteristics and political and psychological issues. These data will help to test hypotheses about the antecedents and consequences of variation in the level of deliberation among the 28 experiments and also at the level of the individual participants. Institutionally the research design had variation in the sense that for half of the groups there was no decision to be made at the end of the experiment, whereas the other half of the groups had to decide on a set of recommendations about the future of Colombia to be sent to the High Commissioner for Reintegration. Half of these decisions had to be made by majority vote, the other half by unanimity. These letters were actually sent out to the High Commissioner so that for half of the experiments the discussions had immediate policy relevance, whereas for the other half the discussions had no immediate outside effect.

For the practical organization of the experiments, at the very beginning Jaramillo and Ugarriza stated the following discussion topic: "What are your recommendations so that Colombia can have a future of peace, where people from the political left and the political right, guerillas and paramilitaries, can live peacefully together?" In contrast to other such experiments, in particular "Deliberative Polling,"[32] no briefing material was handed out beforehand on the topic to be discussed. Also, in contrast to Deliberative Polling, moderators did not intervene to encourage deliberative behavior. It was precisely our research interest to see to what extent ex-combatants were willing and able to behave in a deliberative way without any outside help. If,

---

[32] See below, research design for Europolis.

for example, participants did not speak up during the entire experiment, moderators did not ask them to do so. Or when opinions were expressed without justification, moderators did not ask why they held such opinions. Therefore, the discussion was free-floating within a broadly formulated topic. Not handing out briefing material before the experiments and moderators not intervening in the discussions eliminated two possibly confounding factors for our causal analyses. After about 45 minutes, Jaramillo and Ugarriza brought the discussion to an end.

Research design for Bosnia–Herzegovina

Bosnia–Herzegovina, with its recent internal armed conflict, was also a difficult place to do experiments. For this part of the project, *Simona Mameli* was responsible. She organized a preliminary test experiment in Sarajevo, but came to the conclusion that this was not a good place to do her research. The reason was that she found many ethnically mixed families, so that it was difficult to construct groups with deep divisions. Mameli then chose two places where the civil war was particularly ferocious, Srebrenica and Stolac. In Srebrenica, as is well known, a large number of Muslim men were brutally murdered by Serbs. In Bosnia–Herzegovina, Muslims prefer to be called Bosnjaks, not wishing to be identified with a religion. I will also use this term. Stolac has a deep division between Croats and Bosnjaks. It is located close to the better-known town of Mostar; there was bloody fighting in both places. Mameli chose to do the experiments in Stolac because Mostar has become too much of a tourist destination.

The research design for the experiments in Bosnia–Herzegovina is basically the same as for Colombia, in the sense that no briefing material was handed out beforehand and that the moderators did not intervene to encourage deliberative behavior. In *Srebrenica*, Mameli organized six experiments with altogether 40 participants: 22 women and 18 men. For three experiments, she selected the participants with a method called "random walk." This means that she walked the streets of Srebrenica and approached people in a random way to participate in the experiments. It would have been better to draw random samples from lists of Serb and Bosnjak inhabitants of Srebrenica, but since no such lists exist, random walk was the second-best selection method. With random walk to select participants, Mameli encountered two

difficulties. One was related to the living pattern of the Bosnjak population. It forms the numerical majority in Srebrenica, but many Bosnjaks
are only formally registered in the town and prefer to spend most of
their time somewhere else. Mameli has seen many empty houses belong-
ing to Bosnjaks. It seems that many of them come back only for elections or commemorative events for the genocide, because the traumatic
memories make it hard for them to permanently live in Srebrenica.
It appears that more moderate Bosnjaks tend to live permanently in
Srebrenica. For the experiments, this means that we likely got more
moderate Bosnjaks in our sample. We had such a bias in Colombia
also, where, as we have seen above, the most violent and psychologically troubled ex-combatants had to be excluded from the experiments.
From a research design perspective this is not ideal, but such is life
in societies with an internal armed conflict in the recent past or still
ongoing. A second difficulty in searching for participants through a
random walk was that some, both Serbs and Bosnjaks, were not willing
to participate or, when they did promise to attend, did not show up.

For the other three experiments in Srebrenica, we wanted participants who had been exposed to a program of reconciliation and peace-
building to examine whether participation in such a program made a
difference to the behavior in the experiments. The Nansen Dialogue
Center, a Norwegian NGO, has such a program; its main objective "is
to contribute to reconciliation and peace building through interethnic
dialogue."[33] The staff of the center helped to recruit people who had
participated in their activities, making the selection as randomly as
possible. Among the persons recruited by the Nansen Dialogue Center,
there were also some who did not show up. Thus, as in Colombia, the
six experimental groups in Srebrenica had unequal size and not always
the same number of Serbs and Bosnjaks. Again, this is the best that
we could do in the place where the worst genocide in Europe since
World War II had taken place. It was even somewhat of a surprise
that Mameli could do the six experiments at all, since one might have
expected that it would not be possible to find any Serbs and Bosnjaks
willing to sit together at the same table.

The practical organization of the experiments in Srebrenica was basically the same as in Colombia. Participants had to fill out questionnaires

---

[33] See www.nansen-dialogue.net/content.

before and after the experiments. With the exceptions of some local adaptations, the questionnaires were the same as in Colombia. At the beginning of the experiments, Mameli, assisted by a friend from the region, gave the topic of the discussion, which was to formulate recommendations for a better future in Bosnia–Herzegovina. Participants were asked to agree on a set of recommendations to be delivered to the High Representative for Bosnia and Herzegovina. In contrast to Colombia, such a decision had to be made in all experiments; there were too few experiments to introduce another control variable. Contrary to Colombia, where, for security reasons, discussions were only audio-taped, in Srebrenica experiments were both audio- and video-taped.

In *Stolac*, the experiments were organized in the same way as in Srebrenica. As already mentioned above, the town is deeply divided between Croats and Bosnjaks. The Croats are the majority, and the mayor belongs to a Croatian nationalist party. There is supposed to be some power-sharing with a Bosnjak nationalist party, but it does not work at all well. There are Croatian flags everywhere, causing resentment among the Bosnjaks. Like in Srebrenica, there is a general feeling of fatigue and disillusionment. The High Commissioner did visit the town the year before and listened to the problems of the population, but nothing has changed since this visit. So people in Stolac are not only frustrated with their own local administration but also with the "internationals" who seem to make things even worse. Simona Mameli, again assisted by a friend familiar with the local situation, could also carry out six experiments in Stolac with a total of 35 participants: 20 women and 15 men. Like in Srebrenica, for half of the experiments participants were recruited by the Nansen Dialogue Center, for the other half by random walk in the streets of the town. Again, not everyone who had promised to show up did so, so that the number of participants varied and there was not always the same number of Croats and Bosnjaks. Like in Srebrenica, there was most likely a bias toward moderation among those who attended the experiments.

Research design for Belgium

Belgium has an increasingly deep division between Flemish (Dutch-speaking) and Walloons (French-speaking). In contrast to Colombia and Bosnia–Herzegovina, there has never been an armed conflict between the two language groups, so experiments were easier to organize. It helped, in particular, that *Didier Caluwaerts*, the organizer of the experiments, could rely on a research bureau with experience in sending out Internet surveys for social research.[34] Based on this survey, Caluwaerts selected people to be invited for the experiments, using the method of heterogeneity sampling. He wanted in each experimental group sufficient variation with regard to gender, age, and education. Moreover, he wanted in each group participants who felt either positively or negatively about the other side of the language cleavage. Caluwaerts undertook a total of 9 experiments, inviting 90 persons to participate; 83 actually showed up. In each experiment there were at least eight participants. As in Colombia and Bosnia–Herzegovina, no briefing material was handed out, moderators did not intervene, and participants had to fill out questionnaires before and after the experiments. Three experiments were homogeneous Flemish, three homogeneous Walloon, and three heterogeneous from both sides. Similarly to Colombia and Bosnia–Herzegovina, the discussion topic was formulated in the following broad way: "How do you see the future relation between the language groups in Belgium?" The groups were asked to make a decision on this issue: in three groups by simple majority, in three by two-thirds majority, and in three by unanimity. Combining the language composition of the groups and the decision rules gives a nine-fold table (3 × 3) with one experiment in each field. In a first round of the experiments of only a few minutes, participants had to say in one or two key words what they considered the most important problem or fact in Belgium. In a second round of about an hour-and-a-half, the discussion was free-floating. In a third round, also of about an hour-and-a-half, participants had to discuss specific topics on current Belgian politics with regard to the language issue. A decision had to be made after both the second and the third rounds. The experiments were held on a Saturday at the University Foundation in Brussels, which has no link to any political organization. In the three mixed-language groups there was simultaneous translation. In the Flemish groups Caluwaerts, as a native Dutch-speaker, did the moderation; in the Walloon groups a French-speaker, and in the mixed groups moderation was shared by a French- and a Flemish-speaker.

---

[34] Didier Caluwaerts, "Deliberation across Linguistic Divides: The Case of Belgium," paper presented at the Workshop on the Frontiers of Deliberation, ECPR Joint Sessions, St. Gallen, April 12–17, 2011.

Research design for the Europolis project of the European Union

After three deeply divided nation states, I turn now to the supranational level of the European Union (EU). Historically, the member states of the EU were often deeply divided by war; today also there are deep divisions among some of the member states, for example between Hungary and Slovakia on the status of Hungarians in Slovakia. To do experiments among ordinary EU citizens, our research team was invited to join the *Europolis* project and to code the discussions with our DQI. This project is based on the idea of Deliberative Polling developed by James S. Fishkin and Robert C. Luskin.[35] They raise the questions: "But what if the level of deliberation could be raised, if not for the whole public, at least for a random sample thereof? What if polling could be made deliberative?" Their answer is: "Deliberative Polling explores this possibility by exposing random samples to balanced information, encouraging them to weigh opposing arguments in discussions with heterogeneous interlocutors, and then harvesting their more considered opinions."[36] The idea of Deliberative Polling has been put in practice many times, for example in 2000 in a particularly elaborate way in Denmark ahead of the referendum on the euro.[37]

The Europolis project is organized within the 7th Framework Program of the EU and is coordinated by Pierangelo Isernia of the University of Siena. On May 29–31, 2009, 348 randomly selected persons of all 27 EU member states assembled in Brussels and discussed in 25 small groups first immigration from outside the EU and then climate change. No decisions had to be made at the end of the small-group discussions. There were also plenary sessions with experts and politicians. Participants had to fill out four questionnaires: one back in their home countries, a second one on arrival in Brussels, a third one on departure from Brussels, and a fourth one back in their home countries again. It is important to note that in all projects organized by Deliberative Polling a special effort is made to create conditions favorable for deliberation.

---

[35] James S. Fishkin and Robert C. Luskin, "Experimenting with a Democratic Ideal: Deliberative Polling and Public Opinion," *Acta Politica* 40 (2005), 284–98.

[36] Fishkin and Luskin, "Experimenting with a Democratic Ideal," 287.

[37] Kasper M. Hansen, *Deliberative Democracy and Opinion Formation* (Odensee: University Press of Southern Denmark), p. 2004.

In this sense, the research design is different from the one we used in Colombia, Bosnia–Herzegovina, and Belgium, where we made no special effort to create favorable conditions for deliberation. This was altogether different for the Europolis project. The day before the event, the moderators were trained in long sessions. They were mostly young academics with great language skills from many different EU countries. Although they were told not to intervene in a substantive way in the discussions, they were instructed to make the discussions as deliberative as possible, for example, in encouraging everyone to speak up, to justify their arguments, and to be respectful toward the arguments of others. A further contributing factor to good deliberation in Europolis was the advance briefing of the participants with a brochure of 40 pages containing information on the EU and the two topics to be discussed. Graphically, the key facts and arguments were presented in a professional way; although the participants were not tested as to whether they had read the material, most indicated in the questionnaires that they had done so. In drawing comparisons with Colombia, Bosnia–Herzegovina, and Belgium, we must be aware that the research design for Europolis was quite different. On the one hand, this makes straightforward comparisons problematic. On the other hand, however, it strengthens our conclusions if they are based on two different research designs.

All the discussions of Europolis were audio-taped. A special problem was the multilingual nature of the participants, which necessitated simultaneous translation by professional translators. To make translation manageable, there were only two or three languages represented per group. One language was chosen to be audio-taped in the original voices, the other(s) only in translation. This method has the disadvantage that for the participants for whom only the translation is recorded, the coders cannot hear possible emotions in the original voices. To code and analyze all 25 groups for their discussions on both immigration and climate change will take a long time, with other publications to come. For the current book, I take as a basis the analysis that Marlène Gerber *et al.* did for the ECPR Joint Sessions in St. Gallen, in April 2011.[38] They investigated 9 of the 25 groups, and

---

[38] Marlène Gerber, André Bächtiger, Susumu Shikano, Simon Reber, and Samuel Rohr, "How Deliberative Are Deliberative Opinion Polls? Measurement Tools and Evidence from Europolis," paper presented at the Workshop on the Frontiers of Deliberation, ECPR Joint Sessions, St. Gallen, April 12–17, 2011.

this only for the sessions on immigration and not those on climate change. They chose groups where the recorded language, either in the original or in translation, was German, French, or Polish. For the Polish groups, we could rely on a native Polish speaker; her transcripts were translated into English so that we could check the reliability of her coding. The discussion of immigration came before the discussion of climate change. The first session on immigration in the small groups took place on Friday, May 29, 2009 at 4 p.m. for about an hour; after a coffee break, discussion continued for about another hour. The following day at 9 a.m., there was a plenary session on immigration with experts for an hour-and-a-half. After a coffee break there was another session of small groups, which was short and quickly drifted away from immigration to more general political questions so that we omitted this session from coding.

Research design for Finland

I use Finland as a control case for the three deeply divided countries and the EU as a special case per se. Finland is a homogeneous country with a small Swedish minority, which, however, does not cause any major inter-linguistic problems. Finland can also be characterized as a consensus society. Thus, it serves well as a control case to test to what extent our findings for our deeply divided cases are specific to such cases or apply also to a homogeneous consensus society. As for the Europolis project, we joined the Finnish project while it was already under way. It was initially launched at Åbo Akademi University at Turku by a research group headed by Kimmo Grönland, Maija Setälä, and Kaisa Herne.[39] The coding and analysis with a modified version of our DQI was done by *Staffan Himmelroos*.[40] Participants in the Finnish experiments were a random sample of the Turku region. In November 2006, they discussed in eight groups the question of whether a sixth nuclear power plant should be built in Finland. Each experiment took about three hours and ended with a

---

[39] Kimmo Grönland, Maija Setälä, and Kaisa Herne, "Deliberation and Civic Virtue: Lessons from a Citizen Deliberation Experiment," *European Political Science Review* 2 (2010), 95–117.

[40] Staffan Himmelroos, "Democratically Speaking: Can Citizen Deliberation Be Considered Fair and Equal?," paper presented at the Workshop on the Frontiers of Deliberation, ECPR Joint Sessions, St. Gallen, April 12–17, 2011.

decision either by a vote or by consensus. The number of participants was 90, uttering a total of 1,189 relevant speech acts related to the nuclear issue. As for Europolis, but different from the experiments in Colombia, Bosnia–Herzegovina, and Belgium, in the Finnish project special efforts were undertaken to contribute to favorable conditions for deliberation. Participants received material beforehand on nuclear power and could meet with experts representing different interests on the issue. At the beginning of each group discussion, ground rules were established to remind participants to speak up and to respect the views of others. The discussions were led by trained facilitators who had been instructed not to influence the view of the participants but to intervene if the discussion lost focus or violated deliberative characteristics.

(c) The praxis of deliberation

I wrote this book so that it also has relevance for political praxis. In recent years, deliberation has become prominent in political praxis with efforts to engage ordinary citizens more in the political process. These efforts go under labels such as mini-publics, citizens' juries, consensus conferences, planning cells, and so on. Such efforts in political praxis need to be accompanied by systematic normative and empirical research on deliberation. This is precisely what this book hopes to accomplish. What is the appeal of citizen deliberation for political praxis? An important appeal is to get more legitimacy for political decisions. Many citizens tend not to trust politicians to make decisions for the public good. There is widespread suspicion that many politicians just look after their career interests or are even corrupt. This suspicion is fueled by how the media tend to report politics. Amid such cynicism, there are claims of a democratic deficit. The obvious strategy to counter such a deficit is to involve ordinary citizens more in the political process. In this way, political decisions should become more acceptable to the general public. At least this is a hypothesis worth testing. Another important appeal to let ordinary citizens deliberate political issues is the expectation that fresh ideas are brought into politics, leading to better policy outcomes. Citizens are becoming less willing to accept the authority of politicians to know best. Indeed, the reputation of politicians is in many places at a dismally low level. At the same time, many citizens have expertise from their professional and private lives that is relevant for many political decisions.

The hope to get better and more legitimate policy outcomes has led to many efforts to involve ordinary citizens in a fuller and more systematic way in the political process. I present as an illustration a project of the Regional Council of Tuscany.[41] In 2007, the council enacted Regional Law No. 69, entitled "Rules on the Promotion of Participation in the Formulation of Regional and Local Policies."[42] Key passages for the necessity of such a law read as follows:

- Participation in the formulation and making of regional and local policies is a right. This law pro-actively promotes forms and instruments of democratic participation to render this right effective by making resources available such as money and methodological support.
- The law encourages the autonomous initiative of organized social groups such as local authorities, schools and firms to submit projects to enhance citizen participation.

With such formulations, the law-makers in the Tuscany present a deliberative agenda for their region. They emphasize a participatory form of democracy where ordinary citizens discuss policy issues and communicate their opinions to local authorities. It is also in a deliberative spirit that all interests be heard in the political process and that the political knowledge of citizens be enhanced so that they can give well-developed justifications for their arguments. In sum, a new civic culture should emerge in Tuscany according to the goals of this law. As Antonio Floridia and Rodolfo Lewanski, two deliberative scholars involved in the project, put it:

Tuscany has become a remarkable "laboratory" for empirically testing the validity of deliberative participation in the real world, verifying the effects and possible benefits of institutionalizing it, and applying a specific model aimed at making representative government and mini-publics not only co-exist alongside each other, but actually become complementary and mutually re-enforcing. One way or the other, the results will be of relevance

---

[41] For a description of the project, see Antonio Floridia and Rodolfo Lewanski, "Institutionalizating Deliberative Democracy: The Tuscany Laboratory," paper presented at the Workshop on the Effects of Participatory Innovations, ECPR Joint Sessions, St. Gallen, April 12–17, 2011.

[42] See www.consiglio.regione.toscana.it/partecipazione. The website also has an English version of the law.

to those – be they scholars, practitioners, politicians, or polities – interested in such democratic innovations.[43]

To implement the law, the Regional Council should appoint "an expert in public law and political science of proven experience in the methods and practices of participation." This happened on October 1, 2008, with the appointment of Rodolfo Lewanski, a political scientist at the University of Bologna, who has published widely in the field of deliberation.[44] He heads the Autorità per la Partecipazione (Authority for Participation) with a staff to help him execute his duties. In the three years from 2008 to 2010, grants of 2,138,775 euro were awarded; the average grant was 31,453 euro.[45] To receive a grant, local communities, schools, businesses, and any formal or informal groups of ordinary citizens can apply. It is then the duty of the Authority for Participation to evaluate the applications and to decide who is successful. After a project has been finished, the Authority for Participation has to determine to what extent the stipulated goals of the project have been accomplished.

As an illustration of a concrete project, I use the local community of Piombino, located on the coast of the Ligurian Sea. The issue was the renovation of Piazza Bovio (the town square), located on a rock reaching out to the sea. Instead of leaving the decision to technical experts and the local authorities, the citizens of Piombino were strongly involved in the decision process. Conditions were particularly favorable for deliberation since citizens' preferences were not yet deeply crystallized, did not depend on strong group affiliations, and did not promote identity-based appeals. Later in the book, I will discuss cases where conditions for deliberation were less favorable. By way of introduction, it seems appropriate to begin with a case where conditions are favorable for deliberation and to see what happens under these conditions.

The Piombino project began in April 2008 and ended in December 2008. In April, flyers were distributed in various places such as the main market square to inform the population about the project. On the evening of May 9, an information assembly about the project was held, in the presence of a staff member of the Authority for

[43] Floridia and Lewanski, "Institutionalizing Deliberative Democracy," p. 2.
[44] I know Rodolfo Lewanski personally, so I have good knowledge of his work for the Regional Council.
[45] Floridia and Lewanski, "Institutionalizing Deliberative Democracy," table 1 in Annex.

Participation. Together with the mayor of the town, this staff member presented the goal of the project: in a dialogue with the technical experts, the citizens of the town shall work out the best solution for the renovation of Piazza Bovio. Thereby, all participants shall feel free to express their opinions, and all opinions shall be respected. Discussions took place in small groups of not more than ten participants. On the one hand, participants were chosen randomly from the official lists of the town. On the other hand, townspeople could volunteer to participate. In this way, five groups were formed. Each group met three times between May and October. At these meetings, technical experts of the town (engineers and architects) were available to procure information if the citizens so desired. It was important, however, that these technical experts did not lead the discussions. It was instead one of the citizens who acted as moderator. After each meeting, the discussions were summarized in a report, containing the arguments articulated in the discussions. At the beginning of the group discussions, the participants were asked to say what the Piazza Bovio means for them. The responses were uniformly positive, for example:

- the piazza serves as a linkage among the generations, contributes to the identity of the town, it is our pride;
- on the rock reaching out to the sea, the piazza opens the town to the beauties of nature, it is a window to the infinite wide world;
- the piazza is a social location where townspeople meet, it is particularly fitted for lovers;
- the piazza is a place of tranquility allowing calm self-reflection.

Despite these generally positive reactions to the piazza, the discussion groups had many suggestions for improvement, in particular:

- So that at night the stars can better be seen, the lighting should be dimmer, especially at the outer end of the piazza. To this suggestion it was objected that with dimmer lighting security would be endangered, especially for elderly or handicapped people. To take account of these conflicting arguments, a discussion ensued about lighting methods. It was suggested to allow much light at the ground and less light toward the sky. It was also suggested that solar energy should be used for the lighting of the piazza.
- For the pavement of the piazza different suggestions were made with regard to the color and the material to be used. Participants

went into so much detail as to suggest, for example, the use of a material that would allow chewing gum dropped by children to be washed off.

- A lively discussion took place about the number and kind of trees to be planted. Here again, participants had to consider conflicting criteria. On the one hand, trees should give much shade, but they should not hide the view of the sea. The chosen trees also should not damage the pavement with their roots.

Discussing these topics and many more, the individual groups attempted to reach consensus or at least majority positions. Minority positions, however, were also included in the reports of the groups. Thus, a lonely voice demanded that all benches be removed from the piazza; although this demand did not get any support, it was mentioned in the report of the group. A particularly innovative element of the entire project was the involvement of the schoolchildren of Piombino. After school trips to the piazza, they had to make drawings of how the piazza should look. These often very colorful and joyful drawings were exhibited and also put on the website of the town. In this way, children learned a good lesson about practical politics with a very concrete case of policy-making.

The project came to an end in December 2008 when the entire population of Piombino was invited to be informed about the results of the group discussions. On this occasion, the local authorities promised to take account of the suggestions worked out in the groups, which indeed they did, especially if there was consensus on particular aspects of how the piazza should look. The citizens of the town were also encouraged to continue to be involved in the further planning and execution of the renovation of the piazza. From a deliberative perspective, it is important to note that according to the reports of the groups the discussions were led in a serious and respectful way, with arguments being weighed carefully and people being willing to change their positions if confronted with new information and good arguments. Sometimes, deliberative discussions are organized without any linkage to an ongoing policy debate. As we will see later in the book, such free-floating discussions without end point also have value in contributing to the political self-development of participants. In this chapter, however, I want to present with Piombino a case where citizen discussions are part of an ongoing policy process. In this way I want to emphasize that citizen deliberation can very well have policy relevance.

I have now presented an example to show how ordinary citizens can be involved in deliberative political issues. In recent years, there has been a great wave of such enterprises in many parts of the world. It is obvious that a need is felt to engage citizens more thoroughly in political debate. For the scholarly community, the challenge is to investigate conditions under which such experiments in citizen deliberation can be successful. I will take up this challenge in the chapters to come. In the last chapter, I will come back to the praxis of deliberation.

1 | *Citizen participation in deliberation*

(a) Normative controversies in the literature

There is consensus among deliberative theorists that ordinary citizens should have the opportunity to take part in political deliberation, but there is controversy over how many citizens should actually do so. On the one hand, there is the normative position that ideally all citizens should be involved in political deliberation. In their everyday life, they should discuss political matters in their families, with friends and neighbors, in the workplace, and in their clubs and associations. These discussions should have a deliberative character in the sense that participants should be open to the force of the better argument. As a consequence, opinion-formation at the grass-roots level would take place in a reflective way. These reflected opinions are then communicated to political leaders through a variety of channels like personal encounters, public meetings, the media, and the Internet. This participatory position is advocated by Jürgen Habermas, who argues that all those affected by a political decision should be included in deliberation (*Inklusion aller Betroffenen*).[1] Since important decisions, for example about the environment or health care, affect everyone, the Habermasian position implies that everyone should participate in the deliberation of such issues. Habermas hopes that deliberation among ordinary citizens will have an influence on elections, legislation, and administrative power, since "the flow of communication between public opinion formation, institutionalized elections, and legislative decisions is meant to guarantee that influence and communicative power are transformed through legislation into administrative power." In this way, citizens should be a strong countervailing force against the two traditional influences in politics, "money and administrative power."[2]

[1] Jürgen Habermas, *Ach, Europa* (Frankfurt a.M.: Suhrkamp, 2008), p. 148.
[2] Jürgen Habermas, *Between Facts and Norms: Contributions to a Discourse Theory of Law and Democracy* (Cambridge, MA: MIT Press, 1996), p. 299.

Some theorists consider it as unrealistic that virtually all citizens will ever participate in political deliberation. Therefore, as these theorists argue, one has to think about a more realistic way to involve the grass-roots level in deliberation of political issues. They put their hopes into so-called *mini-publics*, by which they mean groups of randomly selected citizens. James S. Fishkin, a prominent theorist, is at the forefront of this movement with the idea of Deliberative Polling.[3] The crucial question is what deliberation in such mini-publics means for a political system at large. Fishkin hopes that participants in mini-publics get a taste for deliberation and, at home, will engage other citizens in deliberative activities. He also hopes that participants in mini-public deliberations will emerge as opinion leaders so that their reflected opinions will be taken on by other citizens. In all these ways, deliberation in mini-publics should spread to a larger number of citizens.

Maija Setälä also reflects on the role of mini-publics in the political decision process.[4] She cautions that "deliberative mini-publics are often called by public authorities on an ad hoc basis," and this raises for Setälä "questions about the motivations behind them. The recommendations of advisory mini-publics are often ignored or bypassed." According to Setälä, "the impact of mini-publics could be strengthened by the institutionalization of their use and by developing ways in which their recommendations are dealt with in representative institutions."[5] Erika Cellini *et al.* go a step further than Setälä when they warn that the organization of mini-publics can be misused to distract the attention of the public from the arenas where real decision-making takes place.[6] As an example they give health policy decision-making in the Toscana region: while the government organized mini-publics on the distribution of health costs, it decided at the same time on the reorganization of the entire hospital system in the region. In this way, the mini-publics pulled the attention away from where real decision-making occurred.

---

[3] James S. Fishkin, *When the People Speak: Deliberative Democracy and Public Consultation* (Oxford University Press, 2009).

[4] Maija Setälä, "Designing Issue-Focused Forms of Citizen Participation," paper presented at the Conference on Democracy: A Citizen Perspective, Åbo, May 25–27, 2010, p. 15.

[5] Setälä, "Designing Issue-Focused Forms of Citizen Participation," p. 15.

[6] Erika Cellini, Anna Carola Freschi, and Vittorio Mete, "Chi delibera? Alla ricerca del significato politico di un'esperienza partecipativo-deliberativo," *Rivista Italiana di Scienza Politica* 40 (2010), 138: "distrazione dell'attenzione del pubblico dalle sedi dove si negoziano gli interessi."

Cellini *et al.* also demonstrate that these mini-publics that were advertised by the organizers as representative were not so, but had a strong over-representation of highly educated and politically active people. Their general point is that it was not the case that the mini-publics gave ordinary citizens the power to influence health policies in the region. First, ordinary citizens were not duly represented and second, the mini-publics had no influence on the ongoing decision-making of the political authorities.

A special problem for the deliberative criterion of equal participation is how to handle scientific and other experts. Alfred Moore warns "that the ideal of citizen equality to deliberate issues that affect them is in tension with the inequalities of knowledge that are inherently governing complex societies."[7] He considers this tension as unavoidable; therefore, "the question is not *whether* expert authority is part of the deliberative system, but *how* it is integrated and whether this integration is itself subject to deliberative standards."[8] Moore contrasts a technocratic with a democratic model of expert authority. In the former model, judgment is surrendered in deference to the expert authority. The democratic model, by contrast, opens "expert authority to public judgment in a way that challenges some technocratic defences of the role of expertise in politics, yet does not imply a denial of the value of expert authority in politics."[9] By way of example he mentions Aids activists who "developed expertise and were able to force their way into discussions of treatment strategies and experimental design."[10] As a general principle, Moore wants "to enable the kind of criticism that grounds expert authority in the absence of mere blind deference."[11]

John Parkinson warns that with all the focus on mini-publics, we should not forget the macro level. He wants to look "at the public reasoning and decision making that happens in and between democratic societies every day rather than just in the confines of a citizens' jury." Parkinson is concerned that "technocrats have taken over and turned deliberative democracy into just another set of tools for researching,

---

[7] Alfred Moore, "Questioning Deference: Expert Authority in a Deliberative System," paper presented at the annual meeting of the Midwest Political Science Association, Chicago, March 31–April 3, 2011, p. 14.

[8] Moore, "Questioning Deference," p. 14.

[9] Moore, "Questioning Deference," pp. 4–5.

[10] Moore, "Questioning Deference," p. 13.

[11] Moore, "Questioning Deference," p. 14.

even manipulating, the 'user' of public services."[12] As a consequence of this trend, Parkinson sees the danger that deliberative democracy will lose "its larger critical potential."[13] He wants to see how deliberation works not only in mini-publics but in societies at large. Jane Mansbridge *et al.* reinforce the point that one should also look at how deliberation works in societies at large.

> To understand the larger goal of deliberation, we suggest that it is necessary to go beyond the study of individual institutions and processes to examine their interaction in a system as a whole. We recognize that most democracies are complex entities in which a wide variety of institutions, associations, and sites of contestation accomplish political work, including informal networks, the media, organized advocacy groups, schools, foundations, private and non-profit institutions, legislatures, executive agencies, and the courts. We thus advocate what may be called a system approach to deliberative democracy.[14]

Mansbridge *et al.* emphasize that in a deliberative system not all elements need to have a deliberative nature: "for example, highly partisan rhetoric, even while violating some deliberative ideals such as mutual respect and accommodation, may nonetheless help to fulfill other deliberative ideals such as inclusion."[15] To illustrate their approach, Mansbridge *et al.*

take a closer look at protest. Protest often appears to violate several standards of deliberation. First, the slogans protestors use to excite enthusiasm and convey a dramatic message often undermine epistemic subtlety. Second, when protest explicitly or implicitly threatens sanctions or imposes costs, it acts as a form of coercion. Third, protest sometimes involves levels of disruption and contestation that fail to meet deliberative standards of civility and civic respect, [but] protest can begin to correct inequalities in access to

---

[12] John Parkinson, "Conceptualising and Mapping the Deliberative Society," paper presented at the Political Association Conference, Edinburgh, 2010, pp. 14–15.

[13] Parkinson, "Conceptualising and Mapping the Deliberative Society," p. 2.

[14] Jane Mansbridge, James Bohman, Simone Chambers, Tom Christiano, Archon Fung, John Parkinson, Dennis Thompson, and Mark Warren, "A Systemic Approach to Deliberative Democracy," paper presented at the Workshop on the Frontiers of Deliberation, ECPR Joint Sessions, St. Gallen, April 12–17, 2011.

[15] Mansbridge *et al.*, "A Systemic Approach to Deliberative Democracy," p. 3.

influence by bringing more voices and interests into the decision making process.[16]

Thinking of deliberation in systemic terms is a useful exercise, but it makes it more difficult to identify what is deliberative and what not. To take the illustration of Mansbridge *et al.*, a protest action may appear as non-deliberative at the micro level but as contributing to deliberation at the systemic level, but it is not easy to determine whether a particular protest action contributes to deliberation at the systemic level.

Stefan Rummens also takes a systematic look and argues that good deliberation in all kind of forums and networks is not sufficient for deliberative democracy, which must be strongly supplemented with traditional representative institutions. For him, "representative politics provide political debate with a narrative structure which makes the political process particularly visible and accessible to larger audiences."[17]

Despite all the controversies among theorists, there is agreement that citizens should be involved in politics, and as much as possible on an equal level. As Dennis F. Thompson puts it: "Equal participation requires that no one person or advantaged group completely dominate the reason-giving process, even if the deliberators are not strictly equal in power and prestige."[18] Jane Mansbridge puts the same idea as follows: "The deliberation should, ideally, be open to all those affected by the decision. The participants should have equal opportunity to influence the process, have equal resources, and be protected by basic rights."[19] The question is only how many citizens are actually able and willing to participate in this way in politics. While Habermas stresses the ideal of all citizens deliberating on an equal level and without constraints, theorists like Fishkin see this ideal as unrealistic and think of ways to increase the amount and quality of citizen participation in

---

[16] Mansbridge *et al.*, "A Systemic Approach to Deliberative Democracy," p. 25.
[17] Stefan Rummens, "Staging Deliberation: The Role of Representative Institutions in the Deliberative Democratic Process," paper presented at the Workshop on the Frontiers of Deliberation, ECPR Joint Sessions, St. Gallen, April 12–17, 2011, p. 20. Forthcoming in the *Journal of Political Philosophy*.
[18] Dennis F. Thompson, "Deliberative Democratic Theory and Empirical Political Science," *Annual Review of Political Science* 11 (2008), 527.
[19] Jane Mansbridge with James Bohman, Simone Chambers, David Estlund, Andreas Follesdal, Archon Fung, Christina Lafont, Bernard Manin, and José Luis Marti, "The Place of Self-Interest and the Role of Power in Deliberative Democracy," *Journal of Political Philosophy* 18 (2010), 2.

political deliberation. Mansbridge also acknowledges that the ideal that she postulates in the above quotation is unrealistic in the real world of politics: "In a polity of any size, it is impossible to give everyone a 'say' in the literal sense of having one's individual voice heard by all other members of the polity."[20]

Christian F. Rostbøll goes a step further. Although he argues "that we facilitate and encourage participation in deliberation," he is also of the view that citizens should be able to "use their individual rights to take a strategic attitude and withdraw from the obligations involved in deliberation. This follows from the commitment to the dimension of freedom that entails a right to drop out of deliberation (an aspect of negative freedom), and from the idea that it would not contribute to deliberative freedom to force people to deliberate."[21]

The emphasis of deliberative theorists on citizen participation in everyday political discussions contrasts with an elitist model of democracy as advocated in a classical way by Anthony Downs, who articulates the basic premises of the model in the following way: "we borrow from traditional economic theory the idea of the rational consumer ... our homo politicus is the 'average man' in the electorate, the 'rational citizen' of our model democracy ... he approaches every situation with one eye on the gains to be had, the other eye on costs."[22] The notable feature of this formulation is that Downs compares the citizen to a consumer. As the consumer shops for goods and services in the marketplace, the voter shops in the political market for political parties and candidates. The choice that the voter makes is at the individual level. On the basis of a cost–benefit analysis, he or she decides for whom to vote or to not vote at all. The voter is an individual utility maximizer. Down's model of democracy is *election-centered*. Between elections the voters do not need to care much about political issues. It is up to the political leaders to do so. As elections approach, this is the time to judge political leaders, and voters decide whether to keep them in office or to throw them out. By contrast, the deliberative model is *talk-centered* and wants ordinary citizens, or at least many of them,

---

[20] Mansbridge *et al.*, "The Place of Self-Interest," 23.
[21] Christian F. Rostbøll, *Deliberative Freedom: Deliberative Democracy as Critical Theory* (Albany: State University of New York Press, 2008), pp. 206, 162.
[22] Anthony Downs, *An Economic Theory of Democracy* (New York: Harper & Row, 1957), p. 7.

to deliberate political issues on a regular basis. From the perspective of democratic theory, it makes a big difference whether one takes an election-centered or a talk-centered approach to the role of citizens in politics.

(b) Empirical results

Literature review

My literature review reveals that it is not easy to determine to what extent ordinary citizens deliberate about politics in their daily life. First of all, *surveys* are problematic since it is socially desirable in many quarters to say that one talks in a deliberative way about politics. Who wants to admit to not being open to the arguments of others or not considering the public interest? Early in my career, I noticed that many citizens exaggerate their participation in referenda when answering interview questions. I investigated the participation of Swiss citizens in four referenda in the years 1963/4.[23] On the one hand, citizens were asked in interviews about their participation; on the other hand, I could gather official data about their participation. This was possible because Swiss citizens have to put their voting ballots in one box and their voting identity cards in another box. For my research purposes, I got access to the voting identity cards, which allowed me to check whether the interview answers corresponded to the identity cards that were turned in. If citizens answered that they had participated in the referenda but their identity cards could not be found, this was proof that they had not participated. If, by contrast, they answered in the interviews that they had not participated, but I could find their identity cards, this meant that they had participated. On average, in all four referenda, 25 percent answered in the interviews that they had participated when they did not do so according to the identity cards. Only 3 percent were in the opposite situation, declaring in the interviews that they had not participated when they had indeed done so. These data indicate a strong norm among Swiss citizens to participate in referenda, thus they are under pressure to give socially desirable answers. I concluded from this study that surveys may easily exaggerate levels

---

[23] Jürg Steiner, "Interviewergebnisse und amtliche Angaben bei Abstimmungen," *Kölner Zeitschrift für Soziologie und Sozialpsychologie* 17 (1965), 234–44.

of political participation. This is probably true not only for participation in referenda but also for other forms of political participation.

To demonstrate the problem of investigating with mass surveys political deliberation among ordinary citizens, a study by Lawrence R. Jacobs *et al.* serves me well.[24] It is a well-executed study that I do not wish to harshly criticize. It is precisely because it is well executed that it serves my purpose in the present context. A random sample of American citizens were asked to indicate their involvement in the following scenarios (with the percentage of affirmative answers shown):

1. Informal face-to-face or phone conversations with people you know about public issues that are local, national, or international at least a few times a month   68%
2. Tried to persuade someone about your view on a public issue   47%
3. Tried to persuade someone about whom to vote for   31%
4. Attended a formal or informal meeting in the past year to discuss a local, national, or international issue   25%
5. Used email or instant messaging to talk informally about issues of public concern at least a few times a month   24%
6. Participated in the last year in Internet chat rooms, message boards, or other online discussion groups organized specifically to discuss a local, national, or international issue   4%

Jacobs *et al.* conclude from these data that "talk is far more extensive than many political theorists and researchers presumed. Although it does not always conform to the idealized standards posed by the advocates or critics of democratic deliberation, public talking is a vibrant and surprisingly wide-spread process by which citizens form opinions about civic life."[25] I would caution that the data only indicate what Americans *say* about political talking, not about how much they *actually* talk about politics. That the figures are so high reveals that political talking is deeply embedded in the American norm system, if not always in actual behavior. Jacobs *et al.* also claim that the interviewees "consistently report that the forums they attended relied

[24] Lawrence R. Jacobs, Fay Lomax Cook, and Michael X. Delli Carpini, *Talking Together: Public Deliberation and Political Participation in America* (University of Chicago Press, 2009).

[25] Jacobs *et al.*, *Talking Together*, p. 25.

on expert information, reason-giving, and toleration ... These findings are consistent with the optimistic appraisals of deliberation and its democratic potential."[26] Once again, however, one has to be aware that the findings are based on survey questions and not on actual observation of political talk. Jacobs *et al.* also rely on self-reporting to investigate the impact of participating in a public meeting with the following question: "People sometimes follow up their participation in public meetings with other kinds of activities intended to address the problem that was discussed. Have you engaged in any charitable, civic or political activities as a direct result of the last meeting you attended about a public issue?"[27] The formulation of this question makes it particularly obvious that the respondents have an incentive to answer in a positive way, taking account of what is socially desirable. Thus, the results have to be interpreted with caution that participation in public meetings "stimulate and facilitate further political and civic action."[28]

The same caution applies to a survey study by Didier Caluwaerts *et al.* of a random sample of Belgian voters, in which they asked voters whether they have talked within the last month about politics with family, with friends, and with work colleagues.[29] Some 69 percent reported having talked about politics with family, 66 percent with friends, and 55 percent with work colleagues. A breakdown of the studies by Jacobs *et al.* and Caluwaerts *et al.* by education shows in both countries that the incidence of political talk increases with education. In Belgium, men talked more about politics than did women, whereas in the US there was no difference by gender. By age, neither country showed any difference.

How relevant are the survey studies by Jacobs *et al.* and Caluwaerts *et al.* for the normative controversies presented in the first section of the chapter? First of all, it is unclear whether the studies measure deliberation or just talk. This ambiguity is particularly visible in how Jacobs *et al.* titled their book. In the main title they refer to talk,

---

[26] Jacobs *et al.*, *Talking Together*, pp. 77, 81.

[27] Jacobs *et al.*, *Talking Together*, p. 98.

[28] Jacobs *et al.*, *Talking Together*, p. 117.

[29] D. Caluwaerts, S. Erzeel, and P. Meier, "Différences de sexe en discussions politiques et implications normatives pour la démocratie délibérative," in K. Deschouwer, P. Delwit, M. Hooghe, and S. Walgrave (eds.), *Les Voix du Peuple* (Brussels: Editions du ULB, 2010), pp. 159–75.

in the subtitle to deliberation. Therefore, the positive answers to the survey questions seem to include also plain talk and not only deliberation. Second, we must consider that the positive answers may be greatly exaggerated. All this means that Fishkin may be right that one should not expect a high level of deliberation among ordinary citizens, so that one has to look for special means to increase deliberation. Particularly troubling is the finding in both studies that people with a low level of education speak relatively rarely about politics in their daily lives, which violates the deliberative postulate of equal participation. Foreshadowing my normative conclusions in the last section of this chapter, I will propose measures to increase deliberation, particularly among the less educated, in suggesting more deliberative ways in how schoolchildren are taught.

Michael A. Neblo *et al.* combine in a creative way a survey method with an experiment.[30] In a random sample of American citizens, they investigate their "attitudes toward hypothetical opportunities for deliberation."[31] The experimental part consists "of field experiments in which random samples of citizens from 13 congressional districts were offered an opportunity to participate in an online deliberative forum with their member of Congress to discuss immigration policy."[32] Based on both parts of their investigation, Neblo *et al.* find "that willingness to deliberate is much higher than research in political behavior might suggest, and that those most willing to deliberate are precisely those turned off by standard partisan and interest group politics."[33] The groups turned off by traditional politics but willing to deliberate are "younger people, racial minorities and lower-income people."[34] It is also noteworthy that those with lower levels of education are as willing to deliberate as those with higher levels of education, whereas in standard politics those with a higher level of education tend to have a higher level of participation. The study of Neblo *et al.* offers hope that new technologies may contribute to more equal participation in

[30] Michael A. Neblo, Kevin M. Esterling, Ryan P. Kennedy, David M.J. Lazer, and Anand E. Sokhey, "Who Wants to Deliberate: And Why?," *American Political Science Review* 104 (2010), 566–83.

[31] Neblo *et al.*, "Who Wants to Deliberate?," 571.

[32] Neblo *et al.*, "Who Wants to Deliberate?," 575.

[33] Neblo *et al.*, "Who Wants to Deliberate?," 582.

[34] Neblo *et al.*, "Who Wants to Deliberate?," 574.

deliberation. In the normative part of the chapter, I will show how the Internet can be useful for deliberation.

Simone Chambers undertook one of the first attempts to study the level of deliberation among ordinary citizens not with surveys but with direct observations. In the summer of 1992, a number of conferences were set up across Canada to discuss possible solutions to the various constitutional impasses facing the nation. The background for organizing these conferences was the impasse on potential independence for Québec and an upcoming referendum on this thorny issue. Conference participants represented a broad cross-section of Canadians. From the observation of some of these conferences, Chambers concludes that they

> conformed to ideals of deliberation in that there was a conscious attempt to guarantee dialogical equality so that everyone could speak and be heard and to exclude influences, such as money and power that might distort the conversation ... Participants could "afford" to be flexible, open, and cooperative. This in turn led to real movement of positions and convergence on issues.[35]

Chambers is a theorist, and it is noteworthy that quite early in the philosophical debate about deliberation she felt the need for an empirical investigation of how ordinary citizens talk with each other about important political issues. Chambers acknowledges that these conferences had characteristics that were particularly favorable for deliberation.

Not only did participants at the conferences not take any votes or make any internal decisions but their role in the larger constitutional debate was left vague. They had no clear mandate. The outcomes of these conferences did not bind in any authoritative way. The end of the conferences did not represent any kind of closure or decision. It is not quite right to say that nothing was at stake, for it was not an academic conference discussing constitutional options for ancient Athens but rather citizen participants who were aware of the seriousness and urgency of the issues and knew that they had the ear of the public as well as the political elite. Nevertheless, it is correct to say that a binding or authoritative decision was not at stake and this freed participants from the fear of premature or disadvantageous closure.[36]

---

[35] Simone Chambers, "Talking versus Voting: Legitimacy and Deliberative Democracy," unpublished paper, University of Colorado, 1999, pp. 4–6. See also Simone Chambers, "Constitutional Referendums and Democratic Deliberation," in Mathew Mendelsohn and Andrew Parkin (eds.), *Referendum Democracy: Studies in Citizen Participation* (New York: Palgrave, 2001).

[36] Chambers, "Talking versus Voting," pp. 5–6.

These deliberative conferences did not spill over into the actual referendum campaign on Québec independence later in the year. From her normative position as theorist, Chambers expresses

great disappointment ... at the caliber and tenor of the debate. Lacking was the openness and flexibility of the conference participants, that is, the willingness to revise claims, to make them fit with other, now perceived as equally legitimate, claims. Instead, the referendum campaign appeared to harden positions. Furthermore, leaders and spokespersons began to talk in zero sum terms, to the effect that any concessions to other interests would be a loss for their side. Rather than reasonable arguments, fear of being a loser in the deal was played up. All in all, the referendum debate had an effect opposite to what deliberation is supposed to have: it moved participants further apart, heightened distrust, exacerbated misunderstandings and left Canadians in a worse place than when they started.[37]

This early empirical study by Chambers shows that under favorable conditions, citizens are able and willing to talk with each other about serious political matters at a high level of deliberation. The study also shows, however, that it is most difficult to transfer such a deliberative culture to the elite level and to society more generally when actual important decisions have to be made. The hope of Chambers as a theorist was that the leaders would be inspired by the deliberative tone of the discussions at the informal conferences. But she was disappointed that the tone dramatically changed when the decision on Québec independence came closer. It seems to be one thing to talk informally about a political issue at a conference resort and quite another thing to have the same discussion when the stakes are high because a decision has to be made. The study by Chambers reinforces the worry of Maija Setälä that citizens' conferences will be ignored when actual hard decisions have to be made. In the normative part of the chapter, I will present a table showing different functions of citizens' conferences.

Pamela Johnston Conover and Donald D. Searing used focus groups in the UK and the US to investigate to what extent ordinary citizens are able and willing to address political issues in a deliberative way. They claim that "focus groups allow researchers to investigate the meaning of concepts, topics and processes as ordinary citizens understand them. They direct us to the language that citizens use

---

[37] Chambers, "Talking versus Voting," pp. 5–6.

to understand these matters ... Thus, focus groups are an especially useful method for probing the experience of everyday talk."[38] For Conover and Searing, "deliberation entails listening very carefully to the view of others, explaining to them one's own views, and taking time together to think over a matter thoroughly. Thus, deliberation is an exercise in rational reason giving."[39] This definition, according to Conover and Searing,

is certainly much more rigorous than is the everyday informal discussion about public affairs practised by the British and American citizens in our research. We can best characterize what these ordinary citizens actually do ... as discussions or everyday talks, occasionally deliberative but more typically unstructured, spontaneous, and without clear goals. Such discussions involve a wide variety of communication forms – argument, rhetoric, emotion, testimony or storytelling, and gossip – rather than being limited to rational exchange of reasons.[40]

Acknowledging that "everyday political talk may not be rigorously deliberative," Conover and Searing still insist that "it would be premature to dismiss altogether the dialogic function of everyday political talk; [it] helps citizens to work out their preferences, try out justifications for them, and develop confidence about performing in the public arena." Although Conover and Searing see less deliberation in their British and American focus groups than Chambers did in the Canadian citizens' conferences, both studies agree that ordinary citizens have potentially the capacity to address political issues in a deliberative way. However, the caveat that Chambers made for her investigation is also valid for the focus groups of Conover and Searing, namely that conditions for deliberation were particularly favorable since the participants did not have to make any authoritative decisions. If the focus groups were required to decide, for example, the tax rate in their local communities, the level of deliberation may have been quite lower. The study by Conover and Searing, like the study by Chambers, raises once again the question of the value of citizens' conferences for deliberative democracy at large. Reading an earlier version of the book manuscript, Ian O'Flynn is critical in stating "it

[38] Pamela Johnston Conover and Donald D. Searing, "Studying Everyday Political Talk in the Deliberative System," *Acta Politica* 40 (2005), 273.
[39] Conover and Searing, "Studying Everyday Political Talk," 271.
[40] Conover and Searing, "Studying Everyday Political Talk," 271.

seems that these exercises are pretty pointless. Sure, the participants might feel better afterwards. But they are still not engaged in decision making, and, in any case, the numbers involved are absolutely tiny."[41] As I will show in the normative section of this chapter, I consider free-floating citizens' conferences not as pointless as O'Flynn thinks. Participants may not only feel better afterwards, they may also have done something for their self-actualization, which is not a small matter.

Julien Talpin did a qualitative ethnographic study of a real-life experience of citizen involvement in policy decisions.[42] The model was Alegre in Brazil where citizens were involved in the budgeting process. Talpin studied three European communities where this experience was replicated, Morsang-sur-Orge in the Paris banlieue, the eleventh district in Rome, and Seville in Spain. In these three communities ordinary citizens were given the opportunity to be involved in the budget process and, within some limits, to allocate money to the different programs of the community. Talpin was able to observe altogether 124 such meetings, and also did interviews with organizers and participants. From the perspective of participation, the negative finding is that many citizens dropped out, "being disappointed by the narrowness of the power they were given or the manipulations orchestrated by elected officials."[43] The study by Talpin makes us aware that it is difficult to keep participation of ordinary citizens alive over a longer period of time, especially when deliberation is not, or is insufficiently, consequential. The study also speaks to the argument of Rostbøll that citizens should have the freedom to drop out of deliberation. I agree that they should have this freedom and that this is part of their autonomy. The empirical research reported up to this point shows that surveys give a much more positive picture of the level of deliberation than when actual behavior is observed. For my normative conclusions, I will base myself more on direct observations of deliberative efforts than on deliberation as recalled in surveys.

---

[41] Personal communication, August 8, 2011.
[42] Julien Talpin, *Schools of Democracy: How Ordinary Citizens (Sometimes) Become Competent in Participatory Budgeting Institutions* (Colchester: ECPR Press, 2011).
[43] Talpin, *School of Democracy*, p. 4, book prospectus.

New data on deliberative experiments[44]

Colombia is our most challenging case, because at the time of the experiments the internal armed conflict was still going on. Some 342 ex-combatants participated in 28 experiments. For the topic of the present chapter, it is interesting to see how evenly or unevenly participants spoke up. Of the ex-combatants, 115, or 34 percent, did not speak up at all in the experiment they attended. This is indeed a high percentage that needs explanation. The most plausible explanation is that given their traumatic experiences, many ex-combatants were cagey about uttering wrong words and preferred to remain silent. From observing the experiments, Maria Clara Jaramillo and Juan Ugarriza, our researchers for Colombia, had the impression that these mute participants were not completely passive but listened to the discussion; they did not disturb the group by showing signs of lack of interest such as yawning, closing their eyes, and other disruptive behavior. Who were the ex-combatants who were willing to attend the experiments but did not speak up? A binary analysis shows that ex-guerrillas were more reluctant to speak up than ex-paramilitaries.[45] A possible explanation is that, given the Colombian context, guerrillas are more outcasts than the paramilitaries and are therefore cagier about speaking up after demobilization. Those with a low level of education and those recently demobilized also tended more often to remain silent. Gender and age did not differentiate between speakers and non-speakers. As the following data show, participation was also uneven among those who spoke up.

Did not speak up at all	34%
Spoke up once or twice	30%
Spoke up 3–10 times	28%
Spoke up 11–20 times	7%
Spoke up 21–30 times	1%
Total participants	100%

These figures demonstrate that with regard to participation, the experiments with ex-combatants were far from the ideal of the

---

[44] For the research designs, see Introduction, Section (b).
[45] Binary analyses in this chapter will be supplemented in Chapter 9 by multiple regressions.

deliberative model. Constraints were not external in the sense that participants were prevented from speaking up; there were instead internal constraints at play inducing a large number of participants to speak up very little or not at all. It is noteworthy that of the 1,027 speech acts, only 5 were interrupted by other participants, which indicates a calm and not boisterous atmosphere during the experiments. For the characterization of the experiments it is also noteworthy that most interventions were short: 87 percent of the speech acts lasted 1.5 minutes or less.

For *Bosnia–Herzegovina*, I begin with the experiments in *Srebrenica* with Serbs and Bosnjaks. As the following data show, compared with Colombia, fewer participants spoke up only once or twice or not at all. Although in Srebrenica the worst massacres in Europe since World War II had occurred, few participants were so traumatized that they hardly dared to speak up. To be sure, participants were not ex-combatants like in Colombia, which may account for the fact that in Srebrenica there were fewer people who spoke up very little or not at all. And yet, in Srebrenica, too, there was great inequality of participation.

Did not speak up at all	18%
Spoke up once or twice	7%
Spoke up 3–10 times	18%
Spoke up 11–20 times	23%
Spoke up 21–30 times	15%
Spoke up 31–40 times	10%
Spoke up 41–50 times	7%
Spoke up 51 times or more	2%
Total participants	100%

In Srebrenica, there was more of a give-and-take than in Colombia, with 6 percent of the speech acts being interrupted by other participants. But there was only a single case where someone complained of being constrained by the behavior of other participants. The quick give-and-take is also revealed by the fact that virtually all interventions stayed below one minute; thus, the interventions tended to be even shorter than in Colombia. The experiments in *Stolac* between Croats and Bosnjaks were quite similar to those in Srebrenica. Again in contrast to Colombia, there was a quick give-and-take with few participants speaking little or not at all, although participation was very uneven like in Colombia.

In *Belgium*, all participants spoke up, and there were few who spoke up only once or twice. With no political violence caused by the language divide, one would not expect traumatized participants, and this is indeed what seems to have happened. Participants seemed to be at ease to talk about how to handle the thorny language issue. But we must also note that even in Belgium there was great inequality in how much people were involved in the discussion. Breaking down the data by age, gender, and education shows no differences by age and education, but a great difference by gender, with women speaking up much less than men.

Did not speak up at all	0%
Spoke up once or twice	2%
Spoke up 3–10 times	24%
Spoke up 11–20 times	35%
Spoke up 21–30 times	28%
Spoke up 31–40 times	6%
Spoke up 41 times or more	5%
Total participants	100%

Of all the 1,664 speech acts in Belgium, 301, or 18 percent, were interrupted by other participants, much more than in Colombia and in Bosnia–Herzegovina. Does this mean that from this perspective Belgium was less deliberative than Colombia since interruptions prevent the speakers from fully developing their arguments? We should note, however, that in only 2 of the 301 interrupted speech acts did the speaker complain about the interruption. Perhaps sometimes interruptions can be seen as a sign of vivid interactivity, which would indicate good deliberative quality. This discussion shows that it is not easy to interpret interruptions from a deliberative angle. Depending on the context, they may indicate lack of civility but also great interest in what others have to say.

For *Europolis*, one has to consider that the moderators, in contrast to those in Colombia, Bosnia–Herzegovina, and Belgium, were trained to encourage equal participation. If someone did not speak up, he or she was called upon to do so. Despite such encouragement there was still a large amount of unequal participation, with women, the less educated, working class, and people from Central and Eastern Europe speaking up the least. For women, however, more detailed analyses have shown that although they speak up less than men, they are very much part of the discussions in the sense that men interact as much with them as with other men.[46]

In *Finland*, like in Europolis, moderators encouraged equal participation, but here, too, participation was very uneven, with women, the less educated, the very young, and the very old speaking up the least.

In sum, participants in the experimental groups spoke up to a very unequal extent, even in cases when moderators encouraged equal participation. This unequal pattern had little to do with external constraints like undue interruptions but much more with internal constraints of not being able or willing to speak up. These constraints were particularly strong among women and the less educated.

(c) Normative implications of empirical results

The most striking result of the empirical section of this chapter is that citizens participate very unevenly in deliberation of political issues. It is not surprising that we arrive at this result, but for the normative debate about deliberation it is important to know on a firm empirical basis that under quite different conditions there is great inequality in deliberative participation. From a normative perspective, we have to confront this fact head-on. What is really troubling is that there is a systematic bias in the sense that middle-aged men with higher levels of education tend to speak up the most. The empirical world is far away from the Habermasian normative ideal of equal and unconstrained participation. Does this invalidate the Habermasian deliberative model? Not at all. We should remember from the Introduction that the philosophical model of deliberation is meant as a "regulative" ideal in the sense of Immanuel Kant, which means that it is set as a goal for which we should strive but which we will never quite attain. As an anonymous reviewer of an earlier version of this book remarked, we should not fall into the trap of finding normative theorists "impractical"; they set ideals by which reality can be judged. In my view, we should not relax standards with regard to equal participation in deliberation and look for means for encouraging all citizens to take more part in deliberation of political issues. The good news is that from some of the

---

[46] Marlène Gerber, "Who Are the Voices of Europe? Evidence from a Pan-European Deliberative Poll," paper presented at the ECPR General Conference, Reykjavik, August 25–27, 2011.

reported empirical data we can conclude that many citizens have internalized a strong norm that it would be a good thing to be involved in political issues. Thus, the challenge is how to further strengthen these norms, and, more importantly, to help people to put these norms into practice.

I agree with the position of Robert E. Goodin, reported in the Introduction, that deliberative practice can also take place individually. In emphasizing the inter-personal aspect, deliberative scholars should not forget that individuals can also fruitfully deliberate within their own brain. They can reflect on conflicting arguments to solve a problem. They can also discuss with an imagined interlocutor. This happens in particular when they read a book and engage in an imagined dialogue with the author. As Wilhelm von Humboldt argued a long time ago, solitude gives the freedom for creative thinking.[47] This ideal of individual self-reflection should not be neglected in the deliberative model. We cannot constantly think in the company of others. We also need time for ourselves to think through the problems of the world. Such individual deliberation is a precondition for good inter-personal deliberation, which then, in turn, helps to further clarify our own thoughts.

Schools play an important role in developing a deliberative culture, in the sense that children learn to think about different ways to solve a problem.[48] Earlier in my career, I underwent teacher training and taught for a time in middle and high school. Based on this experience, I have great hopes that schools can make a major contribution to the development of a deliberative culture in a society. Beginning as early as kindergarten, students can be taught to listen to each other with respect, to justify their arguments, possibly also with personal stories, and to be open to yield to the force of the better arguments. A good teaching technique to develop these skills is to have students tackle tasks not only individually but often also in small groups. The

---

[47] "Einsamkeit und Freiheit" (solitude and freedom). Wilhelm von Humboldt, *Ueber die innere und äußere Organisation der höheren wissenschaftlichen Anstalten in Berlin*, vol. X (Berlin: Preußischen Akademie der Wissenschaften, 1903 [1810]), pp. 250ff.

[48] See Special Issue on Deliberative Democracy in Higher Education, *Journal of Public Deliberation* 6 (1) (2010). See also Caroline Guibet Lafaye, "Faut-il éduquer à la délibération?," *Archives de philosophie du droit* 54 (2011), 161–76.

challenge with such *group work* is that some students often dominate the discussion while others are free-riding. A good teacher will
be able to remedy this problem in showing students that they will be
more successful in resolving their task if all participate in an equal and
unconstrained way. Groups then report their results to the class, where
they are further discussed. These class discussions should often be
organized in a spontaneous way without interventions by the teacher,
so-called *free student discussions*. Again there is a challenge, because
to speak up in a free student discussion is not easy for many students
who may be too shy or lack the necessary rhetorical skills. Here, too,
a good teacher can create an atmosphere where, perhaps only over a
long period, students feel comfortable speaking to a larger audience.
If the teaching techniques of small-group work, group reporting to
larger audiences, and free student discussions are used in a systematic way from kindergarten to university, key deliberative skills can
be developed that can then be used when participating as citizens in
deliberation of political issues. Of particular importance is that deliberative skills are also taught to children who do not go on to higher
education. These children in many cases do not come from families
with a deliberative culture, so that schools are the most promising way
to bring more equality to deliberation. Special care must also be taken
that girls are not too shy to speak up in class discussions so that later
as citizens they are as active as men are in deliberative discussions. I
will come back in the very last chapter to the importance of schools
for the development of a deliberative culture.

While these teaching techniques can be applied in all fields from
mathematics to art history, a special challenge to develop a deliberative culture confronts teachers in civics classes. They should present to
their students politics both as a strategic power game and as respectful
deliberation, being two different ways to interpret what happens in
politics. Students could then discuss on the basis of concrete political
case studies which interpretation is more plausible. A good teacher can
make them aware that a definite answer to this fundamental question
of political life is not possible. The answer will always depend on the
philosophical perspective. The teacher can show that Machiavelli and
Kant, for example, gave different answers to the role of power and
morality in politics. In this way, students become sophisticated in how
politics can be interpreted. To help civics teachers to orient their teaching in this direction, civics textbooks should be more closely linked

to cutting-edge political science research. Well-researched case studies should be included in the textbooks, preferably case studies that are interpreted from both a power and a deliberative perspective. With such textbooks as background, civics becomes more interesting than is traditionally the case. Students will learn that both power and arguments are important in politics and, as a result of such teaching, will become more sophisticated citizens who feel comfortable participating in a deliberative way in political discussions. They have learned in school that in thinking and talking about political issues they should act not as consumers but as citizens. To learn such role ascriptions early in life is very important.[49]

In order to get more egalitarian and unconstrained citizen participation, one should also further develop the idea of mini-publics, citizens' conferences, or whichever name we want to use for discussion groups of ordinary citizens. Thereby, one has to be aware that mini-publics can easily be manipulated by the political elites for their own purposes, as some theorists such as Erika Cellini, John Parkinson, and Maija Setälä warn. In the Introduction, I have presented the effort of the Tuscany region to work with mini-publics to engage citizens more in the political process. As illustration, I used the town of Piombino where small groups of citizens discussed the renovation of the town square. In order to evaluate the value of such mini-publics for deliberation, we must distinguish between projects where the organizers make special efforts to create favorable conditions for deliberation and projects where no such special efforts are made. Examples of the former projects are Fishkin's Deliberative Polling, where the moderators instruct the participants to follow the basic rules of deliberation and intervene when these rules are not followed.[50] Examples of the latter projects are our own experiments in Colombia, Bosnia–Herzegovina, and Belgium, where the moderators only gave the topic for discussion and then abstained from any further instructions or interventions. Both approaches have merits. We should be aware, however, that the two approaches serve different purposes. People planning to work with mini-publics should carefully consider what purpose they have in mind. If the purpose is purely scholarly, I recommend that the moderators do not give instructions, abstain from

---

[49] This aspect was pointed out to me by Claudia Landwehr.
[50] Fishkin, *When the People Speak*.

A. Mini-publics in civil society, moderators do *not* intervene in discussions	B. Mini-publics in civil society, moderators *do* intervene in discussions
C. Mini-publics as part of formal political decision process, moderators do *not* intervene in discussions	D. Mini-publics as part of formal political decision process, moderators *do* intervene in discussions

Figure 1 Mini-publics by location and role of moderator

interventions, and let the discussion go wherever it goes. Under these experimental conditions, one can see, for example, which participants do not speak up or are disrespectful. If, on the other hand, the purpose of organizing mini-publics is to develop the deliberative skills of the participants, it is beneficial if the moderators intervene, in a similar way to the good teachers discussed above. Interventions by the moderators are also advisable if the discussion groups are to come up with well-reflected policy recommendations. Another distinction with regard to mini-publics is their location either in civil society or as part of the formal political decision process. This distinction cuts across the distinction of whether the moderators intervene or not. Combining the two distinctions results in the above four-field table (see Figure 1).

Mini-publics in Box A are organized in civil society, and discussions are free-floating without intervention by the moderators. Such experiments allow the testing of hypotheses about the antecedents and consequences of variation in the level of deliberation away from any formal political decision process. Mini-publics in Box B are helpful to train participants in deliberative skills, serving as a continuation of the training received in school. With Box C we can test hypotheses about the influence of mini-publics on policy outcomes. Here, discussions in mini-publics are integrated in the formal political decision process. One can investigate, for example, whether the influence of mini-publics is greater the earlier in a decision process they are integrated. Or one can test whether the influence of mini-publics depends on whether their policy recommendations are made public or whether they are only communicated to the responsible decision-makers.

The most interesting, from a practical perspective, but also the most problematic, are mini-publics in Box D. Thanks to the guidance given by the moderators, such mini-publics may attain a high level of deliberation allowing a correspondingly high influence on policy outcomes. But there is also the problem of manipulation that I have discussed earlier in the chapter. Politicians may select participants for mini-publics in such a way that their recommendations correspond to their wishes, and, furthermore, moderators may direct the discussions along a path favored by the politicians. In my view, this is indeed a real danger. But this does not necessarily have to be a major problem. There are also positive cases. A good example are the mini-publics in the Italian town of Piombino, described in the Introduction, which discussed the renovation of the town square. The small discussion groups took up their work before the town authorities had developed any plans for the renovation. The discussions were guided by the professional staff of the Autorità per la Partecipazione in Florence, the state institution to accompany from a research perspective the various mini-publics in the Tuscany region. The final recommendation of the mini-publics in Piombino were taken up and implemented to a large extent, although not universally, by the town authorities. In my view, the Piombino example should be taken as a good model to be followed in other places. For David Friedrich, such mini-publics as part of the formal decision process are not only needed at the local level but also at the European level, which for him "means to establish such forums at a regular basis at different places on different topics and to establish mechanisms that require the EU institutions to justify their policy choices in the light of the outcomes of the deliberative forums."[51]

When working with mini-publics in whatever form, it is important that the participants are drawn in a random way, representing as far as possible the population at large. As Yves Sintomer shows, the use of the lot in politics has a long tradition going back to Ancient

[51] David Friedrich, "European Governance and the Deliberative Challenge," paper presented at the ECPR General Conference, Reykjavik, August 25–27, 2011, p. 18.

Greece and to Early Renaissance Florence and Venice.[52] Thus, it is nothing revolutionary to apply drawing lots to contemporary mini-publics. It is already done on a broad basis for jury selection. Mini-publics should be selected in a similar way. I agree with Sintomer that

> good deliberation needs to include various points of view, so that the range of arguments can be enlarged, and the reasons better balanced. In this line of thought, randomly selected mini-publics tend to be better than participatory devises based on voluntary involvement or on the organized civil society because they rest on a cross section of the people and maximize the epistemic diversity of their deliberation. This is why they can bring something valuable to what is, in fact, a context of increasing complexity.[53]

Sintomer argues further that "these mini-publics embody a counterfactual opinion – what the larger public could think if it could truly deliberate … the counterfactual opinion tends to be more reasonable than the wider public debate."[54] Thus, mini-publics are not expected to give a representative picture of the raw public opinion but on what public opinion could be if it were the result of careful deliberation. In the final chapter, on the praxis of deliberation, I will have more to say on how mini-publics can be made part of the formal decision process and how it tends to be difficult from a practical point of view to implement the rule of randomness.

Emphasizing the importance of participation of ordinary citizens in political deliberation, does not mean, of course, that other forms of political participation are unimportant. I agree with theorists like Mansbridge and Parkinson, reported in the first section of the chapter, that at the system level not everything can and should be deliberative. Involvement of citizens in politics does not mean that they be only deliberative. Sometimes, participation in street protests and strikes is the appropriate thing in order to get heard. And, of course, going to the polls for competitive elections remains an essential element in a deliberative democracy. Hard bargaining is also part of deliberative

---

[52] Yves Sintomer, "Random Selection, Republican Self-Government, and Deliberative Democracy," *Constellations* 17 (2010), 472–87. On randomness, see also Peter Stone, *The Luck of the Draw: The Role of Lotteries in Decision-Making* (New York: Oxford University Press, 2011).

[53] Sintomer, "Random Selection," 482.

[54] Sintomer, "Random Selection," 482.

democracy, as are aggregative votes in parliament and other institutions. How about the position of Rostbøll that citizens should have the negative freedom not to participate in deliberation and, by extension, not to participate in politics at all? Reluctantly, I agree with this position, although any form of democracy depends on widespread citizen participation. But if, for example, a poet is so involved in his or her art that politics is mentally far removed, I would understand that such a poet would stay away from any political involvement. I would have the same understanding for a person overburdened with personal problems, for example terminal illness or long-term unemployment. To be sure, we should develop a strong norm for political participation and in particular political deliberation. But we should also be tolerant of people who are unable or unwilling to follow this norm. Such tolerance shows respect for individual autonomy, also a key element of deliberative democracy.

2 | Rationality and stories in deliberative justification

According to deliberative theory, arguments need to be justified. This element of the theory has two aspects: the form and the substance of justification. This chapter deals with the form, the next chapter with the substance. With regard to the form, the key question is whether in deliberation only rational arguments are allowed or whether personal stories can also be used.

(a) Normative controversies in the literature

In the Habermasian version of deliberation, arguments need to be justified in a rational, logical, and elaborate way. Assertions should be introduced and critically assessed through "the orderly exchange of information and reasons between parties."[1] The arguments must have intrinsic characteristics that make them compelling to others.[2] "Communicative action refers to a process of argumentation in which those taking part justify their validity claims before an ideally expanded audience."[3] Jürgen Habermas, as a normative standard, explicitly excludes narratives and images as deliberative justification.[4] This does not mean, however, as Michael A. Neblo points out, that Habermas excludes narratives and images as a practical matter or considers such discourses as necessarily inferior.[5] There is controversy in

---

[1] Jürgen Habermas, *Faktizität und Geltung: Beiträge zur Diskurstheorie des Rechts und des demokratischen Rechtsstaats* (Frankfurt a.M: Suhrkamp, 1992), p. 370: "den geregelten Austausch von Informationen und Gründen zwischen Parteien."

[2] Jürgen Habermas, *Moralbewusstsein und kommunikatives Handeln* (Frankfurt a.M.: Suhrkamp, 1983), p. 97.

[3] Jürgen Habermas, *Between Facts and Norms: Contributions to a Discourse Theory of Law and Democracy* (Cambridge, MA: MIT Press, 1996), p. 322.

[4] Jürgen Habermas, *Ach, Europa* (Frankfurt a.M.: Suhrkamp, 2008), p. 157: "nicht diskursive Ausdrucksformen wie Narrative und Bilder."

[5] Michael A. Neblo, *Common Voices: Between the Theory and Practice of Deliberative Democracy* (unpublished book manuscript), see especially ch. 2.

the philosophical literature about this focus of Habermas on rationality in the justification of arguments. Theorists like Jane Mansbridge argue that testimonies about personal stories should also count as valid justifications. She justifies this position in the following way: "Stories can establish credibility, create empathy, and trigger a sense of injustice, all of which contribute directly or indirectly to justification."[6]

An anonymous reader of an earlier version of this book criticizes the position of Mansbridge in giving a more limited role to stories in the deliberative model: "Stories might be necessary to constitute the topic and to expand the boundaries of inclusiveness and recognition. But stories, greetings, etc. do not provide, in themselves, justifications." It is ultimately an empirical question that I will address in the second section of the chapter whether stories are successfully used to justify arguments. In the following quotation John S. Dryzek leans more in the direction of Mansbridge in expecting that stories can be effective in inducing reflection: "In some accounts (e.g., Habermas), reasoned argument is privileged, but deliberation can be open to a variety of forms of communication, such as rhetoric, testimony (the telling of stories), and humor. Real-world political communication generally mixes these different forms, and those that do not involve argument can be effective in inducing reflection."[7]

Patrizia Nanz agrees with Dryzek that the deliberative model should have space for personal testimonies, and her formulation implies that personal stories can also serve as justification when she writes that public debate should also allow expressing one's identity and speaking with one's voice. In doing so, one would not only put an issue on the agenda but also express an opinion. More specifically, Nanz argues:

By underlining the conceptions of critical/rational discourse, Habermas neglects the extent to which public communication does not consist in argumentation aiming at consensus, but involves questions of individual interest, social and cultural recognition, power, prestige, etc. Participation in public debates is not simply a matter of formulating contents but also of being

---

[6] Jane Mansbridge with James Bohman, Simone Chambers, David Estlund, Andreas Follesdal, Archon Fung, Christina Lafont, Bernard Manin, and José Luis Marti, "The Place of Self-Interest and the Role of Power in Deliberative Democracy," *Journal of Political Philosophy* 18 (2010), 64–100.

[7] John S. Dryzek, "Democratization as Deliberative Capacity Building," *Comparative Political Studies* 42 (2009), 1381.

able to speak in "one's voice"; thereby, simultaneously enacting one's socio/cultural identity through specific expressive modes or rhetorical features.[8]

Michael E. Morrell adds the argument that personal stories are valuable even if they do not lead to agreement:

If narrative or testimony opens people up to other perspectives, even if they do not then agree with those perspectives, then narrative and testimony can serve an important function by clarifying what different people believe is at stake in deliberation. For example, those opposed to same-sex marriage may never agree that it should be legal, but they may reach a better understanding of what is at stake in the issue after listening to the narratives of same-sex couples and the difficulties they face in society.[9]

Morrell also adds that personal stories have value in themselves.[10] In this way, he takes a counter-position to Dryzek, who argues that personal stories are only relevant for deliberation if they are connected to general issues.[11]

Claudia Landwehr is also sympathetic to storytelling, but cautions that "we have to be careful to consider in how far we can embrace rhetoric and storytelling without giving up what is essential to deliberation: the give-and-take of reasons." She also warns that "narratives can be highly manipulative, and it is difficult to assess their truth. Even if the storytellers are not exactly lying, they may be exaggerating, playing with the audience's emotion." Therefore, "further empirical research is required to find out what the effects of storytelling are, who benefits if we allow storytelling to play a considerable role in discourses." And she hypothesizes "that those who do better at arguing will also do better at storytelling."[12] In a similar way, Kasper M. Hansen is critical of making storytelling a key part of deliberation. He acknowledges that stories may "help establish an intersubjective understanding of the situation. Narratives may also evoke sympathy and reveal the sources of the participant's values, which may serve to explain the underlying

---

[8] Patrizia Nanz, *Europolis: Constitutional Patriotism Beyond the Nation State* (Manchester University Press, 2006), p. 36.

[9] Michael E. Morrell, *Empathy and Democracy: Feeling, Thinking, and Deliberation* (University Park: Pennsylvania State University Press, 2010), p. 142.

[10] Morrell, *Empathy and Democracy*, p. 168.

[11] Dryzek, "Democratization as Deliberative Capacity Building."

[12] Personal communication, March 10, 2010.

premises of a participant's opinion." But like Landwehr, Hansen warns that emotional personal stories may be "strongly manipulative."[13]

As we have seen above, Dryzek also mentions humor as an element of deliberative justification. Sammy Basu spends an entire article discussing why humor helps deliberation. He sees humor as a virtue.[14]

Humor provisionally suspends decorum, putting the mind at liberty to hear all sides. It allows one to temporarily suspend one's cherished beliefs and contemplate the implications without treachery ... Humor finds ambiguities, contradictions and parables in what is otherwise taken literally ... Humor keeps the process of reasoning open-ended ... humor can be a social lubricant. It breaks the ice and fills awkward silences ... Comedy permits frankness to be less threatening.[15]

By contrast, Habermas wishes to have deliberation free of humor when he writes that "jokes, fictional representations, irony, games, and so on, rest on intentionally using categorical confusions."[16] So we are back at the Habermasian insistence on rationality as the only acceptable way to justify arguments in the deliberative model. This Habermasian position is criticized in a systematic way by Sharon R. Krause.[17] Starting from David Hume, Krause asserts that Habermas and theorists like him put too much emphasis on rationality, and that more attention should be given not only to stories but to sentiment and passion in general. She argues that "deliberation, as Hume conceives it, is not devoid of intellect, but it involves more than merely intellect. The process of practical reasoning is a holistic one, in which cognition and affect are deeply entwined."[18] From this Humean position, Krause criticizes Habermas for being insufficiently aware that all reasons also have an affective element. "To have a conception of the good therefore is to have an affective attachment to it or a desire to realize it; when we are rational, we are also desiring."[19] According to Krause, Habermas includes much more

---

[13] Kasper M. Hansen, *Deliberative Democracy and Opinion Formation* (Odensee: University Press of Southern Denmark, 2004), p. 121.

[14] Sammy Basu, "Dialogic Ethics and the Virtue of Humor," *Journal of Political Philosophy* 7 (1999), 385.

[15] Basu, "Dialogic Ethics and the Virtue of Humor," 385–92.

[16] Quoted in Basu, "Dialogic Ethics and the Virtue of Humor," 398.

[17] Sharon R. Krause, *Civil Passions: Moral Sentiment and Democratic Deliberation* (Princeton University Press, 2008).

[18] Krause, *Civil Passions*, p. 103.

[19] Krause, *Civil Passions*, p. 30.

affect in his concept of rationality than he is willing to acknowledge. To demonstrate that pure rationality is impossible, Krause refers to neuroscience and approvingly quotes Antonio Damasio, whose research suggests that "the cool strategy advocated by Kant, among others, has far more to do with the way patients with prefrontal damage go about deciding than with how normals usually operate."[20]

Krause does not necessarily advocate more passion in politics, since she is well aware that uncontrolled passion may have devastating consequences. Her point is rather that we should treat passion as part of deliberation as long as it has a moral dimension. "Expressions of sentiment can contribute in valuable ways to public deliberation even when they do not take an explicit argumentative form."[21] Krause sees a great range of emotional expressions with the potential of having a moral dimension: "By allowing informal, symbolic, and testimonial types of deliberative expressions, it can enrich citizens' reflection on public issues and thereby improve public deliberation. Such expressions are also tremendously important for the cultivation of moral sentiment."[22] Krause, however, is aware that she runs into the problem of concept-stretching in including too many emotions into the concept of deliberation: "To be sure, it is important to distinguish between deliberative and nondeliberative forms of expression. Not every expression is deliberative, and we risk losing the clarifying power of analysis if we define the category too broadly."[23] To count for Krause as deliberative, emotional acts must "represent (a) efforts to change the minds and hearts of the public, (b) on some matter of law or policy, and (c) with a view to justice."[24] Krause summarizes her overall position in the following way.

Our minds are changed when our hearts are engaged … we cannot be the passionless, disengaged deliberators that we think we ought to be, even when we succeed in deliberating impartially. If this book advances our basic understanding of ourselves, our reflective passions, and our deliberative practices, it will have fulfilled its ambition. What it suggests is that any policy initiatives undertaken on behalf of impartial justice should aim not for the transcendence but for the civilizing of passions in public life.[25]

[20] Krause, *Civil Passions*, p. 54.
[21] Krause, *Civil Passions*, p. 118.
[22] Krause, *Civil Passions*, p. 122.
[23] Krause, *Civil Passions*, p. 119.
[24] Krause, *Civil Passions*, p. 119.
[25] Krause, *Civil Passions*, pp. 125, 203.

Hans Joas argues that it is a different matter whether one deliberates about fundamental values or only about social norms.[26] Whereas a purely rational discourse may be appropriate when social norms are discussed, emotions and stories are crucial when values are involved.

This means that our communication about values is oriented toward a communication about feelings and experiences in ways that are different from rational discourse ... We cannot make plausible and defend our value commitments without telling stories – stories about the experiences from which our commitments arose, about other people's experiences or about consequences a violation against our values had in the past. Biographical and historical narration in this sense is not just a matter of illustration for didactic purposes, but a necessary part of our self-understanding and of our communication about values.[27]

For Susan Bickford, emotions are also an important part of the deliberative model when she writes that "knowing about people's emotions ... is knowing something about how to communicate with them."[28] The crux of her argument is that it is important how we talk about emotion.

[How we do it] is one of the central ways in which people negotiate and dispute meaning and value in political communication ... emotional expressions are interpreted, reacted to, given meaning by ourselves and by others in a context of difference, conflict, and inequality. This context also supplies multiple interpretative frames – ways of talking – about emotion ... these multiple frames lead us to read emotion one way or another, and those readings have particular worldly effects on our ability to communicate democratically.[29]

These reflections of Bickford are of particular interest when we wish to empirically study the effect of emotions in a political discussion. It is no longer sufficient to investigate the influence of emotions per se. One has instead to investigate how emotions are interpreted in a particular context. As an illustration, Bickford mentions that the expression

---

[26] Hans Joas, "Values versus Norms: A Pragmatist Account of Moral Objectivity," *The Hedgehog Review: Critical Reflections on Contemporary Culture* 3 (2001), 42–56.

[27] Joas, "Values versus Norms," 55.

[28] Susan Bickford, "Emotion Talk and Political Judgment," *Journal of Politics* 73 (2011), 1024–37.

[29] Bickford, "Emotion Talk and Political Judgment," 1029, 1032.

of anger by women is often interpreted as hysterical, which it is not if men express anger.

Gary Mucciaroni and Paul J. Quirk bring yet another controversy to the literature about justification. They argue that political decision processes must be led in an *intelligent* way and that this does not only depend to what extent a decision process fulfills criteria of formal logic. They want to compare the claims of legislators "to the best empirical evidence and analysis bearing upon those claims from qualified scholars, researchers, consultants and other experts that was available to legislators at the time the debate takes place. We judge claims to be more realistic, or at least defensible, the more consistent they are with the evidence and informed opinion." Mucciaroni and Quirk "do not think that experts are always correct or that democratically elected legislators should adopt experts' views and dismiss those of their constituents, but we assume that deliberation will be better informed and public policy better served in most cases if legislators follow those who are generally presumed to be most knowledgeable about a topic."[30] With this view of a good justification, Mucciaroni and Quirk argue that it is not enough to have logical linkages between reasons and opinions; these linkages must also be supported by solid empirical research. With this approach, they go beyond the Habermasian notion of rationality in adding a substantive aspect. Mucciaroni and Quirk apply their approach to the US Congress and come up with the result "that debate in Congress included a considerable amount of distortion, misleading information and outright falsehood." They "found particularly discouraging that legislators persistently reassert inaccuracies even after they have been corrected multiple times."[31]

Bernard Reber follows the line of reasoning of Mucciaroni and Quirk in emphasizing the importance of scholarly research for deliberation, particularly when technological projects with long-term consequences are involved. According to Reber, deliberation is most useful when scholarly research shows great uncertainties in what will happen in the far-off future. Deliberation should not be limited to situations where the facts are well established; it is particularly suited for sorting

[30] Gary Mucciaroni and Paul J. Quirk, "Rhetoric and Reality: Going Beyond Discourse Ethics in Assessing Legislative Deliberation," *Legisprudence: International Journal for the Study of Legislation* 4 (2010), 42.
[31] Mucciaroni and Quirk, "Rhetoric and Reality," 49.

out situations with great uncertainties.[32] Thereby, discussion should not be limited to possible alternatives, because some alternatives may be judged impossible by some but possible by others. The very feasibility of alternatives should be deliberated.[33]

Finally, one should also consider that any justification may be utilized for purely strategic reasons. Giovan Francesco Lanzara draws our attention to this possibility when he writes that particular justifications may be used instrumentally in the competition for power.[34] All these controversies in the normative literature about what kinds of justification are best for deliberation cry out for empirical studies, to which we now turn.

(b) Empirical results

Literature review

For rationality and stories as deliberative justifications, the review of the literature brought a rich harvest of useful empirical studies. Let me begin with our earlier investigation of parliamentary debates in Germany, Switzerland, the UK, and the US.[35] At the time, we did not yet include stories, but relied on the Habermasian rationality of justification. Accordingly, our Discourse Quality Index (DQI) defined a sophisticated level of justification as having a certain complexity in the sense that an argument is justified with more than one reason and that these reasons are logically linked with the postulated outcome. The most striking result was the strong difference between plenary sessions

---

[32] Bernard Reber, "Argumenter et délibérer entre éthique et politique," *Archives de Philosophie* 74 (2011), 292–3: "La délibération ne se limite pas aux conflits entre des interprétations qui semblent fondées, assurées et complètes. Elle peut s'appliquer également à ses incertitudes descriptives et normatives."

[33] Reber, "Argumenter et délibérer entre éthique et politique," 293: "il ne faut pas restreindre la discussion aux seuls possibles puisque, par exemple, certaines conséquences sont jugées possibles par les uns et impossible par les autres. La possibilité est l'objet même du débat."

[34] Giovan Francesco Lanzara, "La deliberazione come indagine publicca," in Luigi Pellizzoni (ed.), *La deliberazione publicca* (Rome: Meltemi editore, 2005), p. 55: "giusticare decisioni che hanno solo una motivazione politica, la competizione per il potere."

[35] Jürg Steiner, André Bächtiger, Markus Spörndli, and Marco R. Steenbergen, *Deliberative Politics in Action: Analysing Parliamentary Discourse* (Cambridge University Press, 2005), pp. 98–137.

in the public eye and committee meetings behind closed doors. We analyzed 3,086 speech acts in 52 debates. For plenary debates, 76 percent of the speech acts revealed a sophisticated justification, for committee meetings only 30 percent. If we reduce the level of required complexity, allowing also arguments with a single reason as long as this reason is logically connected to the postulated outcome, 88 percent of the speech acts in plenary sessions and 60 percent in committees fulfill this less-demanding criterion. Thus, the difference still remains between public and non-public meetings. To what extent do these findings correspond to the rationality postulated by Habermas? Discussions in committee meetings behind closed doors were far removed from the Habermasian ideal. Robert E. Goodin gives a good explanation why this may be so:

In ordinary discourse, we generally proceed on the assumption that others are pretty much like ourselves. We merely gesture toward arguments, expecting others to catch the allusions, rather than belabouring points. We talk principally in terms of conclusions, offering in ordinary discussion only the briefest argument-sketch describing our reasoning leading to those conclusions. We do so precisely so as not to belabour the point needlessly.[36]

If we apply this explanation to parliamentary committee meetings behind closed doors, one could say that its members are engaged in ordinary discussion so they can afford to take the shortcuts described by Goodin. What about the debates in plenary sessions with the public looking on? Did they have the intrinsic characteristics that make them compelling to others, as demanded by Habermas? Could one say that it was "a process of argumentation in which those taking part justify their validity claims before an ideally expanded audience,"[37] to use the words of Habermas? In our coding, we only judged whether arguments contained logical chains linking reasons to postulated outcomes. We did not judge, however, how good these reasons were. Some of them were not of a stellar nature in the Habermasian sense. Why not also judge the logical stringency of the arguments? This would not be an impossible task but would involve great measurement problems, so that for the time being we decline to enter this field of measuring

---

[36] Robert E. Goodin, "Talking Politics: Perils and Promise," *European Journal of Political Research* 45 (2006), 253.

[37] Habermas, *Moralbewusstsein und kommunikatives Handeln*, p. 97.

the logical quality of arguments. This means that we can say only that in plenary sessions the overwhelming majority of the speech acts contained some kind of rational reasoning while only very few cases offered no reasoning at all.

Although our initial DQI did not include stories as ways to justify arguments, Bächtiger *et al.* went back to the data and investigated stories for two debates in Switzerland, one on a language article in the constitution, the other on a labor law.[38] For the language article, 30 percent of the speech acts in the plenary sessions contained a personal story, in the committee meetings 19 percent. In the discussion of the labor law, personal stories were rarer: 10 percent in the plenary sessions and 4 percent in committee meetings. These data indicate that storytelling depends on the issue under discussion. Language issues being close to home stimulated more personal stories than the more technical aspects of labor law. It is also noticeable that personal stories are more often told in the public arena of plenary sessions than behind closed doors in committee meetings. The explanation may be that personal stories are particularly useful for making an argument to the voters through the windows of the parliament building. Another result of the analysis of Bächtiger *et al.* is that personal stories are more often told at the beginning of a decision process. This was true for the discussion of the language issue in two plenary sessions: 34 percent personal stories in the first session, dropping to 22 percent in the second session. The committee met eight times, with the number of personal stories evolving from 33 percent to 29, 20, 17, 0, 5, 7, and 8 percent. For the labor law, with its low number of personal stories, the pattern was less clear.

Using an expanded version of our DQI, Dionysia Tamvaki and Christopher Lord investigated 32 plenary sessions of the European Parliament for the period 2004–2009.[39] Compared with the plenary sessions of our national parliaments, sophisticated justifications were much fewer in the European Parliament: 17 percent against 76 percent

[38] André Bächtiger, Susumu Shikano, Seraina Pedrini, and Mirjam Ryser, "Measuring Deliberation: Standards, Discourse Types, and Sequenzialization," paper presented at the ECPR General Conference, Potsdam, September 2009.
[39] Dionysia Tamvaki and Christopher Lord, "The Content and Quality of Representation in the European Assembly: Towards Building an Updated Discourse Quality Index at the EU Level," paper presented at the IPSA International Conference, Luxembourg, March 18–20, 2010.

for the national parliaments. If we reduce the level of required complexity, also allowing arguments with a single reason as long as this reason was logically linked with the postulated outcome, 58 percent in the European Parliament fulfilled this criterion, and 88 percent in the national parliaments. These 58 percent for the European Parliament are comparable to the committee meetings of the national parliaments where the corresponding figure was 60 percent. Why would the debates in the European Parliament with regard to justification be more similar to committee meetings than plenary sessions of national parliaments? One could speculate that plenary sessions of the European Parliament get little public attention, so its members take more shortcuts in their justifications, similar to what happens in committee meetings of national parliaments.

Having looked at parliamentary debates in four Western democracies and the EU, I turn now to the level of ordinary citizens. How rational are their political arguments and to what extent do they rely on personal stories to support their points? There is empirical evidence that ordinary citizens often use personal stories to support their arguments. This depends, however, on the issue under discussion. I begin with a research finding in which storytelling was not prominent. Francesca Polletta and John Lee studied an online discussion of New York citizens about how to rebuild the World Trade Center site.[40] In a forum sponsored by rebuilding authorities and civic groups, participants were asked to make recommendations about housing, transportation, economic development, and a memorial for the victims of the disaster. There were 26 groups participating in this online forum. Participants registered in advance and could post their opinions only to their own group. Polletta and Lee chose 12 of these groups for their study. In general, people were more likely to advance their opinions by way of reasons than personal stories. Narrative claims accounted for only 11 percent of all claims. Women were more likely than men to tell personal stories. There was no variation in storytelling by income, education, and race. Polletta and Lee wanted to know: "What responses do stories elicit compared to reasons? Does storytelling foster or impede the unconstrained give-and-take, flexibility of agenda, and uncoerced

---

[40] Francesca Polletta and John Lee, "Is Telling Stories Good for Democracy? Rhetoric in Public Deliberation after 9/11," *American Sociological Review* 71 (2006), 699–723.

agreement that are the hallmarks of good deliberation?"[41] The results show that "a narrative claim was three times as likely as a non-narrative claim to be responded with agreement or disagreement, a request for clarification or elaboration, doubt about the claim's generalizability or relevance, corroboration, or alleged misinterpretation."[42] Polletta and Lee conclude from this finding that "storytelling is able to secure a sympathetic hearing for positions unlikely to gain such a hearing otherwise ... These assets are especially important for disadvantaged groups insofar as their perspectives are more likely to be marginal to mainstream policy debate."[43] More generally, Polletta and Lee argue that

stories' creation of an alternative reality makes it possible for audiences to identify with experiences quite unlike their own while still recognizing those experiences. Stories' dependence on a cultural stock of plots enables storytellers to advance novel points of view within the familiar form of canonical storylines. Stories' openness to interpretation encourages tellers and listeners to collaborate in drawing lessons from personal experience ... stories may be effective insofar as their normative conclusions are ambiguous. Stories' openness to interpretation makes it possible for deliberators to suggest compromise on their positions without antagonizing fellow deliberators.[44]

These are strong claims for the helpfulness of stories for good deliberation. Of particular importance in the research of Polletta and Lee is that storytelling helps the disadvantaged societal groups, since equality in being heard is a key ingredient of good deliberation.

Jennifer Stromer-Galley reports on another online discussion where she pays attention to storytelling.[45] The basis of her study is the Virtual Agora Project at Carnegie Mellon University in Pittsburgh, which brought together residents to discuss in small groups problems of the city's public schools. More specifically, the issue to be focused on was what to do with underutilized schools.[46] Participants were assigned to 23 online discussion groups. In this context, storytelling was much more frequent than in the New York study about how to rebuild the

---

[41] Polletta and Lee, "Is Telling Stories Good for Democracy?," 705.
[42] Polletta and Lee, "Is Telling Stories Good for Democracy?," 714.
[43] Polletta and Lee, "Is Telling Stories Good for Democracy?," 718.
[44] Polletta and Lee, "Is Telling Stories Good for Democracy?," 718.
[45] Jennifer Stromer-Galley, "Measuring Deliberation's Content: A Coding Scheme," *Journal of Public Deliberation* 3 (2007), 1–35.
[46] The project included also face-to-face discussions but because of equipment malfunctioning these discussions were not recorded.

World Trade Center site. Indeed, in the Pittsburgh study, "personal anecdotes were used most frequently ... Participants in deliberations primarily use their personal experiences as a basis from which to reason."[47] Some 33 percent of all arguments were supported by personal stories. When participants gave non-personal reasons, they relied in particular on the briefing materials handed out to the groups and the media. Why were personal stories so much more frequent in Pittsburgh than in New York? An obvious reason is that personal experiences with schools are much more common than experiences with rebuilding the site of the World Trade Center. In a critical way, Stromer-Galley notes "a high amount of off-topic talk."[48] One can easily imagine that personal stories did not always strictly focus on the assigned topic of what to do with underutilized schools. Does such off-topic talk necessarily have to be seen in a negative way, as Stromer-Galley does? As we have seen above, Polletta and Lee take another view in considering the ambiguous nature of storytelling as helpful for deliberation in that it reduces the risk of antagonizing fellow deliberators. From this perspective, someone may tell a funny story about his or her schooldays that has little or nothing to do with underutilized schools but helps to lighten the atmosphere. Are such off-topic stories an unnecessary and harmful waste of time or a facilitating factor for better deliberation in further discussions? This is an interesting issue to ponder when I come to my normative conclusions in the last section of the chapter.

Elzbieta Wesolowska addresses the function of storytelling for good deliberation in a study of Polish parents of school-age children discussing the issue of sex education in schools.[49] This is once again a topic very much amenable to telling personal stories. This was particularly the case when the groups consisted only of women. For these situations, Wesolowska summarizes her findings as follows:

Common experiences and emotions accompanying them were shared. These experiences included the discovery of individual sexuality at a young age and later, motherhood. Women told each other about their anxieties, curiosities, hopes and other feelings accompanying these experiences, communicating

[47] Stromer-Galley, "Measuring Deliberation's Content," 15, 19.
[48] Stromer-Galley, "Measuring Deliberation's Content," 19.
[49] Elzbieta Wesolowska, "Social Processes of Antagonism and Synergy in Deliberating Groups," *Swiss Political Science Review* 13 (2007), 663–80.

them quite often through story telling. The main protagonists in these stories were mostly disputants themselves. Some of the stories were very personal and intimate. Quite often a story told by one person was followed by a similar story told by another. Thus, a sort of "chain exchange of stories" was observed. Participants conveyed their knowledge, feelings and convictions in an easy to understand and memorable way concluding their stories with practical recommendations concerning proper sex-education at schools.[50]

Wesolowska concludes from her investigation that "effective deliberation need not be the exchange of rational argumentation ... The narrative mode of communication, where values, experiences and knowledge are passed in the form of storytelling, lead to agreement."[51]

Marli Huijer offers another set of data demonstrating the beneficial effects of storytelling for deliberation.[52] She studied the political debate in the Netherlands about embryo selection for hereditary breast cancer (pre-implantation genetic diagnosis, PGD). On May 26, 2008, the State Secretary of Health of the Labor Party announced that embryo selection for hereditary breast cancer would henceforth be permitted. Her argument stressed patient autonomy so that female carriers of a serious hereditary disease should have the option of PGD to protect their children. This argument was opposed by the Reformed Christian Party, who warned of a slippery slope: since we are all genetically at risk for something, in the end this decision would be used for all kind of potential hereditary diseases. Good health should not be of higher priority than human life itself. At the beginning of the debate, the two positions were presented in stark contrast, not leaving space for compromise. Then ordinary people with hereditary breast cancer in their families began to tell their stories in the media, taking positions on both sides of the issue. Huijer characterizes these stories in the following way:

Rather than providing simple answers, [the stories] emphasized the moral complexity of the situation. A clear plot was often lacking. Moreover, their style of speaking was more emotional and less rhetorical; it was more aimed at reaching understanding than persuading others ... [the stories] were more

---

[50] Wesolowska, "Social Processes of Antagonism," 674.
[51] Wesolowska, "Social Processes of Antagonism," 676.
[52] Marli Huijer, "Storytelling to Enrich the Democratic Debate: The Dutch Discussion on Embryo Selection for Hereditary Breast Cancer," *BioSocieties* 4 (2009), 223–38.

ambiguous than those of the politicians ... The stories had the power to complement and open up the arguments used in the PGD discussion.[53]

Huijer's analysis identifies a strong effect of these stories on the debate among politicians:

In sum, after listening to the ambiguous stories of women and men who directly experienced the anguish of living with hereditary breast cancer, the unambiguous and principled way the Labour Party and the Reformed Christian Party started the public discussion on PGD for hereditary breast cancer came across as disrespectful. The stories helped to transform the public sphere, where politicians and the public generally act and speak, into a realm where people were prepared to listen to each other and reach mutual understanding.[54]

This understanding involved a compromise solution with which both political parties could live: "each request for PGD was to be separately evaluated. Assisted by a multidisciplinary team of experts, in each case the patient and physician are to take into account the severity and nature of the disease, the treatment options, additional medical criteria, and psychological and moral factors."[55] Huijer concludes from her research that "more than any reasoned argument the stories of the carriers demonstrate the moral complexity of their situation. In a democracy, where most political leaders and private citizens prefer clear-cut positions to ambiguity, that is a huge accomplishment."[56]

As Nevin T. Aiken reports, storytelling has also had a positive influence in deeply divided Northern Ireland.[57] He studied groups in local communities engaged in programs designed to encourage cross-community contact and dialogue.[58]

Such dialogues have tended to take the form of carefully mediated "storytelling" forums in which a small number of nationalists and unionists are brought together to share their personal experiences of past conflict and hear those of the other community ... such processes may be essential to

---

[53] Huijer, "Storytelling to Enrich the Democratic Debate," 234.
[54] Huijer, "Storytelling to Enrich the Democratic Debate," 236.
[55] Huijer, "Storytelling to Enrich the Democratic Debate," 235.
[56] Huijer, "Storytelling to Enrich the Democratic Debate," 237.
[57] Nevin T. Aiken, "Learning to Live Together: Transitional Justice and Intergroup Reconciliation in Northern Ireland," *International Journal of Transitional Justice* 4 (2010), 166–88.
[58] Aiken, "Learning to Live Together," 184.

reconciliation as they allow people a chance to look beyond their political narratives and stereotypes to individualize and humanize the Other ... storytelling can lead not only to a greater willingness to reconcile in the present but also to a more nuanced and empathetic understanding of the past.[59]

By contrast, Aiken finds that storytelling in the frame of legal investigations may even inflame intercommunity tensions. "One of the most prominent of these [cases] was the 1998 decision by British Prime Minister Tony Blair to establish an independent judicial inquiry into the events of 'Bloody Sunday', an incident in which 14 Catholics were killed by British soldiers on 30 January 1972 in the city of Derry."[60]

For many of those family members who came forward to provide testimony, the adversarial process of cross-examination by state lawyers during the inquiry led to a highly antagonistic rather than cathartic experience ... the inquiry has largely served to inflame rather than reduce intercommunal tensions ... it's not a very good way of building better relationships between communities – in fact it's quite confrontational.[61]

With his investigation of storytelling in Northern Ireland, Aiken makes the important point that the effect of storytelling on intercommunity reconciliation depends to a great extent on the context in which stories are told. It seems that the more informal and relaxed the context, the more likely it is that storytelling will have a positive effect. This review of the literature gives a rich picture of the role of storytelling, so that I will have a solid basis in the last section to say something on the normative controversies concerning storytelling in the deliberative model raised in the first section.

New data on deliberative experiments[62]

In contrast to our earlier investigation of parliamentary debates, we have now also included stories in our DQI. As we have seen earlier in the chapter, not all stories have a deliberative character. It is difficult, however, to distinguish in a reliable and valid way categories of deliberative and non-deliberative stories. Therefore, for the time being, we

---

[59] Aiken, "Learning to Live Together," 185–6.
[60] Aiken, "Learning to Live Together," 178.
[61] Aiken, "Learning to Live Together," 178.
[62] For the research designs, see Introduction, Section (b).

have not yet coded stories on this basis, but have preferred qualitative analyses. I begin with such a qualitative analysis that Maria Clara Jaramillo has done for experiments with ex-combatants in *Colombia*. She looked at the internal dynamic of how the discussions evolved in the experiments. She was particularly interested in whether there were *transformative moments* when the discussions became more deliberative. A good example of such a transformative moment based on a personal story occurred in an experiment with 17 participants from both the left-wing ex-guerillas and the right-wing ex-paramilitaries. At first, the two sides talked across each other, not reacting to what previous speakers had said. A necessary precondition for any deliberation is that a dialogue takes place in which the participants engage with each other. When the participants speak only in a monological way, one cannot talk of deliberation. In this particular experiment, the change from a monological to a dialogical pattern occurred with the sixth speaker, Javier, who presented his personal story of why he had joined the guerillas.[63] To get a good sense of what he said, I present his entire story:[64]

I finished high school in 2002. I'm from Valle del Cauca.[65] My father is a truck driver. I used to like being around him. He gives a very bad life to my mother as he drinks a lot. I then decided to go out on my own. I made some money and left for Meta.[66] In Meta I did very well. I had learned how to drive when I was thirteen years old, with my father. He taught me. In Meta, I found a job driving a car. It was the first time for me to go to a guerrilla area. The first time that I saw the guerrilla people, I was very scared. They would ask me why I was so scared. They told me not to be scared. They told me to join the organization. There was this guy who died later on. His name was Omar. He showed me a little device and a computer and he asked me to locate where we were. As I properly pointed the exact place in which we were located in Meta, he told me I was smart and that I could be of use for them. I said that I was afraid of fire arms. He promised that I could move forward in life, if I decided to join them. I don't know. I thought it was something good and I told him I was going to think about it. After that, he

---

[63] Names in this section have been changed.
[64] Translation from Spanish by Maria Clara Jaramillo.
[65] Valle del Cauca is one of the 30 political divisions that Colombia is divided into, located southwest of Bogotá.
[66] Another Department in Colombia, located east of Bogotá and with great presence of the guerrillas.

would contact me every twenty days. He would send a girl, a boy, even he himself would come. I would often go to their camp and talk to him. He would talk a lot to me about politics. He had so many books. One day, we arrived at a place and Omar had died. There was someone new in charge. I tried to put some distance, to move away from them and they kept calling me, trying to convince me to join them. I would answer that I didn't like that, that I was afraid of fire arms. He told me whether I wanted to come to Bogota and study. I studied for a semester but then had to leave because a girl from another FARC front who was also at the university was caught. I then joined the regular Colombian army, where I had to see so many things. They humiliate you. They mistreat you. Life in the army is such a terrible life. It is like a dog's life. I thought that in the guerrillas they never treat you as badly as in the army. They would never hit you with a stick or kick you. This is definitely not life as it should be.

Javier's story of why he ultimately joined the guerrillas does not seem to have a clear point for the discussion topic assigned to the participants of the experiment. When he tells his story, he does not put forward any argument as to what his definition of the Colombian conflict is or what he thinks the solution should look like. He starts with his story right away in a process that can be interpreted as setting up his identity; he tells us who he is, where he was born, the kind of family life he had, the relationship between his mother and father. Then he leads us into his own personal route into the FARC guerilla. He tells us how he first met guerrilla people, how he eventually decided to join. The next speaker was Fernando, and he was the first one to refer to a previous speaker. He asks Javier how his personal story related to the discussion about the future of Colombia. Fernando puts this question in a respectful way, showing genuine interest in why Javier had told the group his personal story. Javier tries to answer but is obviously taken aback by the question and mumbles "that the people in Colombia are very, very intelligent, very important, people worth a great deal and that Colombia is a very rich country." This answer hardly answers the question of why he joined FARC; he is not making a logical connection between people in Colombia being intelligent and worthwhile and his joining the guerillas. But somehow this exchange between Javier and Fernando broke the ice. From then on, participants talked with each other, taking up arguments that others had brought up. The exchange between Javier and Fernando was a transformative moment, building up trust so that the monological talking could change into a dialogical pattern.

As we have seen in the literature review, not all stories have a deliberative character. Jaramillo has also found stories that acted as deliberation stoppers. In another group of ex-combatants, deliberation began at quite a high level. Thus, the first speaker makes a reasoned argument that giving more social and economic opportunities to the poor will be a step to overcome violence. The following speakers keep up the good level of deliberation in pursuing the discussion of previous speakers. A transformative moment comes with the sixth speaker, who at first does not see any hope for solving the violent conflict in Colombia. Referring to the example of himself, he states that it is about time for people to think about the fact that some day they are going to die so they should strengthen their faith, and, contradicting his earlier position, faith would after all solve the violence issue. How to react to this very personal and also very confusing statement? The following speakers are taken aback and do not follow the interactive path of the beginning of the discussion. The sixth speaker apparently has derailed the deliberative thread with his personal experience with faith.

We looked at the Colombian data not only from a qualitative but also from a quantitative perspective. This task was taken on by Juan Ugarriza. In the 28 experiments, a total of 1,027 speech acts were made. In 41 percent of all speech acts no opinion was expressed; an example of such a speech act reads as follows: "When we talk about violence, we are dealing with the topic as if it were only guerrillas and paramilitaries, and it is not so. Because there is also domestic violence, violence against children."[67] This statement does not imply an opinion of what should or should not be done. I exclude such speech acts, taking only speech acts where an opinion was expressed as 100 percent and present how these opinions were justified.

No justification at all	36%
Justification with an illustration	34%
Reason given, but no connection with opinion	17%
Reason given, connection with opinion	10%
More than one reason, connections with opinion	3%
Total speech acts with opinion	100%

---

[67] "Cuando se habla de violencia estamos manejando como el tema que no es sino que ... como guerrilla y paramilitares, y no es así. Porque hay violencia intrafamiliar, hay violencia contra los niños."

In order to give some feeling for the coding categories, here are illustrations for each category.[68]

An opinion without any justification: "My proposal is that everyone is given a house, everyone from a low social class. Sure, and education."[69] In order to emphasize that this proposal does not need any particular justification, the speaker exclaims "claro," a commonly used expression in Colombia.

Justification with an illustration: "We also ask for more security for ourselves. I have been victim of three attempts here in Bogota. I have been shot. I have been wounded. Because I was a commander."[70] The speaker uses in an effective way his personal story to justify more security measures for ex-combatants.

Reason given but no connection with opinion: "We need more investors in Colombia. It is just that we need rich people so there is employment."[71] The speaker claims that more rich people will lead to more employment but the causal linkage between the two items is not explained.

Reason given, connection made with opinion: "If there was not drug trafficking, there would not be armed groups. If coca is legalized, it all becomes legal commerce. The only thing that can put war to an end, so there is peace is that drug trafficking ends."[72] The speaker argues that making drugs legal would lead to legal commerce, thus making drug trafficking and armed groups redundant and therefore causing peace.

More than one reason given, connections made with opinion: "Another very good proposal for this country is to build more roads. This is the richest of countries. But what happens? People want to have more economic development, but have no roads. People should have a way to send out livestock, fish, pigs, everything, crops. Where I come from there are no access roads. And hence people are forced by

---

[68] Translation by Juan Ugarriza.
[69] "La propuesta mía es que den vivienda a todos los ciudadano de estrato bajo. ¡Claro! Y educación."
[70] "Nosotros pedimos acá también más seguridad para nosotros ... A mí me han hecho tres atentados acá en Bogotá. Me han dado balín. Me han herido, ... porque uno fue comandante."
[71] "Necesitamos más inversionistas en Colombia. Es que nosotros necesitamos de los ricos para que haya empleo."
[72] "Si no hubiera narcotráfico no habría de pronto grupos armados. Se legaliza la coca y entonces eso ya se vuelve ... comercial ... Lo único para acabar ... o sea, que haya paz acá, es que no haya más narcotráfico."

nature's law to grow coca. And from there, violence increases. Coca, marijuana, opium, all of that. By the law of nature, a kilo of coca can be carried for five, six days and does not weigh much. But a sack of yucca or potato has to be abandoned after three hours."[73] The speaker links building roads with reducing violence and offers more than one reason to make this causal connection. He also presents a personal story, but only to reinforce the general argument and not as sole justification. This is an illustration of the highest level of justification that we found for the ex-combatants in Colombia. Looking at the vocabulary and the sentence structures in the original Spanish, this is certainly not the most elegant speech, but with regard to substance, the argument has quite a high complexity.

How shall we evaluate the level of justification for these Colombian ex-combatants? Compared with the parliamentary debates in Germany, Switzerland, the UK, and the US, the level of justification of opinions was very low. Whereas the ex-combatants reached the highest level of justification in only 3 percent of speech acts, we remember from earlier in this section that in the national parliamentary debates the corresponding figures were 76 percent for plenary sessions and still 30 percent for committee meetings. We should acknowledge, however, that ex-combatants attempted to justify their opinions in some way or another in 64 percent of the cases. To be sure, in most instances this was not done in a sophisticated way, either only with an illustration or a reason not clearly linked to the expressed opinion. I conclude that given the little formal education of most ex-combatants and their traumatic recent past, it was rather good how they tried to justify their opinions and thus to be interactive. We should not operate with a uniform standard of what constitutes good justification but always

---

[73] "Otra propuesta muy buena de pronto para este país es por lo menos vías de comunicación, vías de penetración. Porque en estos momentos hay ... este país es el más rico de los países. ¿Pero qué pasa? O sea, de pronto donde la gente quiere tener un desarrollo económico pero no tiene las vías ... Que la gente tenga cómo poder mandar de pronto ganadería, pescadería, marranerías, de todo, agricultura ... De donde yo vengo es una tierra de la que es en realidadmente no hay vías de penetración ..., entonces la gente por ley de naturaleza tiene que sembrar coca. Y de ahí la incrementación de la violencia. La coca y la marihuana, el opio, de todo eso ... Por ley de naturaleza: porque un kilo de coca usted anda cinco o seis días y eso no le pesa nada. Mientras usted con un bulto de yuca para sacarlo, y a las tres horas tiene que dejarlo abandonado."

consider the context. Thus, it is unfair to compare the level of justification of Colombian ex-combatants with that of parliamentarians in mature democracies. We might have expected that ex-combatants would be reluctant to express any opinions at all. Thus, it is not too bad that 59 percent of the speech acts contained an opinion and that it was in about two-thirds of these speech acts that the opinions were justified in some way or another.

I now report binary analysis for the level of justification.[74] Ex-combatants had very different levels of education: 7 percent had no formal education at all, 32 percent 1–5 years, 51 percent 6–11 years, and 10 percent 12 years or more. We have already seen in Chapter 1 that those with a low level of education more often did not speak up during the entire experiment. When they actually did speak up, it was often without expressing a specific opinion. Thus, the opinions of those who were least educated entered the discussion the least often. When they did express an opinion, however, it is remarkable that they justified it about as well as the better educated. One would expect that with a higher level of education and therefore better cognitive skills, sophisticated justifications would become more prevalent. But this was not the case. Perhaps those with little or no formal education felt under particular social pressure to justify their arguments. It is puzzling why those with university education did not use their cognitive skills more often to justify their arguments in a sophisticated way. A possible explanation could be that participants with a high level of education often did not bother to justify their opinions in a sophisticated way because they took it as self-evident that their opinions were correct. But it could also be that those with a university education did not wish to show off their intellectual skills to those with little or no education.[75] This is a good example of how often in the social sciences empirical data can be interpreted in a conflicting way. Further analyses have not shown any significant differences by age and gender.

Like in Colombia, Simona Mameli found for *Bosnia–Herzegovina* instances where stories functioned as transformative moments to make the discussion more interactive. An illustration is from one of the experiments in Srebrenica with Serbs and Bosnjaks (Muslims). Almost

---

[74] Binary analyses in this chapter will be supplemented in Chapter 9 by multiple regressions.

[75] This interpretation was pointed out to me by Christiane Lemke.

at the beginning of the discussion, a Bosnjak man proposed that "someone should try to push through a law on the protection and welfare of animals that would, for example, shelter dogs, cats, and others. I cannot send my child to walk to school. I have to drive her." The problem of stray dogs concerned everyone, both Serbs and Bosnjaks. After the Bosnjak man had spoken, he immediately received support from a Serbian man and then from a Serbian woman. Everyone had stories to tell about the nuisance of stray dogs. A quick back-and-forth developed in the conversation. A Serbian woman told the story of a dog in front of the supermarket; a Bosnjak woman enquired whether she meant the one with a broken leg. A Serbian man warned that the problem with stray dogs will become worse with the first snow falling. And more such stories followed. Based on all these stories, it was easy to agree that shelters are needed for stray dogs. Across the deep divide between Serbs and Bosnjaks, stray dogs were a common problem. It was not raised as an abstract policy issue but by the story of the Bosnjak man saying that he was so worried about stray dogs that he did not dare to make his girl walk to school. This was a story with which everyone could identify, a *transformative moment* making the conversation interactive in a deliberative sense.

Later in the same experiment in Srebrenica, again personal stories helped interactivity and to reach consensus, this time to clean the river. A Bosnjak man told the group, "I walk there every day, a willow tree fell in the river bed, and people throw everything away, sofa, trash, garbage." A Serb woman gave support, "you know, the problem is garbage." A Serb man added, "people throw trash, throw all the garbage." As we saw in the discussion on stray dogs, garbage in the river has no ethnic connotation and is of concern for both Serbs and Bosnjaks. Stories are offered from both sides and help mutual understanding of the problem.

Still later in the experiment, a Bosnjak woman expressed concern "about wild pigs that come down into the city." Again this stimulates storytelling. A Bosnjak man reports that "down in Black River one wild pig literally came in the courtyard." A Serb woman remembers that "one night one came down and got stuck in the fence." At this point a Serb woman joked that "pigs also want to learn a little culture here." A Serb man continued the joke, "where we live is also wilderness so that for pigs it is all the same." Half-jokingly, a Serb woman proposed, "here is a hunter, let him solve the problem." Everyone had to laugh at all these jokes, showing how jokes can relax the atmosphere, an argument made by Sammy Basu, as we have seen earlier in the chapter. The multitude of stories and jokes about wild pigs contributed to an easy-going interactive conversation. Like stray dogs and garbage, wild pigs helped to transcend the ethnic divide between Serbs and Bosnjaks.

If, for the Srebrenica experiment, we look at the speech acts from a quantitative perspective, we see that in 37 percent of the speech acts no opinion was expressed, about the same as the 41 percent in Colombia. If we take for Srebrenica, as we have done for Colombia, only the speech acts where an opinion was expressed, we get the following results:

No justification at all	79%
Justification with an illustration	12%
Reason given, but no connection with opinion	3%
Reason given, connection with opinion	6%
More than one reason, connection with opinion	0%
Total speech acts with opinion	100%

Compared with Colombia, in Srebrenica a much higher percentage of opinions were not justified, which does not look deliberative at all. Yet, we also noticed, as shown above, that stories helped to create an easy-going atmosphere. As we remember from Chapter 1, virtually all speech acts in Srebrenica lasted less than a minute and there was a quick give-and-take, not leaving much space for justifications. This pattern in the conversation may have contributed to the easy-going atmosphere. Stating in quick order opinions without justifications perhaps avoided contentious arguments. To be sure, such a pattern is not deliberative according to the usual standards, but in a traumatized place like Srebrenica the first priority must be that people across the deep ethnic divide begin to recognize each other as human beings. To reach this goal, telling stories, even funny ones, and not much attempting to justify one's opinions, may be an appropriate way to have a conversation. From a longitudinal perspective, this may be a good basis to develop later on more deliberative patterns. This is a good example to demonstrate that one should look at deliberation not only from a micro level of individual speech acts but also from a macro systemic level. In war-torn countries, beginning a conversation with stories and not much justification may be a good thing from the perspective of developing in the long run a deliberative system. In the experiments in *Stolac* with Croats and Bosnjaks, the situation was basically the same as in Srebrenica with many colorful stories but few rational justifications.

In *Belgium*, Didier Caluwaerts did nine experiments with 1,664 speech acts altogether. In 13 percent of the speech acts no opinion was expressed, much less than in Colombia and Bosnia–Herzegovina. Living in an advanced democracy, and, particularly, not being traumatized by an internal armed struggle, Belgians felt very much at ease to express their opinions. Taking only speech acts with an expressed opinion as 100 percent, we get the following distribution for the level of justification:

No justification at all	18%
Justification with an illustration	27%
Reason given, but no connection with opinion	12%
Reason given, connection with opinion	38%
More than one reason, connection with opinion	5%
Total speech acts with opinion	100%

This level of justification is much higher than in Colombia and Bosnia–Herzegovina, but lower than among parliamentarians. In Belgium, 43 percent of the speech acts contained at least one reason connected with the expressed opinion. As we have seen earlier in the section, the corresponding figures are 88 percent for plenary sessions of national parliaments, 60 percent for committee meetings of national parliaments, and 58 percent for plenary sessions of the European Parliament. Although the figures are lower for ordinary Belgian citizens, it is remarkable that they are not so much lower than for committee meetings of national parliaments and plenary sessions of the European Parliament, which indicates that one should not underestimate the capacity of ordinary citizens in advanced democracies to justify their opinions in a logically coherent way. While it is no surprise that parliamentarians have a higher level of justification than ordinary Belgian citizens, neither is it surprising that the latter have a higher level than traumatized participants in Colombia and Bosnia–Herzegovina. This difference can be interpreted as a hopeful sign that with increased democratization ordinary citizens learn to justify their arguments in a more coherent way, which augurs well for Colombia and Bosnia–Herzegovina if they make progress in a democratic direction.

As we remember from the research design discussed in the Introduction, in Belgium the participants in one-third of the experiments were homogeneous Flemish, one-third homogeneous Walloon, and one-third mixed between the two groups. We expected that the level of deliberation would be highest in the two homogeneous groups; with regard to justification, however, this is not the case. On the contrary, arguments were more coherently justified in the mixed groups. Post hoc, one may argue that being among members of the same language group, one feels less need to extensively justify one's arguments than when being confronted with members of the other language group. In the latter case, participants risked less often taking shortcuts in their justifications so that the other side did not miss their arguments.

A binary breakdown by age, gender, and education shows that younger participants, men, and the highly educated more often use rational justifications. We have also data on whether participants used stories from their personal experiences. Some 20 percent of all speech acts contained such stories. In 2 percent the stories were unrelated to an argument, in 11 percent they were the sole justification for an argument, and in 7 percent they helped to strengthen a rational argument. In the mixed groups stories were more often used than in the homogeneous groups, which reinforces the point made above that in the mixed groups a special effort was made to justify one's position to the other side of the language divide. Women used stories more often than men; there were no significant differences by age and education.

For *Europolis* the level of justification is similar to Belgium. While in Belgium 18 percent of the speech acts contained no justification, for Europolis it was 19 percent. At the other end, in Belgium 43 percent gave at least one reason connected with the expressed opinion, in Europolis 41 percent.

No justification at all	19%
Reason given, but no connection with opinion or only with illustration	40%
Reason given, connection with opinion	30%
More than one reason, connection with opinion	11%
Total speech acts with opinion	100%

For the interpretation of the great similarity between Belgium and Europolis one must consider that participants in Europolis were encouraged by the moderators to justify their arguments, while in Belgium moderators did not give any such encouragement. This may mean that without encouragement the level of justification would have been lower for Europolis than for Belgium; it may also mean, however, that the encouragement did not have any effect. There is no way to know which interpretation is more valid, which points to the problem when moderators intervene in the discussion.

For the eight *Finnish* experiments on nuclear power, there were 1,189 speech acts expressing a view on the topic.

No justification at all	12%
Reason given, but no connection with opinion	47%
Reason given, connection with opinion	35%
More than one reason, connection with opinion	6%
Total speech acts with opinion	100%

Looking at the speech acts where one or more than one reason was connected with the expressed opinion, the data are virtually the same as in Belgium and Europolis: 43 percent for Belgium and 41 percent each for Europolis and Finland. One has to consider that in Finland, like for Europolis, participants were encouraged by the moderators to justify their opinions so that the results for Europolis and Finland are most comparable, and it is remarkable that there are no significant differences between the two data sets. One could perhaps have expected that in a homogeneous country like Finland, participants would have taken shortcuts more often than in Europolis, where people would have felt more need to justify their opinions to strangers from other countries. One could also have expected differences in the opposite direction in the sense that, being in a foreign environment, participants in Europolis may have felt less at ease to justify their arguments than people in Finland who were meeting in familiar surroundings. None of these two hypotheses turns out to have any validity since there were no differences in the level of justification between Finland and Europolis. Has Europeanization so much progressed that it does not make a big difference whether one meets in a national or a European context, at least not in how one justifies one's opinion? Binary analyses of the Finnish data show no significant differences by gender and age, while those with the lowest level of education had the lowest level of rational justification.

(c) Normative implications of empirical results

Stories were an important topic in the first two sections of this chapter.[76] What can empirical data tell us about the role of storytelling in the deliberative model of democracy? First of all, storytelling is prevalent at both the elite and the mass level. Members of parliament and ordinary citizens often use stories to justify their arguments. Sometimes, this happens in combination with a rational justification, sometimes stories are used as sole justification. It seems to me that quite often storytelling is compatible and even helpful for the values postulated by the deliberative model. This was most clearly revealed in the experiments with ex-combatants in Colombia. Given their traumatic memories and their reluctance to participate in the experiments, they had the tendency to shy away from engaging each other in an interactive way. Often, it was a personal story with a human touch that broke the ice. After such a story, ex-combatants tended to be more willing to engage each other and to recognize each other's identity and problems. The practical lesson is that personal stories are particularly helpful to encourage deliberation if the atmosphere is tense and frozen, as among ex-combatants in a war-torn country. Appeals to rational arguments are much less helpful in such situations for people to engage each other in a deliberative interactive way. Personal stories may often be the only hope to loosen up the atmosphere. Stories also helped in Bosnia–Herzegovina to create a climate of deliberation. We have seen how in Srebrenica stories about stray dogs, wild pigs, and trash in the river helped Serbs and Bosnjaks to see that they have common problems across the deep ethnic divide.

The interactive potential of storytelling is not only revealed in our own research but also in the research of other deliberative scholars. The online discussion of New York citizens about the rebuilding of the World Trade Center site has shown that stories have a high chance of being responded to. Storytellers are asked to elaborate and to clarify the implications of their stories. Thus, stories encourage a give-and-take in the discussion. The Polish project of parents discussing sex

---

[76] See also the experiments of Baccaro *et al.* reported in Chapter 10 where they found that moderators of mini-publics should not put too much emphasis on structure and rationality but also allow some loose bantering with storytelling and emotions.

education also reveals the interactive potential of storytelling. Quite often a story told by one person was followed by similar stories by other persons so that an entire chain of stories resulted. Such chains of stories often concluded with practical recommendations concerning proper sex education. From the perspective of the deliberative model, another beneficial effect of storytelling is that it helps the socially disadvantaged to get a better voice. This was visible in the Colombian experiments where ex-combatants with no or little formal schooling could use personal stories to get the attention of other participants. That personal stories help the disadvantaged is also reported from the online discussion of New York citizens about the rebuilding of the World Trade Center site. Still another possible advantage from the perspective of the deliberative model is that stories do not tend to antagonize other participants. This finding is also reported from the discussion about the World Trade Center site where it was found that stories usually have an ambiguous character and are open for interpretation, which takes a sharp edge off the discussion. If one agrees with the conclusions resulting from stories, often it may not be altogether clear to what extent the storytellers actually agree with each other. This vagueness may indeed contribute to an atmosphere of less antagonism, but it may, of course, also have the disadvantage that the ambiguity of the discussion prevents a clear-cut decision.

There are still other possible problems with storytelling. In the first section of the chapter, we have seen that some theorists fear that stories are used in a manipulative way to one's own advantage. There is some basis for such fear when we recall that parliamentarians use stories more often in plenary sessions than in committee meetings. In plenary sessions, members of parliament often speak to the viewing public, and then it is tempting to use stories in order to manipulate public opinion. Behind closed doors in committee meetings, by contrast, stories are less effective for manipulation, which could explain why in this context they are less often used. Another problem with storytelling occurred when citizens of Pittsburgh discussed what to do with underutilized schools and often went off-topic. It is certainly a problem when stories are unrelated to the issue under discussion, because participants may lose interest and the discussion begins to drift away. One should also consider, however, that off-topic stories, in particular in the form of good and not offensive jokes, may loosen up the atmosphere, which, in turn, may help to increase the level of deliberation. In this context, I want to address the controversial issue among theorists of whether stories always need to connect the particular to the general in order to be valuable. As we recall, Dryzek answers the question in the positive, Morrell in the negative. From the experience with stories in our experiments, I take a middle position. It is legitimate that someone tells a story related only to particulars of his or her life. During the further discussion, however, other participants should make an effort to relate this particular story to a more general level.

When we consider all positive and negative consequences of storytelling, how well does it fit the deliberative model when participants in a political discussion try to justify and strengthen their arguments with stories? In my view, the fit is not too bad. If indeed the empirical analyses hold up that storytelling contributes to increased reciprocity, to more equality, and to less animosity, the picture looks favorable from a deliberative perspective. To be sure, the negative sides are that stories may be used in a manipulative way and that they can take the discussion away from the issue under discussion. When mini-publics such as citizen juries are organized, moderators need to take account of these possible shortcomings. They must take care that the discussion remains focused and that stories are not misused in a manipulative way. We have also seen that stories are more useful at the beginning of a discussion and that not all issues are equally suitable for storytelling. Moderators of mini-publics need to take account of these findings in encouraging stories more at the beginning of a discussion and to consider for which issues stories are appropriate. Moderators should also be aware that women tend to put more emphasis on storytelling than men and that the highly educated more often use rational arguments than the less educated.

There is currently in the deliberative literature great enthusiasm for the positive role of storytelling. I agree with the remark of Landwehr, quoted in the first section of the chapter, that "we have to be careful to consider in how far we can embrace rhetoric and storytelling without giving up what is essential to deliberation: the give-and-take of reasons." I could demonstrate that reason-giving even occurs to some extent among Colombian ex-combatants with little or no formal education. Therefore, we should not let the deliberative model drift too far into storytelling. Not only professional politicians but also ordinary citizens tend to be quite capable of supporting arguments with reasons. Moderators in mini-publics should not hesitate to insist that arguments are presented in a rational form with reasons, conclusions, and clear linkages between the two. To be sure, critics of pure rationality are correct that we also need an affective element to encourage action, and stories are a good vehicle to give emotion and empathy to political discussions. What we need is a good balance between rationality and affect, and this balance depends very much on the context. A discussion on sexuality in schools needs more affect than a discussion about an economic stimulus package, where rationality is more in demand.

The need for rationality in discussing issues such as an economic stimulus package brings me to the last point in this chapter, namely the argument of Gary Mucciaroni and Paul J. Quirk that rationality is needed not only in a formal but also in a substantive way in the sense that the arguments are supported by good evidence, in particular evidence based on the best available research. Whether, for example, an economic stimulus is needed in a particular situation must be based on solid economic knowledge. As Mucciaroni and Quirk demonstrate for the US Congress, such knowledge is often lacking. For such complex issues, we come to the limits of rationality not only for ordinary citizens but also for professional politicians. Given such limits, I agree with Bernard Reber who argues that uncertainties in the current world are often so overwhelming that the principle of *prudence* is in order in deciding political issues.[77] The principle of prudence fits well the deliberative model of democracy. In politics, we often do not have clear answers of how to handle complex issues such as immigration and climate change. We can never be quite sure how our justifications for specific policy decisions will hold up in the long run. These uncertainties should open us to listen to the arguments of others and not to ram through our own preferences. In this sense, deliberative leaders should be prudent. But they should also, as Reber further argues, be willing to think about scenarios that look at first sight impossible in the real world of politics.

---

[77] Bernard Reber, "La délibération des meilleurs des mondes, entre précaution et pluralisme, monographie inédite en vue de l'obtention d'une habilitation à diriger des recherches," Université Paris IV, Sorbonne, 2010.

3 | Common good and self-interest in deliberative justification

(a) Normative controversies in the literature

With regard to the substantive aspect of deliberative justification, the main controversy has to do with the question of whether in good deliberation only references to the common good are appropriate or whether self-interest also has a legitimate place. As Jane Mansbridge *et al.* summarize the literature, "deliberative democracy has traditionally been defined in opposition to self-interest."[1] Jürgen Habermas represents this traditional view in a classical way when he postulates the necessity of "overcoming" one's "egocentric viewpoint."[2] Habermas, however, does not completely exclude the articulation of self-interest, but it must always be justified from a larger point of view. Bruce Ackerman and James S. Fishkin demand that the good citizen should not ask "What's good for me?" but "What's good for the country?"[3] The two theorists see a fundamental difference between a consumer in the market and a citizen in politics. As they put it: "When entering a marketplace, it is generally acceptable for the consumer to limit herself to a single question when choosing amongst competing products – and that is 'Which product do I find most pleasing?'" But, according to the two theorists,

this is not true for citizenship. When you and I get together to choose a new set of leaders, we are not engaged in a private act of consumption, but a collective act of power – one that will profoundly shape the fate of millions of

[1] Jane Mansbridge with James Bohman, Simone Chambers, David Estlund, Andreas Follesdal, Archon Fung, Christina Lafont, Bernard Manin, and José Luis Marti, "The Place of Self-Interest and the Role of Power in Deliberative Democracy," *Journal of Political Philosophy* 18 (2010), 64.

[2] Jürgen Habermas, "Morality and Ethical Life: Does Hegel's Critique of Kant Apply to Discourse Ethics?," *Northwestern University Law Review* 83 (1989), 45.

[3] Bruce Ackermann and James S. Fishkin, "Deliberative Day," *Journal of Political Philosophy* 10 (2002), 143.

our fellow citizens, and billions more throughout the world. With the stakes this high, it is morally irresponsible to choose the politician with the biggest smile or the biggest handout.[4]

Ackermann and Fishkin acknowledge that "there may be many occasions when what is good for the country is also good for me personally. But the good citizen recognizes, as the good consumer does not, that this convergence is by no means preordained, and that the task of citizenship is to rise above self-interest and take seriously the nature of the common good."[5] But how can we know what the common good is? Here, Ian O'Flynn presents a nuanced position.[6] For him, the common good or public interest "is fundamentally a moral idea, one that is principally concerned with the proper conduct of political life in general and the proper ways of making collectively binding decisions in particular."[7] The basic claim of O'Flynn is "that deliberative democracy is well placed to deliver the public interest ... Deliberative democracy obliges us to take a broader or more encompassing view of important decisions of law or policy than merely consulting our own special interest in them."[8] The position of O'Flynn is nuanced in the sense that although deliberation is helpful to find the public interest, it would be too easy to say that the public interest is whatever results from deliberation; "even after deliberation we may still not have a clear preference about the matter ... This means, of course, that the public interest may be controversial – with the best will in the world, different people may arrive at different conclusions about what is best for the entire society."[9] For O'Flynn, such controversies about the content of the public interest do "little to undermine the idea of the public interest *per se.*"[10] It makes sense to him to think about the public interest, although there may not always be agreement on what it is.

The argument that special interests have a place in deliberative democracy is forcefully put by Mansbridge *et al.*; for them, self-interest "ought to be part of the deliberation that eventuates in a democratic

---

[4] Ackermann and Fishkin, "Deliberative Day," 143.
[5] Ackermann and Fishkin, "Deliberative Day," 143.
[6] Ian O'Flynn, "Deliberating about the Public Interest," *Res Publica* 16 (2010), 299–315.
[7] O'Flynn, "Deliberating about the Public Interest," 300.
[8] O'Flynn, "Deliberating about the Public Interest," 301, 307.
[9] O'Flynn, "Deliberating about the Public Interest," 302–3.
[10] O'Flynn, "Deliberating about the Public Interest," 313.

decision." They qualify this postulate, however, in saying that self-interest must be "suitably constrained."[11] This is an important qualification, which leads them to a nuanced position with regard to self-interest and deliberation. Mansbridge *et al.* begin their analysis with a careful distinction between interest as a general concept and self-interest as one of its sub-categories. By the general term they mean "both material and less tangible interests, including other-regarding and ideal-regarding interests."[12] For self-interest, however, they exclude "other-regarding and ideal-regarding interests."[13] How can self-interest be justified as compatible with good deliberation? Mansbridge *et al.* argue that "including self-interest in deliberative democracy reduces the possibility of exploitation and obfuscation, introduces information that facilitates reasonable solutions and the identification of integrative outcomes, and also motivates vigorous and creative deliberation. Including self-interest in the regulative ideal of deliberative democracy embraces the diversity of human objectives as well as the diversity of human opinions."[14] The essence of this justification is that making self-interest part of good deliberation allows the less powerful also to have a significant say in bringing their grievances more easily into the discussion. Mansbridge *et al.* illustrate their position with an anecdotal case where a weak member of a group brought his self-interest into play and thereby could swing the decision of the group in another direction. Mansbridge *et al.* consider this case as compatible with good deliberation. The case warrants elaboration:

One evening in 1965, forty-six faculty members at the University of Michigan who wanted to protest the Vietnam War met until four AM to decide between two proposals: a day-long anti-war moratorium with faculty calling off their classes, which would break the faculty members' contracts with the university, or an alternative new idea of a 24-hour session on the war with no cancelled classes. A young assistant professor eventually said, "I'm in favor of the alternative but it's not because I think it is more or less effective as a protest against the Vietnam War. It's because I'm scared. I'm afraid of losing my job. I could repeat some of the arguments for switching that others have given, but that's not the real reason." A majority emerged for the alternative proposal, the disappointed pledged their support, and

---

[11] Mansbridge *et al.*, "The Place of Self-Interest," 64.
[12] Mansbridge *et al.*, "The Place of Self-Interest," 68.
[13] Mansbridge *et al.*, "The Place of Self-Interest," 68.
[14] Mansbridge *et al.*, "The Place of Self-Interest," 72–5.

the "teach-in" was born. Teach-ins spread rapidly across the universities in America, at least in part because that solution accommodated self-interests that a more restrictive interpretation of a deliberatively justified argument would have excluded from the discussion. In this case, the deliberation had been framed to decide which strategy was the most effective protest. The decision was supposed to be not about what was best for "us," the deciding group, but what was best for the anti-war cause. The young assistant professor, trying to maintain authenticity but undoubtedly also worrying that the remark showed him insufficiently committed to the cause, offered his self-interest as information about himself, not as a justification. Yet that information turned out to be highly relevant, as what was best for the anti-war cause turned out to include the cost of anti-war activity for potential participants.[15]

This is a nice illustration of how the expression of self-interest of the young assistant professor ultimately resulted in a good outcome. However, Mansbridge *et al.* argue that not all expressions of self-interest are compatible with good deliberation:

In the ideal of deliberative democracy, the expression and pursuit of self-interest must be curtailed both by the universal constraints of moral behavior and human rights and by the particularly deliberative constraints of mutual respect, equality, reciprocity, fairness and mutual justification. Thus many forms of self-interest are ruled out, not as desires but as justifications. "The desire to be wealthier come what may," for example, is in most instances not compatible with mutual respect, equality, reciprocity, fairness and mutual justification.[16]

Mansbridge *et al.* have used two extreme examples of what kind of self-interests should be included or excluded from good deliberation. It is easy to see why the anxiety of the assistant professor over potentially losing his job should be included and why the desire to be as wealthy as possible should be excluded. But what about the many cases in between? Where should the line be drawn? Mansbridge *et al.*'s answer is that "the question of which kinds of claim are appropriate in any deliberation must itself be subject to deliberation and mutual justification."[17] This should be valid not only for what counts as self-interest compatible with good deliberation but also for what counts as

---

[15] Mansbridge *et al.*, "The Place of Self-Interest," 74.
[16] Mansbridge *et al.*, "The Place of Self-Interest," 76.
[17] Mansbridge *et al.*, "The Place of Self-Interest," 77.

common good. The ultimate conclusion of the analysis of Mansbridge *et al.* is that "participants need not be fully neutral or detached in the deliberative process."[18]

Christian F. Rostbøll agrees with Mansbridge in stating that "we need to know the interests of everybody to determine what is in the equal interest of all." He stresses, however, that many lower-class people have false class consciousness and do not know what their true interests are. From the perspective of critical theory, Rostbøll sees the task of deliberation to contribute to more self-reflection.

The greatest strength of deliberative democracy is ... to politicize and initiate reflection about beliefs, policies, and institutions that are uncritically accepted by most people, and hence not discussed at all ... Deliberation has the great advantage that it can challenge uncritically accepted forms of oppression and inequality without being paternalistic or setting up external standards of true and false interests. Because of its requirement of non-domination and its procedural nature, public deliberation cannot impose anything on anyone but can only aim at emancipation by encouraging and provoking processes of self-reflection.[19]

Rostbøll mentions as an example of an uncritically accepted form of oppression and inequality the capitalist system with its emphasis on the benefits of the free market. Deliberation should help workers to become aware of their false class consciousness.[20] With theorists like Rostbøll, deliberative theory gets a critical edge. In conclusion, one can say that there is great controversy among theorists about the role of self-interest in the deliberative model of democracy.

(b) Empirical results

Literature review

The literature review on empirical research about the topic of this chapter confronts the difficulty that both politicians and ordinary citizens may not always be truthful when they argue using the common good to justify their position. They may use common-good arguments

[18] Mansbridge *et al.*, "The Place of Self-Interest," 78.
[19] Christian F. Rostbøll, *Deliberative Freedom: Deliberative Democracy as Critical Theory* (Albany: State University of New York Press, 2008), p. 220.
[20] Rostbøll, *Deliberative Freedom*, p. 38.

in a strategic way to defend their self-interests. But words may still matter. As Jon Elster argues, hypocrisy may have a "civilizing" effect, in the sense that it may not be so important *why* an appeal to the common good is made, what matters is that it *is* made because once an actor appeals to the common good, he or she can be held accountable to that standard.[21] In a recent paper, Elster adds the caveat that in his earlier work he "mostly assumed that the desire to promote the public good is at the top of the hierarchy and that individuals will be motivated to present themselves as motivated by that desire." He now acknowledges that this assumption may not always hold, so "the effect of hypocrisy is not always civilizing."[22]

I begin with our earlier research on parliamentary debates in Germany, Switzerland, the UK, and the US.[23] Once again, we discovered interesting differences between plenary sessions and committee meetings. Let us look first at the expression of group interests. Here is an illustration from a plenary session:

On June 2, 1997, the House debates an education bill whose goal is to reduce class size in schools. The bill is introduced by David Blunkett, the Labour Secretary of State for Education and Employment. During his speech Labour MP Anne Campbell rises and Blunkett yields to her for the following statement: "Is my right hon. friend aware how important the Bill is to my constituency, especially to parents at Milton Road infant school, which had an excellent Ofsted report earlier this year but now has to implement 25,000 pounds of cuts imposed by the previous Government?"[24]

Surprisingly, only 9 percent of all speech acts in plenary sessions of all four countries contained such references to group interests, and in committee meetings only 5 percent. Why would members of parliament so rarely refer to group interests, and less so in committees than in plenary sessions? The reason seems to be that they like to take shortcuts, especially when they are out of the public eye. As we have seen

---

[21] Jon Elster, "Introduction," in Jon Elster (ed.), *Deliberative Democracy* (Cambridge University Press, 1998), pp. 1–18.

[22] Jon Elster, "Deliberation, Cycles, and Misrepresentation," paper presented at the Conference on Epistemic Democracy in Practice, Yale University, October 20–22, 2011, p. 3.

[23] Jürg Steiner, André Bächtiger, Markus Spörndli, and Marco R. Steenbergen, *Deliberative Politics in Action* (Cambridge University Press, 2005).

[24] Steiner *et al.*, *Deliberative Politics in Action*, pp. 173–4.

in Chapter 2, Robert E. Goodin forcefully makes the argument for the utility of shortcuts.[25] Also, it may not always seem proper to refer constantly to group interests. This argument is made by Julien Talpin and Laurence Monnoyer-Smith for citizen experiments on climate change in the French region of Poitou-Charentes.[26] The experiments were done both face-to-face and online. The authors report "that we hardly ever observed self-interested justifications both on-line and face-to-face. Even for debates most centered on actors' personal experience, self-interest was hardly ever opposed to environmental reasons."[27] Talpin and Monnoyer-Smith see social norms at play that concern "a grammar of public life, making the public expression of both personal and partisan interests pragmatically difficult for actors, otherwise risking symbolic sanctions or depreciation of their reputation."[28] However, they qualify this explanation, noting that these experiments were not decision-making bodies, so that

discussions would not have any impact on participants' daily life; they had no personal interests to defend. Risking losing face publicly in a pro-environmental environment, participants had little interest in voicing arguments that, in the end, would not change their life. Defending one's interests in public is costly, and actors are only ready to do it when the latter are at stake.[29]

It has also to be considered that climate change involves a sensitive public good, so it is particularly inappropriate to use self-interest arguments. For other issues like taxes and subsidies, there is less of a social norm against using self-interest as an argument, especially where actual policy decisions have to be made. This discussion shows that it is a delicate matter to interpret data on the expression of self-interest in political discussions.

For the expression of the common good in our investigation of parliamentary debates, we encounter the opposite problem in the sense

---

[25] Robert E. Goodin, "Talking Politics: Perils and Promise," *European Journal of Political Research* 45 (2006), 253.

[26] Julien Talpin and Laurence Monnoyer-Smith, "Talking with the Wind? Discussion on the Quality of Deliberation in the Ideal-EU Project," paper presented at the IPSA International Conference, Luxembourg, March 18–20, 2010.

[27] Talpin and Monnoyer-Smith, "Talking with the Wind?," p. 14.

[28] Talpin and Monnoyer-Smith, "Talking with the Wind?," p. 14.

[29] Talpin and Monnoyer-Smith, "Talking with the Wind?," p. 15.

that there is a social norm to express arguments in terms of the common good. Here, we distinguish two categories. On the one hand, we define the common good in utilitarian terms, which means the greatest benefits for the greatest number of people.[30] The following case in the British House of Commons illustrates this category. On February 27, 1998, the House discusses governmental priorities for women. Harriet Harman, Labour Secretary of State for Social Security and Minister for Women, refers in the following way to the common good: "Child care must not be a poor service for poor families but an excellent service for all families. It must be universal."[31] With this statement she postulates the best solution for the highest number of families, and she also refers to the good of society at large. The other common-good category is based on the so-called difference principle as postulated by John Rawls.[32] This principle states that in a political decision the most disadvantaged social groups should profit the most. In the debate just mentioned on priorities for women, Ms. Harman also refers to the difference principle when she says: "The government's priority must be to help those who have the greatest difficulty in paying rather than spreading it evenly across the range."[33] If we look first at the two common-good categories combined, there is a striking difference between plenary sessions and committee meetings. In the former, 31 percent of the speech acts refer to the common good, in the latter only 9 percent. If we distinguish between the two categories of the common good, in plenary sessions 17 percent is articulated in utilitarian terms, 14 percent in terms of the difference principle; in committee meetings, 6 percent in utilitarian terms and 3 percent in terms of the difference principle.

How do these results match up with the philosophical literature presented in the first section of the chapter? The discussions in the committee meetings are far away from good deliberation as postulated by the philosophical literature. It happened rarely that committee members explicitly referred to the common good and engaged each other in how to define the common good. The picture does not improve if we include references to group interests compatible with

---

[30] John Stuart Mill, *Utilitarianism* (Oxford University Press, 1998).
[31] Steiner *et al.*, *Deliberative Politics in Action*, p. 174.
[32] John Rawls, *A Theory of Social Justice* (Cambridge, MA: Harvard University Press, 1971).
[33] Steiner *et al.*, *Deliberative Politics in Action*, p. 175.

good deliberation as postulated by Mansbridge *et al.* As we have seen above, only 5 percent of the speech acts in committee meetings referred to group interests. More importantly, we find it hard to empirically distinguish between group interests compatible and non-compatible with good deliberation. Mansbridge *et al.* give two extreme examples on either side, which does not help to classify the many cases in the middle. Mansbridge *et al.* merely say that, in good deliberation, participants should mutually justify what group interests are appropriate. We could not find any efforts by members of parliament to discuss the appropriateness of group interests for their deliberation.

Summing up, members in parliamentary committees very often take shortcuts in their discussions and do not bother to refer in an explicit way to arguments concerning the common good or group interests. As Goodin writes, they do not wish to belabor points that seem quite obvious and would only take time away from more detailed substantive discussions. References to the common good or group interests may often be considered as unnecessary distractions in committee meetings since time is always a scarce resource in politics. The situation is different in plenary sessions under the scrutiny of the public eye. Here, as we have seen, about one-third of the speech acts refer to the public good, although such references may not always be meant in a sincere way.

The question of the common good was also studied by Dionysia Tamvaki and Christopher Lord for the European Parliament.[34] They looked at debates on the Lisbon Treaty, the EU budget, climate change, the work program for the Commission, security and defense policy, and crime liability. For the individual speech acts, they examined whether they refer to (1) a national interest, (2) an intergovernmental interest, (3) a European interest, (4) a global interest. A fifth category was for speech acts without reference to any particular interest. There were very few references to a national interest; the highest number occurred for the discussion of the Lisbon Treaty, with 14 percent of the speech acts referring to a national interest. By contrast, a common European interest was mentioned very frequently, ranging from 42 percent for the security and defense policy to 75 percent for the work program of

---

[34] Dionysia Tamvaki and Christopher Lord, "The Content and Quality of Representation in the European Assembly: Towards Building an Updated Discourse Quality Index at the EU Level," paper presented at the IPSA International Conference, Luxembourg, March 18–20, 2010.

the Commission. References to global interests depended very much on the issue, ranging from a high of 36 percent for climate change to only 3 percent for crime liability. Tamvaki and Lord see from these results an indication "of a cosmopolitan post-national deliberative order."[35] It is indeed striking how few references are made to national interests and how European arguments and even global ones dominate the debates. A direct comparison with the national parliaments is not possible since Tamvaki and Lord used a different methodology for this aspect of their investigation than we did with our Discourse Quality Index (DQI). But it still seems that in plenary sessions of the European Parliament references to the common good are more frequent than in the plenary sessions of the national parliaments.[36] Perhaps this is due to the fact that in the European Parliament, which is a new and still-fragile institution, parliamentarians feel more of an obligation to stress common interests than in the long-established national parliaments, where it may seem more appropriate to take shortcuts in formulating arguments. It is also possible that people running for the European Parliament are more common-good-oriented than persons attracted to play a role in national parliaments where power considerations are more important.

What are the arguments that ordinary citizens use when they discuss political issues? The study by Elzbieta Wesolowska of Polish parents of school-age children discussing sex education in schools is useful.[37] The following statement by one of the participants is of particular interest: "I care first of all about the good of my own children." When other participants remind him that the task of the group is to prepare common recommendations for all Polish public schools, he replies: "Everyone should have the right to bring up his or her own children the way he or she considers right and nobody else should interfere."[38] This is clearly an expression of self-interest. Is it compatible with good deliberation in the sense of Mansbridge *et al.*? There was some objection from other participants but no thorough deliberation with mutual justifications of whether this expression of self-interest was compatible with good deliberation. This is a good illustration of how difficult

---

[35] Tamvaki and Lord, "The Content and Quality of Representation," p. 29.
[36] Committee meetings were not studied for the European Parliament.
[37] Elzbieta Wesolowska, "Social Processes of Antagonism and Synergy in Deliberating Groups," *Swiss Political Science Review* 13 (2007), 663–80.
[38] Wesolowska, "Social Processes of Antagonism," 671.

it is to put the idea of Mansbridge *et al.* in empirical terms to distinguish deliberative and non-deliberative self-interest. At an analytical level, the distinction makes sense, but is not very helpful for empirical investigations. Susan Stokes argues that, for elections in the UK and the US, over time the narrow self-interests of voters play less of a role. She cites research that, in nineteenth-century America, voting had been "a social transaction in which they handed in a party ticket in return for a shot of whiskey, a pair of boots, or a small amount of money." In the UK in the nineteenth century, political parties sent out brokers to the neighborhoods and workplaces to find out "the needs of individual voters." Such behavior is no longer considered appropriate, or is even outlawed. Stokes sees "a widespread norm that democratic decisions ought to transcend economic self-interest ... Voters get at least as worked up by arguments about what's right as by arguments about what's in their group's interest."[39]

New data on deliberative experiments[40]

In *Colombia,* of the total of 1,027 speech acts, in 31 percent the speaker referred to potential benefits and costs for his or her own group. But there were also 9 percent of the speech acts where the speaker referred to the common good and 5 percent to moral principles such as social justice and peace. Once again, as in previous chapters, I offer illustrations for the categories to give some feeling for the coding categories.

Reference to common good: "If access to education was really free of charge our children or grandchildren could see a better country."[41]

Reference to moral principles: "In order to reduce a little the violence figures, it is necessary to count on clear policies to reach social justice or equity."[42]

How do we evaluate the data? As we have seen for the parliamentary debates in Germany, Switzerland, the UK, and the US, 31 percent

---

[39] Susan Stokes, "A Rational Theory of Epistemic Democracy," paper presented at the Conference on Epistemic Democracy in Practice, Yale University, October 20–22, 2011, pp. 6, 8.

[40] For the research designs, see Introduction, Section (b).

[41] "Que realmente el acceso a la educación fuera gratuita ... de pronto nuestro hijos o nuestros nietos podrían ver un país mejor."

[42] "Para disminuir un poco los índices de violencia hay que haya unas políticas claras de justicia social, o de equidad."

of the speech acts in plenary sessions and 9 percent in committee meetings referred to the common good. Thus, the data for the ex-combatants are comparable to the committee meetings. In plenary sessions, there were many more references to the common good, but one has to consider that in the public eye parliamentarians are under social pressure to make references to the common good, whether they mean it sincerely or not. In the experiments, ex-combatants were under no such pressure, so it is remarkable that they referred as often to the common good as did national parliamentarians in committee meetings. We did some binary analyses by gender, age, and education and found that the youngest participants refer least often to specific group interests and that references to moral principles increase with more education.[43]

In *Bosnia–Herzegovina*, in the experiments in *Srebrenica* with Serbs and Bosnjaks, 5 percent of the speech acts contained references to the common good and 1 percent to abstract moral principles, which are both somewhat lower than in Colombia. One has to consider, however, as we have seen in the last chapter, that in the experiments in Srebrenica participants often told stories about such matters as stray dogs, wild pigs, and the polluted river, where the common good was not explicitly mentioned and thus not coded but was implicitly more or less present. For Srebrenica, it is also remarkable that, in contrast to Colombia, virtually no participants referred to benefits and costs for their own group, Serb or Bosnjak. When they told stories, it would have been easy, for example for the garbage in the river, to blame the other side, but this almost never happened. Thus, although the common good was rarely mentioned in an explicit way, the atmosphere in Srebrenica had some sense of the common good binding the participants together, more so than among Colombian ex-combatants. The explanation seems to be that in Srebrenica people certainly had bad memories about the massacres but had not been actively involved in military combat like the ex-combatants in Colombia. In the experiments in *Stolac* with Croats and Bosnjaks, there was also some atmosphere of the common good, although it was rarely expressed in an explicit way.

In the experiments in *Belgium*, 7 percent of the 1,664 speech acts referred to the common good and 9 percent to abstract moral

---

[43] Binary analyses in this chapter will be supplemented in Chapter 9 by multiple regressions.

principles. These results correspond to what we found for Colombia and Bosnia–Herzegovina. One would have expected that in Belgium, as an advanced democracy, references to the common good and moral principles would have been much higher than in war-torn Colombia and Bosnia–Herzegovina. One should also note, however, that in only 3 percent of the speech acts did Flemish and Walloons refer to costs and benefits of their own group. Looking closer at the Belgian data, we get the surprising result that participants in the linguistically mixed experimental groups refer more often to the common good than participants in the linguistically homogeneous groups. The interpretation could be that in homogeneous groups one takes the liberty of shortcuts more often since one assumes that almost everyone in the group thinks in terms of the common good. Binary analyses show that the younger and the highly educated refer more often to the common good.

In Colombia, Bosnia–Herzegovina, and Belgium, participants in the experiments were asked to discuss the future of their deeply divided countries. Thus, the discussion was framed in such a way that references to the common good virtually always meant their own country. For *Europolis* the situation was different. Having the task of addressing the issues of immigration from outside the EU and worldwide climate change, participants had a multi-level framework for thinking about the common good. They could think about their own country, other EU countries, the EU at large, and the world community. The following data show how the speech acts were distributed among these categories:

Reference to interests of own country	8%
Reference to interests of other EU countries and/or EU as a whole	10%
Reference to interests of world community	4%
None of these references	78%
Total of all speech acts	100%

In the context of a discussion with people from all EU countries, a reference to the interests of one's own country cannot be considered as a reference to the common good but rather as a special interest. By contrast, the 14 percent of references to the interests of other EU countries, the EU as a whole, and the world community are common-good-oriented. If we add for Belgium references to the common good and to abstract moral principles, the resulting 16 percent are very similar to the 14 percent for Europolis. For the *Finnish* experiments on nuclear power, only 8 percent of the speech acts contained references to the common good.[44] This may mean that in a homogeneous country like Finland one takes shortcuts more often in not explicitly referring to the common good, whereas in Belgium as a divided society and also in the still very heterogeneous EU one feels more of a need to emphasize common interests.

(c) Normative implications of empirical results

Empirically, we have seen that participants in a discussion often take shortcuts and, in order to save time, do not spell out self-interests on which their arguments are based. Are such shortcuts allowed in a discussion that wants to be deliberative? Time is a scarce resource, so there are good reasons not to refer to self-interests if everyone knows what these interests are. Deliberation should not be boring but spirited so that everyone stays attentive. If speakers constantly refer to their self-interests, this becomes tedious and indeed boring. If farmers, for example, each time they speak up on a farm issue, mention that they have a personal interest in the issue, it becomes trivial so shortcuts are appropriate. The caveat is, however, that other participants must have the right and even the obligation to ask for the interests behind an argument if these interests are not self-evident. Saving time can never be used as an excuse in good deliberation not to reveal interests if other actors ask for them. In many cases, it is less self-evident than in the farm example what the interests behind an argument are so they must be revealed, at least the first time the issue is raised in a discussion. In my view, shortcuts with regard to interests should be used with great caution and not too often. We must acknowledge that good deliberation is time-consuming; it is not the most efficient way to organize a debate. Good deliberators must not be time pressured so that they are able to spell out in a clear way the interests behind their arguments. However, they must be aware of when these interests have become clear enough to everyone, in case repetition becomes tedious. In this sense, good deliberation is quite an art form.

---

[44] In utilitarian terms, 4 percent, and 4 percent in terms of the difference principle. A breakdown by gender, age, and education does not reveal any significant differences.

The next question is whether the expression of self-interest is compatible with good deliberation. Empirically, the experiments in Colombia, for example, offer clear cases where, in my view, it was in a deliberative spirit that ex-combatants expressed their self-interest in getting housing, health care, education, and job opportunities. After all, they were willing to give up arms and to participate in the government program of reintegration. In this way, they rendered a service to the common good of Colombian society. To be sure, ex-combatants did not often make the linkage between their self-interests and the common good, but given their traumatic situation one cannot reasonably expect them to be able and willing to articulate how their self-interests may fit the common good. Not making this linkage should not exclude the self-interests of these traumatized ex-combatants from a deliberative discourse. Such exclusion would be wrong since the interests of some of the poorest and most suffering members of society would not be considered.

From the experiments in Poland, we have an interesting borderline case of whether the expression of self-interest should be considered deliberative or not. As we saw above, Polish parents of school-age children discussed sex education in school, with one father making the following provocative statement: "I care first of all about the good of my own children … Everyone should have the right to bring up his or her own children the way he or she considers right and nobody should interfere." This statement looks egocentric and does not leave space for dialogue; the father wants to decide himself what is good for his children and is not open to listening to the arguments of others. A careful reading of the statement shows, however, that the father cares "first of all" about his children, which leaves open the possibility that he still cares about children of other parents. This should have been an occasion for other discussants to ask the father to reveal what he means by "first of all." Since no one did follow up in this way, we have a case that is ambivalent whether it is inside or outside deliberative limits. It is certainly not a shining example of good deliberation. My normative implications are that in good deliberation people should be encouraged to put their interests on the table. Thereby, almost all interests should be allowed to enter the deliberative discourse. Rare exceptions would be if someone expresses a crude self-interest and explicitly states that he or she is unwilling to submit it to the arguments of other participants.

Having established my position with regard to the role of self-interest in the deliberative model, I address now the question of to what extent arguments should be formulated in terms of the common good. The empirical data indicate that when common-good arguments are made, they are often not much more than empty words in flowery language. To be useful in a deliberative discourse, common-good arguments must be expressed in very specific ways. It is only under this condition that other discussants can react to such arguments. If someone simply says that his or her proposal is good for the country, this is no basis for a continuing dialogue. By contrast, if the argument is, for example, that a proposal helps to increase Gross Domestic Product (GDP), another discussant can respond that GDP has little validity in measuring quality of life and may propose quality-of-life indicators such as clean air and low crime rates. On such a basis, a spirited discussion about various definitions of the common good may follow. Thereby, the common good should not only be seen in terms of the nation state but should also consider neighboring states and, for an increasing number of issues, even the world at large. Such a discussion may reveal that at a fundamental level people may differ much more than they are aware. But this is healthy for good deliberation. I agree with Rostbøll that deliberation should help to bring into the open fundamental differences. At first, this may easily lead to increased polarization. In the long run, however, thanks to good deliberation, people may learn to accept that they have different notions of the common good. Such an outlook is particularly welcome in deeply divided societies such as those studied in this book. If in Colombia, for example, ex-guerrillas accept that ex-paramilitaries define the common good in terms of law and order, and ex-paramilitaries accept that social justice is of prime importance for ex-guerrillas, much would be gained. The goal of deliberation is not necessarily that everyone agrees on a definition of the common good, but that one learns to live peacefully, respecting the different ways people define the common good.

4 | *Respect in deliberation*

(a) Normative controversies in the literature

There is agreement in the normative literature that mutual respect in the sense of *reciprocity* is a key element of good deliberation. This holds for both speakers and listeners. As Jane Mansbridge *et al.* put it, "participants should treat one another with mutual respect and equal concern. They should listen to each other and give reasons to one another that they think the others can comprehend and accept."[1] Such mutual respect requires, in the words of Amy Gutmann and Dennis Thompson, "an effort to appreciate the moral force of the position with which we disagree."[2] There is controversy, however, about the exact definition of respect and whether respect should be extended to all arguments or whether there are arguments that are so distasteful that they do not merit respect. Jürgen Habermas takes the position that all arguments should be considered and that good reasoning will allow the cutting of distasteful arguments from further discussion.[3] This Habermasian position is forcefully articulated by Christian F. Rostbøll who shares with Habermas a background in critical theory of the Frankfurt School. For Rostbøll, a "basic assumption underlying deliberative democracy, as I see it, is that no one has privileged access to truth or to the true interests of others. The only way to arrive at judgments that have the presumption of having right on their side is

---

[1] Jane Mansbridge with James Bohman, Simone Chambers, David Estlund, Andreas Follesdal, Archon Fung, Christina Lafont, Bernard Manin, and José Luis Marti, "The Place of Self-Interest and the Role of Power in Deliberative Democracy," *Journal of Political Philosophy* 18 (2010), 2–3.

[2] Amy Gutmann and Dennis F. Thompson, "Moral Conflict and Political Consensus," *Ethics* 101 (1990), 85. See also Rainer Forst, *Das Recht auf Rechtfertigung* (Frankfurt a.M.: Suhrkamp, 2007).

[3] Jürgen Habermas, *Between Facts and Norms: Contributions to a Discourse Theory of Law and Democracy*, trans. William Regh (Cambridge, MA: MIT Press, 1996), especially pp. 104ff.

through public process of deliberation where everyone is free and able to participate."[4] Italo Testa, another theorist, sets out his position in the title of his paper, "Limits of Respect in Public Dialogue," arguing that not anything goes in political debate:

Respect for the legitimacy of values, beliefs, and preferences should not be conferred *a priori*, as unconditional and un-retractable. Were it so, we would have as a consequence that *anything* goes: there would be no way to distinguish between legitimate and illegitimate claims, and dialogue would defeat itself and its validity structure ... there will always be some views that we won't hold as respectable: and this is not a bad thing in itself.[5]

Testa makes the distinction between respect for arguments and respect for persons making arguments. He is of the opinion that there are not only arguments but also persons that do not merit respect. For this claim, he gives the following illustration:

let's take the case of a political context where we need to listen to the opinion of an expert about how to dispose of refuse. If we later discover that the expert was not impartial as he had not publicly revealed having shares in a firm specializing in waste disposal in just the way that he proposes, then a personal attack would be rather reasonable.[6]

From this illustration, Testa concludes that "there can be occurrences where the moral authority of the claimer is relevant to judge the degree of credibility ... this is what happens in the refuse case, where the alleged hidden agenda justifies the doubt that this person may not be an objective arguer."[7] Testa continues, however, that the lack of moral authority of a speaker has no impact on the legitimacy of his or her arguments if the two elements are not related. In this case, we should not say, "since you are not worthy of respect, then your argument is not either."[8] Testa uses the concept of respect in a complex way with respect for arguments and persons being intertwined in a multifaceted way.

---

[4] Christian F. Rostbøll, *Deliberative Freedom: Deliberative Democracy as Critical Theory* (Albany: State University of New York Press, 2008), p. 103.

[5] Italo Testa, "Limits of Respect in Public Dialogue," paper presented at the Conference on Rhetorical Citizenship, University of Copenhagen, October 9–10, 2008, pp. 16–17.

[6] Testa, "Limits of Respect in Public Dialogue," pp. 9–10.

[7] Testa, "Limits of Respect in Public Dialogue," p. 11.

[8] Testa, "Limits of Respect in Public Dialogue," p. 10.

James Bohman and Henry S. Richardson, another two theorists, also see limits to respect in political debate. To be sure, they hope "that citizens will civilly engage with one another on the basis of the reasons that each actually accepts ... ideally, deliberative civility demands that one is willing to consider anyone's arguments."[9] They acknowledge, however, the "difficulties about being civil to the uncivil."[10] They wonder whether one has "to listen to Ann Coulter's rants or Al Franken's satirical riffs,"[11] the former being at the extreme right, the latter at the extreme left of the American political spectrum. Bohman and Richardson conclude that "sometimes, indeed, the pursuit of justice requires engaging with others uncivilly."[12] For Kasper M. Hansen, arguments challenging equality and freedom of expression should be banned from deliberation, "because otherwise the theory violates its own theoretical foundation as an *unconstrained* deliberation, which would limit the opinions voiced during the deliberative process ... it seems impossible to question equality or freedom of expression without questioning the entire concept of deliberative democracy."[13] A very concrete discussion about acceptable and non-acceptable arguments occurred in Norway after the gruesome massacre in July 2011. According to Sverre Midthjell, a close observer at the scene, it was the hottest topic after the massacre. How should extremist anti-Islam rhetoric be dealt with? "Should we take action to suppress it? Do we need to engage their arguments, or can we merely condemn them?"[14]

A controversy concerns the question of whether religious arguments have a legitimate place in deliberation. The prevailing view among theorists is that arguments based on religious doctrine can be introduced in a deliberative discourse but that they must be translated into secular terms. John Rawls, for example, writes that religious arguments "may be introduced in public political discussion at any time, provided that in due course proper political reasons ... are presented."[15] Stephen

---

[9] James Bohman and Henry S. Richardson, "Liberalism, Deliberative Democracy, and Reasons That All Can Accept," *Journal of Political Philosophy* 17 (2009), 272, 274.

[10] Bohman and Richardson, "Liberalism, Deliberative Democracy," 272.

[11] Bohman and Richardson, "Liberalism, Deliberative Democracy," 272.

[12] Bohman and Richardson, "Liberalism, Deliberative Democracy," 271.

[13] Kasper M. Hansen, *Deliberative Democracy and Opinion Formation* (Odensee: University Press of Southern Denmark, 2004), p. 105.

[14] Personal communication, September 7, 2011.

[15] John Rawls, *Political Liberalism* (New York: Colombia University Press, 1993), p. 217.

L. Carter challenges this position in postulating that "our political culture cannot be truly deliberative unless we let ourselves be tested by religiously grounded moral beliefs."[16] Jürgen Habermas initially sided with Rawls, but has recently softened his position in worrying that religious citizens may be forced to publicly state reasons which do not conform to their true religious convictions.[17] Therefore, in his later writings, he is less opposed to religious people using a religious vocabulary to justify their arguments. Thus, this controversy about the validity of religious arguments in deliberation has quite fluid borders. Another controversy concerns the question of what exactly is meant by the concept of respect. The classical definition is that the exchange of arguments should take place in a calm, polite, and non-confrontational manner. André Bächtiger forcefully puts forward the argument that this definition is "overly respectful,"[18] and considers

questioning, disputing, and insisting as core but frequently overlooked and undervalued elements of a desirable and effective deliberative process. *Questioning* refers to a process of critical interrogation and cross-examination; *disputing* refers to a process of argumentative challenges and counterchallenges; *insisting* refers to a sustained process of questioning and disputing, inducing a thorough and rigid inquiry of the matter under consideration.[19]

In this way, deliberation gets an "adversarial and confrontational" character.[20] Bächtiger cautions, however, "that a questioner or challenger cannot stay confrontational and adversarial throughout the process. He or she must strike a careful balance between confrontational and respectful acts."[21] If such a balance is struck, Bächtiger sees the following beneficial effects:

Questioning, disputing and insisting can unearth new facts and tacit assumptions as well as unravel inconsistencies and holes in the argumentation ...

---

[16] Stephen L. Carter, *The Culture of Disbelief: How American Law and Politics Trivialize Religious Devotion* (New York: Basic Books), p. 240.
[17] Jürgen Habermas, "Religion in the Public Sphere," *European Journal of Philosophy* 14 (2006), 1–25.
[18] André Bächtiger, "On Perfecting the Deliberative Process: Questioning, Disputing, and Insisting as Core Deliberative Values," paper presented at the annual meeting of the American Political Science Association, Washington, DC, September 2–5, 2010.
[19] Bächtiger, "On Perfecting the Deliberative Process," p. 2.
[20] Bächtiger, "On Perfecting the Deliberative Process," p. 2.
[21] Bächtiger, "On Perfecting the Deliberative Process," p. 17.

truthfulness can emerge out of a critical and thorough process of inquiry ... questioning, disputing and insisting allows disadvantaged groups to unravel dominant frames and demonstrate that there are different ways of seeing things ... Sustained critical interrogation and argumentation can unravel new dimensions of the topic under discussion, elicit reasons from other participants, and set in motion a process of reflection, foster respect and eventual preference change.[22]

The benefits of adversarial debates for the quality of deliberation are also stressed by Bernard Manin, for whom "it is the opposition of views and reasons that is necessary for deliberation, not just their diversity."[23] For Manin, "the benefits of deliberation critically depend on the confrontation of opposing arguments."[24] He fears, however, that in everyday life such debates will not occur sufficiently often, because "one cannot expect adversarial debates to arise spontaneously ... as people tend to avoid the psychic discomfort of face-to-face disagreement."[25] Therefore, according to Manin, "on a practical level, adversary debates on issues of public concern need to be actively promoted."[26] For such promotion, he makes the following suggestion:

Citizens' organizations, foundations, debating societies or other voluntary groups should organize these debates. Such voluntary groups would gradually establish their civic reputation and commitment to public interest. The key point is that these debates should be left to private – although not for profit – initiative ... on this principle, speakers should primarily be policy experts, group leaders, activists, moral authorities.[27]

In sum, the concept of respect is more controversial in the philosophical literature on deliberation than it may appear at first sight. It is controversial whether respect should be extended to all arguments and persons and to what extent confrontation is compatible with respect.

---

[22] Bächtiger, "On Perfecting the Deliberative Process," p. 3.
[23] Bernard Manin, "Democratic Deliberation: Why We Should Promote Debate Rather Than Discussion," paper presented at the Program in Ethics and Public Affairs Seminar, Princeton University, October 13, 2005.
[24] Manin, "Democratic Deliberation."
[25] Manin, "Democratic Deliberation."
[26] Manin, "Democratic Deliberation."
[27] Manin, "Democratic Deliberation."

(b) Empirical results

Literature review

In my review of the literature, I found only a few scattered empirical studies on the deliberative aspect of respect. The difficulty of empirically investigating respect in political discussions is that sometimes respect may not be meant truthfully but is instead used strategically to further one's interests. Respect then becomes flattery. If in a parliamentary debate one member calls another "my respected friend," this often may be pure flattery. Jean de La Fontaine has famously exposed such flattery in his fable "Le Corbeau et le Renard" (the crow and the fox).[28] Although crows are not known to be great singers, the fox expressed great respect for the singing skills of the crow, who sat high up in a tree. In order to show off his skills, the crow began to sing, dropping the cheese in his beak. By then it was too late for the crow to realize that he had fallen for a shrewd trick of the fox, who was only eager to get the cheese. The crow would have been better off knowing that the respect shown by the fox was nothing but strategic flattery. To distinguish flattery from true respect may be as difficult in politics as it was for the crow.

Let me begin with our earlier investigation of parliamentary debates in Germany, Switzerland, the UK, and the US.[29] We distinguished respect for the demands of others, respect for counter-arguments, and respect for groups to be helped. Each speech act by a member of parliament was coded for all three aspects on a scale from no respect to explicit respect. There was great variation in the level of respect. An illustration of high respect comes from a debate in the Swiss Council of States on amending the constitution with a language article. In the committee stage, German-speaking René Rhinow proposed establishing in the amendment the abstract principle of freedom of language, analogous to other freedoms like freedom of religion. He withdrew his proposal in the plenary session in deference to the opposition of many French-speakers, and in doing so he referred to the importance

---

[28] Online: www.poesie.webnet.fr/lesgrandsclassiques/jean_de_la_fontaine/ lecorbeau_et_le_renard.
[29] Jürg Steiner, André Bächtiger, Markus Spörndli, and Marco R. Steenbergen, *Deliberative Politics in Action: Analysing Parliamentary Discourse* (Cambridge University Press, 2005).

of peaceful relations among the language groups. From a deliberative perspective, it is important that Rhinow was willing to listen
with respect to the arguments of the French-speakers that establishing
the principle of freedom of language could lead to German-speaking
schools in the French-speaking regions, which would violate the long-
held principle of territoriality for school issues. There was no bargain
in the sense that Rhinow would have received something in return for
withdrawing his proposal. It was simply out of respect for the arguments of his colleagues from the French-speaking regions that Rhinow
withdrew his proposal. An extreme example of low respect occurred in
an abortion debate in the German Bundestag, when Claus Jäger interrupted another member of parliament, shouting: "For this you deserve
a slap in the face."[30] With this rude remark, Jäger demonstrated a total
lack of respect for the argument of his parliamentary colleague. In this
way, he signaled that the argument had no merit so it was not worth
considering.

To get an overall picture of the degree of respect in these parliamentary debates, we constructed a summary index of respect ranging from
0 to 9, with 9 expressing the highest level of respect. Once again, we
found an interesting difference between plenary sessions and committee meetings. This time, committee meetings were more deliberative
than plenary sessions. The mean on our index with regard to respect
was 3.67 for committee meetings and 3.36 for plenary sessions. There
seems to be a trade-off happening among the various deliberative
elements. In Chapters 2 and 3, we have seen that in committee meetings justifications of arguments are less elaborate and references to
the common good less frequent than in plenary sessions; now we see
that respect is higher in committee meetings than in plenary sessions.
Sitting face-to-face around a table seems to generate more respect than
the formal setting of plenary sessions.

In their study of plenary debates in the European Parliament,
Dionysia Tamvaki and Christopher Lord also looked at respect, once
again using our Discourse Quality Index (DQI).[31] Some 25 percent of
all speech acts showed no respect for the demands and arguments of

---

[30] Steiner *et al.*, *Deliberative Politics in Action*, pp. 1–2.
[31] Dionysia Tamvaki and Christopher Lord, "The Content and Quality of
Representation in the European Assembly: Towards Building an Updated
Discourse Quality Index at the EU Level," paper presented at the IPSA
International Conference, Luxembourg, March 18–20, 2010.

other participants, 20 percent were neutral, and 55 percent revealed implicit or explicit respect. In the plenary sessions of our national parliaments, the corresponding figures are 26 percent for no respect, 60 percent neutral, and 14 percent for implicit or explicit respect. Thus, debates at the European level were more respectful than at the national level. Tamvaki and Lord stress that compared with the national level, relatively few speech acts at the European level were neutral, which indicates that "genuine engagement in the discussion characterizes EP deliberative politics."[32] Why these differences between the European and the national level? My discussion in the previous chapter with regard to references to the common good may also apply to respect, in the sense that both elements attain a high level because the European Parliament is still a fragile institution with not much power, so the debates tend to be more civilized than in the long-established and more power-oriented national parliaments. Nicole Doerr's findings in her study of the European Social Forum may also be relevant: preparatory meetings took place at the national level and were less respectful than later meetings at the European level.[33] The explanation that Doerr offers may also apply for the difference between the European Parliament and the national parliaments, namely that the necessity of simultaneous translation in the European Parliament leads to more careful listening and, as a consequence, to a higher level of respect.

Sverre B. Midthjell looked at a particular kind of parliament, the student parliaments at the University of Oslo and the Norwegian University of Science and Technology in Trondheim.[34] Using our DQI, he investigated four debates in Oslo and two in Trondheim; they all dealt with internal university matters such as the creation of a separate faculty for university research centers. Only 11 percent expressed disrespect toward the arguments of other student representatives, much lower than the figures for the national parliaments and the European Parliament.[35] This finding seems to indicate that professional

---

[32] Tamvaki and Lord, "The Content and Quality of Representation," p. 24.
[33] Nicole Doerr, "Activists Beyond Language Borders? Multilingual Deliberative Democracy Experiments at the European Social Forums," paper presented at the ECPR General Conference, Potsdam, September 2009.
[34] Sverre B. Midthjell, "Deliberating or Quarrelling? An Enquiry into Theory and Research Methods for the Relationship Between Political Parties and Deliberation," Master's thesis, Department of Sociology and Political Science, Norwegian University of Science and Technology, 2010.
[35] Midthjell, "Deliberating or Quarrelling?," p. 71.

parliamentarians tend to be more cynical about the motives of their colleagues than members of student parliaments. Perhaps being involved for a long time in full-time politics does contribute to such cynicism, while students involved in university politics still have a certain optimism about the motives of their colleagues.

With regard to discussions among ordinary citizens, rather than professional parliamentarians, James S. Fishkin *et al.* undertook a study in a situation where respect seems particularly difficult to obtain, namely between Catholics and Protestants in a deeply divided Northern Ireland.[36] In the Omagh district, a random sample of both Catholic and Protestant parents were gathered to discuss local school issues; the method of investigation was Deliberative Polling.[37] Those agreeing to attend had to fill out a questionnaire before the experiment and were sent briefing documents conveying relevant factual information, outlining the various options for delivering education, and sketching the arguments for and against each option. The discussion took place in randomly assigned groups of about ten participants led by trained moderators. Participants were encouraged to be respectful to each other. After the discussions, participants again completed the questionnaire. The research question was whether opinions changed from the pre-experimental to the post-experimental questionnaire. The result was that "the participants acquired much more positive views of the other community and of inter-community relations."[38] For example, for the item of how trustworthy the other side is, using a scale from 0 to 1, Protestants moved from 0.646 to 0.751, Catholics from 0.621 to 0.709.[39] This study is of particular interest because it gives a dynamic aspect in asking how respect can be changed. If encouraged to be respectful, respect indeed increases, even in such a deeply divided society as Northern Ireland. For Fishkin *et al.*,

these results are all the more impressive in light of the modesty of this intervention. The Deliberative Polling entailed just a few days to a few weeks of heightened learning and casual discussions in the interval between the initial

---

[36] James S. Fishkin, Robert C. Luskin, Ian O'Flynn, and David Russell, "Deliberating across Deep Divides," paper presented at the 5th General Conference of the European Consortium of Political Research, Potsdam, September 2009.

[37] For more on Deliberative Polling, see the discussion of the research designs in the Introduction, Section (b).

[38] Fishkin *et al.*, "Deliberating across Deep Divides," p. 11.

[39] Fishkin *et al.*, "Deliberating across Deep Divides," table 6, p. 23.

interviews and the deliberations, and just one day of organized deliberation in heterogeneous discussion groups – this in a context marked by decades of tension and inter-group hostility, at times scarred by intense violence. In this light, the changes in policy attitudes related to inter-group relations and in attitudes toward the other group are striking.[40]

Elzbieta Wesolowska also did experiments on school matters with parents of schoolchildren.[41] Her study was carried out in Poland and dealt with the issue of sex education in schools. With regard to the aspect of respect, she found some instances of mutual respect, especially when a group was composed only of women, who could share common experiences of sexuality and motherhood. The topic also lent itself, however, to strongly disrespectful behavior. The most glaring example is a strongly Catholic man, who in his very first statement presented his stance in the following way: "I would request from school ... and not only request but simply demand that teachers should present human sexuality from the Catholic Church perspective ... Otherwise I would not allow for any kind of teaching."[42] Wesolowska comments that "his expectation that other disputants should accept the Catholic Church perspective as the sole guidance for their children's education is contradictory to the reciprocity principle."[43] When this speaker in the further debate "heard arguments undermining the legitimacy of his point of view, he attacked the others with rough and offensive words. Those attacked tried to avoid the discussion at first. However, finally, the discussion became so laden with emotion that all participants engaged in a fierce exchange of words."[44] This is indeed an episode of very low respect ending in a shouting match.

Julien Talpin did a qualitative ethnographic study of a real-life experience of citizen involvement in policy decisions.[45] The model he

---

[40] Fishkin *et al.*, "Deliberating across Deep Divides," p. 14.
[41] For more information on the entire project, see Janusz Reykowski, "Deliberation and Human Nature: An Empirical Approach," *Political Psychology* 27 (2006), 323–46.
[42] Elzbieta Wesolowska, "Social Processes of Antagonism and Synergy in Deliberating Groups," *Swiss Political Science Review* 13 (2007), 670. For Wesolowska's study, see also Chapter 2.
[43] Wesolowska, "Social Processes of Antagonism," 670.
[44] Wesolowska, "Social Processes of Antagonism," 671.
[45] Julien Talpin, *Schools of Democracy: How Ordinary Citizens (Sometimes) Become Competent in Participatory Budgeting Institutions* (Colchester: ECPR Press, 2011).

followed was that of Alegre in Brazil where citizens were involved in the budgeting process. Talpin studied three European communities where this experience was replicated: Morsang-sur-Orge in the Paris banlieue, the eleventh district in Rome, and Seville in Spain. In these three communities ordinary citizens were given the opportunity to be involved in the ordinary budget process and, within an upper limit, to allocate money to the different programs of the community. Talpin was able to observe altogether 124 such meetings, and also did interviews with organizers and participants. There was low reciprocity; discussions consisted mainly of monologues without many reactions by other participants. As Talpin puts it: "Most of the people voice arguments, diagnose problems and evoke possible solutions in a monological way. Personal interventions do not answer each other and hardly ever end up in a constructive exchange of arguments and counterarguments."[46] Based on his observations and interviews, Talpin sees the main reason for the low reciprocity in the reluctance of ordinary citizens to express disagreements:

The public expression of disagreement is a difficult move. Most of the people consider their opinions to be private matters, which do not need to be discussed, justified and eventually modified after a discussion with strangers. It seems that there is, in most public arenas, a strong cultural force pushing people to respect the opinions of others, therefore refusing to contradict or convince them.[47]

New data on deliberative experiments[48]

In *Colombia*, among the ex-combatants one would expect very low levels of respect because only a short while ago they were shooting at each other in the jungle. Would ex-combatants not use the occasion of these experiments to express disrespect, animosity, and even hatred toward the other side? The data of the 28 experiments give a complex picture. On the one hand, of the total of 1,027 speech acts, only eight contained respectful language toward other participants. Here are two examples:

---

[46] Talpin, *Schools of Democracy*, p. 308.
[47] Talpin, *Schools of Democracy*, p. 311.
[48] For the research designs, see Introduction, Section (b).

An ex-paramilitary man, aged 31, nine years of education: "You are absolutely right in what you say. Very good."[49]

An ex-guerrilla man, aged 44, five years of education: "What the fellow says is true."[50]

On the other hand, however, foul language was used also very rarely, in only nine speech acts. Again two examples:

An ex-paramilitary man, aged 27, eleven years of education: "Do not be stupid! Crap, man! If you work, fuck, you do not fucking starve! Obviously! Do not wait for the Government to give away houses for free. Go work!"[51]

An ex-guerrilla woman, aged 35, five years of education: "Are you next? Come down to earth. No opinion. The gentleman here is next. No opinion either. This group of you, neither. Yeah, well! As you do not want to give an opinion."[52]

How do we interpret these puzzling results that ex-combatants are generally neither respectful nor disrespectful? My interpretation is that they are extremely cautious and cagey. Given their recent history, this makes sense. Coming out of an armed conflict, they are traumatized and do not wish to take any risks by using the wrong words. As we have seen in the Introduction, they were reluctant to participate in the experiments, revealing their cautiousness. How deliberative shall we characterize their behavior, with regard to the element of respect and disrespect? Here again, we see that standards of deliberation depend on the context. Given their situation as ex-combatants, one can consider it as appropriate behavior to show great caution in interactions with the other side. One could argue that such cautious behavior may prepare participants for more respectful interactions at a later time when the memories of the war experiences are slowly fading away. There is, however, also the plausible counter-hypothesis that with more time having elapsed since the war, ex-combatants may feel less hesitation in articulating disrespect toward those who fought on the other side.

---

[49] "Usted tiene toda la razón en lo que dice. Muy bien."
[50] "Lo que dice el compañero es verdad."
[51] "No seamos estúpidos, hombre no joda! Si tu trabajas, hijueputa! No es que te cagas de hambre. ¡Obvio! No se pongan a esperar que el gobierno les regale casas: trabajen!"
[52] "Sigues tú? ¡Aterriza! No opina ... Sigue el señor aquí ... ¡Tampoco opina! El grupo de ustedes ... ¡Tampoco opina! Y ustedes ... ¡Tampoco...! ... Sí, pues. ¡Como no quieren opinar!"

Having looked in these first four chapters at the aspects of participation, justification, common good, and respect, this is a good time to do an *interim analysis*. Up to now, the focus was at the micro level of individual speech acts. I will next take a *systemic* view attempting to evaluate the behavior of the Colombian ex-combatants as part of a potentially deliberative system in the country at large.[53] Taking this approach, one has to take into account that ex-combatants met for the first time to talk about political matters. From a systemic perspective, it is remarkable that they did meet at all, although other ex-combatants refused to take part in the experiments. Overall, the tone of the conversation was civilized with very few expressions of disrespect, although explicit respect was also very rare. The atmosphere was characterized by great cautiousness. Ex-combatants articulated ideas of how Colombia could become a more peaceful country; to be sure, many did not speak up, but seemed to be attentive listeners. Arguments were rarely justified with an appeal to the public interest; most often they were only justified with stories or not at all, but such stories helped to lighten the atmosphere. It seems to me that the behavior of the ex-combatants can be evaluated in a positive way from a systemic perspective. If more group conversations across the deep Colombian divide were to take place in this way, the consequence for the country would be positive. One cannot expect that ex-combatants, meeting for the first time on political matters, would have a spirited discussion with full participation, high mutual respect, and elaborate justifications with frequent references to the common good. For an initial meeting, the discussions of the ex-combatants were good enough and augur well for further, more deliberative conversations.

In *Bosnia–Herzegovina*, the results with regard to respect are similar to those in Colombia. In the experiments in *Srebrenica* with Serbs and Bosnjaks, only one speech act contained foul language of disrespect toward other participants, and only two speech acts showed explicit respect. There was, however, much foul language directed at the local authorities in Srebrenica. Both ordinary Serbs and Bosnjaks complained about corruption and bribery among all members of the local authorities. One complaint was, for example, that scholarships only go to children whose families work for the municipality. Considering the deep ethnic division of the town it is remarkable that

---

[53] For the concept of a deliberative system, see Chapter 1.

one participant complained that the local authorities want to separate the ethnic groups, to "prevent us from living together," so that they can keep their power. Given this negative attitude toward the local authorities, a certain solidarity emerged among the participants in the experiments. Such internal solidarity based on hostility toward the authorities also emerged in the experiments in *Stolac* with Croats and Bosnjaks. This solidarity prevented disrespect among participants but did not go so far as to stimulate explicitly respectful language.

An interim analysis for Bosnia–Herzegovina based on the first four chapters from a systemic perspective looks even more positive than for Colombia. Almost all participants took part in the discussions and were involved in a rapid give-and-take with both sides listening to each other. To be sure, explicit references to the common good were rare and arguments were either not justified at all or only justified with stories. Expressions of explicit respect were rare, as were expressions of explicit disrespect. What was striking was that, even more than in Colombia, stories were used to lighten the atmosphere. Thereby, participants talked only in broad terms about issues like stray dogs, not addressing the question of how exactly such issues should be resolved. In this way, they avoided the danger pointed out by Rostbøll of attaining merely false consensus. Creating a relaxed atmosphere with jokes and laughter seemed a good way to initiate a conversation across the deep ethnic divides in Srebrenica and Stolac. More such group meetings would indeed be good from a systemic perspective. Participants in the experiments were wise enough not to address in a concrete and detailed manner all the serious problems confronting their towns. First, one has to prepare the terrain in creating a "common life world," as Habermas uses the term, and this the participants were able to do. They became aware that irrespective of their ethnic background they were confronted with stray dogs and other very concrete daily problems.

In *Belgium*, of the 1,664 speech acts 10 percent showed respect and 4 percent disrespect toward others. Disrespectful language was rarer than in the national parliaments and the European Parliament and corresponded more to what we found among ex-combatants in Colombia. For the latter, my interpretation was that, given their traumatic past, they were cagey about offending other participants. Such an interpretation does not make sense for ordinary Belgian citizens since they are not traumatized like the ex-combatants in Colombia. Perhaps attacking arguments of others with disrespectful language is a behavior typical of parliamentarians but not of ordinary citizens, not even of ex-combatants. After all, members of parliament want to be re-elected and therefore have an incentive to put others down. Citizens do not have such an incentive, and, as suggested by Talpin, they are reluctant to express disagreements. The Belgian data also reveal that ordinary citizens are somewhat reluctant to express explicit respect, with only 10 percent of the speech acts falling into this category. Showing respect for one particular position may indicate that one disagrees with other positions, and, as Talpin argues, for ordinary citizens "public expression of disagreement is a difficult move."[54]

Looking closer at the Belgian data, we find once again, as we already have for rational justification and references to the common good and moral principles, that with regard to respect the linguistically mixed groups were more deliberative than the homogeneous groups. Indeed, when Walloons and Flemish sat together, only 2 percent of the speech acts were disrespectful and 19 percent respectful. These high levels of respect are all the more remarkable since at the time of the experiments Belgium was in turmoil with regard to the language issue. A binary analysis by gender, age, and education shows no differences between men and women, but higher respect was expressed by highly educated and younger age groups. For Belgium we also have data about interactivity measuring to what extent participants listened to each other and how they reacted to what they heard:

The speaker ignores arguments and questions addressed to him or her	12%
The speaker does not ignore arguments and questions addressed to him or her but intentionally or unintentionally distorts these arguments and questions	13%
The speaker does not ignore arguments and questions addressed to him or her and engages these arguments and questions in a correct and undistorted way	64%
As yet no arguments and questions addressed to this speaker	11%
Total speech acts	100%

These data show a high level of interactivity. Omitting the cases where as yet no questions or arguments had been addressed to a

---

[54] Talpin, *Schools of Democracy*, p. 311.

speaker, in 72 percent the reactions were deliberative in the sense that the speaker acknowledged the arguments and questions in a proper way. For the mixed groups the corresponding figure is as high as 84 percent, reinforcing the point that Flemish and Walloons are more deliberative when they come together than when they meet among themselves. Binary analysis shows here, too, that there are no differences between women and men and that the highly educated and the younger age groups are more deliberative.

I also provide an interim analysis for Belgium based on the first four chapters from a systemic perspective. For a valid comparison with Colombia and Bosnia–Herzegovina, the groups of particular interest are those where Walloons and Flemish met. In these linguistically mixed groups, according to all criteria, deliberation was higher than in the two war-torn countries. What does this mean from a systemic perspective? Did Belgian participants make a greater contribution to a deliberative system than those in Colombia and Bosnia–Herzegovina? In my view, not necessarily. Belgium is a mature democracy without political violence. Therefore, expectations must be higher that Belgian citizens are able and willing to deliberate. Even given the higher democratic standards than in Colombia and Bosnia–Herzegovina, it is still remarkable how deliberative the linguistically mixed groups were, especially when during the same period political leaders were not deliberative at all, being unable to put together a stable cabinet across the linguistic divide. Thus, linguistically mixed groups like the ones we analyzed could have a positive effect from a systemic perspective.

In *Europolis*, in 17 percent of the speech acts the speaker reacted in a positive way to arguments addressed to him or her, in 5 percent in a negative way. The number of respectful speech acts are thus higher than in Belgium in general, but about the same for the mixed groups of Walloons and Flemish. This is a remarkable similarity; in both the mixed Belgian groups and the Europolis groups people who speak different languages met and showed particular respect toward participants speaking another language. Although these data are a hopeful sign for respectful communication across language lines, one should also consider that simultaneous translation was done in both situations, and this technical aspect may have helped mutual respect since participants could only speak up when their microphone was on, which made rude interruptions less likely. With less of a quick give-and-take there were more impediments to making disrespectful statements.

Until the microphone was on, participants had time to check their anger. Europolis also has data about interactivity, which was lower than in Belgium. In 41 percent of the Europolis speech acts the speaker did not react to previous arguments, whereas the corresponding figure was 12 percent in Belgium, as seen above. It seems that EU citizens are still not sufficiently familiar with each other, so they are more reluctant than at the national level to engage each other in a continuing conversation. One may say that EU citizens are cautiously respectful to each other. A hopeful sign for the potential for deliberation in the EU is that participants with extreme views on immigration interacted as much with moderates as among themselves.[55]

Considering also what we found in the first four chapters, the level of deliberation in Europolis was quite similar to Belgium. As an interim analysis, I ask what this similarity means from a systemic perspective. Since the countries of the EU have been at peace for a long time, deliberative standards should be higher than in Colombia and Bosnia–Herzegovina, perhaps at the same level as in Belgium; after all, both the EU and Belgium have deep divisions, though not ones causing political violence. Like in Belgium, ordinary citizens in the EU are remarkably deliberative; more so, it seems to me, than is often the case with EU politicians. Therefore, events like Europolis can make a contribution to a deliberative system at the EU level.

For the *Finnish* experiments on nuclear power, 7 percent of the speech acts contained disrespectful statements, slightly higher than in Belgium and Europolis. A breakdown by gender, age, and education shows that the highest number of disrespectful statements occurred among men, older participants, and those with lower levels of education.[56] The Finnish project also has data on reciprocity: 32 percent of the speech acts contained no references to arguments uttered in previous speech acts. Younger people were more interactive than older people, whereas there were no significant differences by gender and education. The Finnish level of interactivity is lower than in Belgium but higher than in Europolis. The high level of interactivity in Belgium may have been stimulated by the urgency of the language issue in Belgian politics and

---

[55] Marlène Gerber, "Who Are the Voices of Europe? Evidence from a Pan-European Deliberative Poll," paper presented at the ECPR General Conference, Reykjavik, August 25–27, 2011.

[56] The Finnish coders found it too difficult to distinguish between respectful and neutral statements.

the willingness of the participants to find solutions. Doing an interim analysis for Finland from a systemic perspective, we note that the level of deliberation is slightly lower than in Europolis and Belgium. Perhaps one might have expected that a homogeneous country with a consensus culture would have a higher level of deliberation. From a systemic perspective, however, more deliberation in Finland may not be needed; on the contrary, more vigorous competition would be desirable. The Finnish case is a good illustration to discuss to what extent more deliberation is always better. From this view, participants in the Finnish experiments were perhaps well served not to overdo deliberation. Our interim analyses for all five cases have shown that the context must be taken into account if one wishes to evaluate the level of deliberation; there are no absolute standards against which the level of deliberation in different contexts can be evaluated.

Finally, there are some relevant results in the current context of how religious actors in *Switzerland* express arguments on abortion and immigration. As we remember from earlier in the chapter, there is controversy among theorists whether religiously expressed arguments have a place in deliberation. André Bächtiger *et al.* of our research group have investigated for national referenda on abortion and immigration to what extent religious groups and individual religious actors presented their arguments in secular or religious terms. Their results are that "religious actors in the Swiss context use far less religious arguments than one might commonly surmise. When going public, religious actors largely abide by the secular norms of public discourse."[57] This is an important finding that will help me in the next section to develop my normative position with regard to the place of religious arguments in deliberative discourse.

(c) Normative implications of empirical results

The normatively relevant question is how deliberatively minded actors should deal with disrespect. As we have seen in the first section of the chapter, there is great controversy among theorists. Some theorists

---

[57] André Bächtiger, Judith Könemann, Ansgar Jödicke, Roger Husistein, Melanie Zurlinden, Seraina Pedrini, Mirjam Ryser, Kathrin Schwaller, and Dominik Hangartner, "Religious Reasons in the Public Sphere: An Empirical Study of Religious Actors' Argumentative Patterns in Swiss Direct Democratic Campaigns" (unpublished paper, 2010).

argue that even disrespectful arguments have a place in deliberation and should be dealt with, while other theorists are of the opinion that some arguments are so distasteful that they should not be addressed at all. I side with the latter position, having found in empirical studies some arguments that are so disrespectful that they should not be considered at all. I offer three examples from the second section of this chapter to make some general points. During an abortion debate in the German Bundestag, Claus Jäger interrupted a female member, saying that for her argument she deserved a slap in the face; this is a distasteful way to express a disagreement that the female member rightly did not react to. Although Jäger did not mean the slap in the face in a literal way, he still violated the human dignity of his parliamentary colleague. He implied that it would have been better had she not spoken up, thus denying her equal status and freedom of expression. This is exactly what Hansen has in mind when he argues that challenging equality and freedom of expression is not acceptable because it undermines the very foundation of deliberation.

The second example has to do with a Colombian ex-combatant who made the argument that ex-combatants should not get free housing with government money. This is a perfectly legitimate argument that this ex-combatant had every right to make. However, he put it in such foul language that the argument itself lost its credibility. Let me repeat what he said: "Do not be stupid! Crap, man! If you work, fuck, you do not fucking starve! Obviously! Do not wait for the Government to give away houses for free. Go work!" Such wording is not acceptable in parliaments where there are rules about proper language, and rightly so. In my view, such rules, in an informal way, should also apply to political discourse outside parliament. For a good deliberative culture it is important that proper language be used. Arguments may be put in forceful and tough ways, but without such offensive language as the ex-combatant used. He could have said simply that free governmental housing is unnecessary if ex-combatants are willing to work, without underlining the argument with foul language. In my view, in good deliberation other participants should take the liberty to point out that such language is not acceptable. Like parliaments, political parties, interest groups, local school boards, etc. should work out their own rules of proper language.

The third example I draw from the Polish experiments on sex education in schools. As we remember, a fiercely Catholic man made the following statement: "I would request from school ... and not only request but simply demand that teachers should present human sexuality from the Catholic Church perspective ... Otherwise I would not allow for any kind of teaching." In my view, such a statement should not be acceptable in good deliberative discourse because it does not leave any space for reciprocity. The man says, in effect, that either you do the teaching my way or you don't do it all, and I am closed to all other alternatives. Such language should not be tolerated. Other participants should tell the man to adopt a more open position if he wishes to continue to be part of the discussion.

Having set limits on language in deliberative discourse, these limits do not imply that language should always be overly polite. On the contrary, I like a spirited discussion where arguments are put forward in a forceful way. The ex-combatants in Colombia, for example, were often too restrained in the way they put forward their arguments. As a consequence, the discussion was often not very lively. In my view, it is proper to characterize other arguments in negative terms. For example, if an argument appears to a listener as incoherent and logically flawed, this listener should say so and ask for clarification. Such a critical reaction does not imply a lack of respect. On the contrary, it shows that the argument of the other is taken seriously and that one wishes to understand it fully. With this position, I support the idea of Manin that in civil society adversarial debates should be organized where disagreements are not suppressed but forcefully articulated and discussed. Good deliberation should be respectful but at the same time lively and spirited.

The question remains of religious arguments in deliberative discourse. Here the issue is that purely religious arguments cite as justification holy persons, texts, or symbols that non-religious people are not willing to accept as justification. Is it a lack of respect if non-religious persons do not accept religiously based arguments, or is it, on the contrary, a lack of respect if persons insist on their religiously based arguments? To clarify my position, let me take the hypothetical example of a political discussion on a bill deliberating whether in divorce proceedings adultery should be taken as a negative element, for example when deciding on child custody. A participant in the discussion may answer this issue in the affirmative with the justification that the Ten Commandments treat adultery as sin. Should this statement be accepted as valid justification from a deliberative perspective?

I do not think so. I would, however, still allow that this religiously based argument be put forward in deliberative discourse. It should be treated with respect and not a priori be dismissed. Other participants, however, should help to put the argument in secular terms, for example in terms of fairness and social justice. The religiously oriented actor may resist such translation into secular terms, insisting that the only basis for his or her judgment are the Ten Commandments. Under these conditions, in the interest of civility, other participants should not push further because this may put the religiously oriented participant in an uncomfortable position. But other participants are entitled not to enter the substance of the argument with regard to the Ten Commandments.

It is an entirely different matter if many participants, even a majority, take the Ten Commandments as basis for their judgment. I would not consider such a discussion as deliberative because it is based on a doctrinal assumption that cannot be put in question. In my view, in good deliberation all assumptions must be open to being challenged. The research of Bächtiger *et al.* shows that many religious actors are willing and able to translate their religious arguments into secular terms. This means that in the real world of politics religiously oriented people may very well participate as full members in deliberative discourse if they do not insist that their religiously based arguments are unquestionable. I hold the same opinion for any doctrine that is presented as unquestionable. If, for example, someone presents an argument based solely on Marxist or free-market doctrines, this violates deliberative spirit. In true deliberation any position must be open to being challenged. As Sverre Midthjell pointed out to me, logically this principle should also apply to the deliberative model itself. I accept this point and agree that we as deliberative scholars should be willing to deliberate about the worth of deliberation; otherwise deliberation risks becoming an unchallenged dogma.[58]

[58] Personal communication, September 7, 2011.

5 | *Public openness of deliberation*

(a) Normative controversies in the literature

Jürgen Habermas has insisted throughout his career that good deliberation should be public and transparent. He still very much emphasizes this point in a recent publication where he demands "publicity and transparency for the deliberative process."[1] He justifies the logic of publicity in claiming that this is a necessary condition to "generate legitimacy."[2] This Habermasian view was for a long time shared by virtually all deliberative theorists, and many of them still stress the importance of publicity and transparency as a key element of the deliberative model. Claudia Landwehr, for example, argues:

> The strongest incentive for actors to name generalizable reasons and engage in argumentation of them exists where interaction is public ... publicity forces actors to give the best possible justification for their premises and decisions ... Accessibility could be guaranteed if doors remain ajar, for example if a committee meeting that is not organized for a large audience is nonetheless open to interested members of the public, journalists or researchers.[3]

Although Landwehr adheres to the logic of publicity, she acknowledges that in practice publicity may be relative. Her point is that even if doors are not fully open but only ajar, the logic of publicity should still apply in the sense that reasons should be "generalizable and transferable."[4]

There are now, however, theorists who acknowledge that sometimes deliberation is facilitated when it does not take place in the public eye.

[1] Jürgen Habermas, "Political Communication in Media Society: Does Democracy Still Enjoy an Epistemic Dimension? The Impact of Normative Theory on Empirical Research," *Communication Theory* 16 (2006), 413.

[2] Habermas, "Political Communication in Media Society," 413.

[3] Claudia Landwehr, "Discourse and Coordination: Modes of Interaction and Their Roles in Political Decision-Making," *Journal of Political Philosophy* 18 (2010), 105–6.

[4] Personal communication, March 10, 2010.

Simone Chambers was one of the first to raise this issue in asking: "Is it better for public deliberation to go behind closed doors and to insulate deliberators from the harmful effects of the glare of publicity? Or should deliberation be in open forums to insure maximum transparency and citizen scrutiny?"[5] Chambers acknowledges that "all normative theories of deliberative democracy contain something that could be called a publicity principle. The principle has many forms but almost always involves a claim about the salutary effects of going public with the reasons and arguments backing up a policy, proposal or claim."[6] She sees "general agreement among most deliberative theorists about what is salutary about [publicity]: having to defend one's policy preferences in public, leans one towards using public reason ... that this public at large can accept."[7] Although Chambers agrees with the prevailing view among deliberative theorists that publicity has many beneficial effects, she is also concerned that the glare of publicity may lead to what she calls a plebiscitory debate. By this she means "demagoguery, misinformation, inflammatory rhetoric, and flattery put in the service of a predetermined agenda," and also that "the speaker says what the audience wants to hear."[8] The question then is under what conditions publicity has good or bad effects. Chambers hopes "that normative theory can learn something from empirical research. Normative theory needs a more nuanced idea of publicity and its effects on speakers. Empirical research can help build a new typology of publicity that in turn helps us understand the conditions under which openness enhances deliberation and the conditions under which it might harm the quality of debate."[9] As an example, Chambers refers to our empirical research with the Discourse Quality Index (DQI) and finds remarkable "the finding that players in competitive systems are more likely to attempt to discredit their opponent in order to score points with an audience than in consensus-oriented systems."[10]

Robert E. Goodin is another theorist who sees limits to the publicity principle. To be sure, he concedes "that the 'ideal speech situation' would

---

[5] Simone Chambers, "Measuring Publicity's Effect: Reconciling Empirical Research and Normative Theory," *Acta Politica* 40 (2005), 255.
[6] Chambers, "Measuring Publicity's Effect," 256.
[7] Chambers, "Measuring Publicity's Effect," 256.
[8] Chambers, "Measuring Publicity's Effect," 262.
[9] Chambers, "Measuring Publicity's Effect," 255.
[10] Chambers, "Measuring Publicity's Effect," 264.

be best. The very best deliberation, let us suppose, would indeed be a cooperative game among all players in which all the deliberative virtues would be simultaneously and continuously on display."[11] Goodin's

point is simply that politics is not like that, at least not in the sorts of representative democracies that now predominate. But while we cannot seriously expect all the deliberative virtues to be constantly on display at every step of the decision process in a representative democracy, we can realistically expect that different deliberative virtues might be on display at different steps of the process.[12]

According to Goodin, this would hold for the virtue of publicity. For good deliberation it would not be necessary that all phases of a decision process would be completely open to the public. Political parties could "work out their positions behind closed doors. [Their] arguments are then put to the maximally expansive deliberative body, the public at large, at an election … Once voters have electorally determined the distribution of power in parliament, party leaders convene a probably only semi-public session to cut deals."[13] Goodin's "larger point is simply that a staged deliberative process, with different deliberative virtues on display at different stages, might add up to a good enough deliberation."[14] With respect to the publicity principle, this means that it can be tolerated from a deliberative perspective that some parts of a decision process take place behind closed doors as long as other parts are truly open to the public eye. John S. Dryzek also takes such a sequential view of the publicity principle when he writes of "the paradox that effective deliberation sometimes benefits from moments of secrecy [as long as] publicity can enter later or elsewhere in the deliberative system."[15]

(b) Empirical results

In my review of the empirical literature, I found very few studies on deliberation where the research design controlled for public visibility.

---

[11] Robert E. Goodin, "Sequencing Deliberative Moments," *Acta Politica* 40 (2005), 193.
[12] Goodin, "Sequencing Deliberative Moments," 193.
[13] Goodin, "Sequencing Deliberative Moments," 193.
[14] Goodin, "Sequencing Deliberative Moments," 193–4.
[15] John S. Dryzek, "Democratization as Deliberative Capacity Building," *Comparative Political Studies* 42 (2009), 1385.

Our own experiments in Colombia, Bosnia–Herzegovina, Belgium, the EU, and Finland do not shed light on the aspect of public visibility because there was no variation with regard to this element since all experiments took place behind closed doors. For our earlier investigation on parliamentary debates in Germany, Switzerland, the UK, and the US, however, we had a quasi-experimental situation in the sense that we could compare public debates in plenary sessions and committee meetings behind closed doors.[16] In the three preceding chapters, I have shown that plenary sessions were characterized by high levels of logical justification and frequent references to the common good, but little respect for the arguments of others, while committee meetings had exactly the opposite characteristics, high levels of respect, but low levels of logical justifications and infrequent references to the common good. These findings fit the argument of Goodin that realistically we cannot expect to have all deliberative virtues simultaneously all the time. A weakness of the above findings is that committee meetings and plenary sessions vary not only in the level of publicity but also in other important aspects. Most obviously, committee meetings are much smaller in size than plenary sessions. Committee meetings also have quite different functions in the parliamentary decision process than plenary sessions; most notably, committees do not make any final decisions on bills while plenary sessions do. Therefore, we cannot exclude the possibility that at least part of the variation in deliberative virtues is due not to the difference in publicity between committee meetings and plenary sessions but to some other differences between the two types of parliamentary institutions.

Ellen Meade and David Stasavage were able to remedy this weakness in profiting from a quasi-experimental situation in real-life politics. In 1993, the US Congress decided that the verbatim minutes of the US Federal Reserve's Open Market Committee (FOMC) must be published, although only after five years in order not to create financial market volatility. As was subsequently revealed, all pre-1993 meetings had been taped, and contrary to the expectations of participants, these earlier records had been preserved and had to be published as well. Meade and Stasavage describe this quasi-experimental situation

---

[16] Jürg Steiner, André Bächtiger, Markus Spörndli, and Marco R. Steenbergen, *Deliberative Politics in Action: Analysing Parliamentary Discourse* (Cambridge University Press, 2005).

as follows: "As a result, the FOMC transcripts provide a rare opportunity to compare decision-making in two environments: after 1993, when officials knew that their statements would eventually become public, and before 1993, when officials believed (erroneously as it turned out) that their statements would remain private."[17] The FOMC is the committee of the Federal Reserve that has the responsibility for setting short-term interest rate policy. It has 8 regularly scheduled meetings per year and 12 voting members: the 7 members of the Board of Governors of the Federal Reserve and 5 of the 12 presidents of the regional reserve banks. During the period studied by Meade and Stasavage (1989–97), the meetings were always chaired by Alan Greenspan, Chairman of the Federal Reserve, who at the beginning of each meeting made an interest rate policy recommendation. The other committee members then had the opportunity to express dissent. Meade and Stasavage make the reasonable assumption that the higher the number of such dissents, the higher the level of deliberation because a wider range of views is expressed. Controlling for factors like inflation and productivity during the period under study, Meade and Stasavage indeed found a strong effect of publicity. They

estimate that a Fed Governor would have had a 10% likelihood of verbally dissenting before the 1993 change and only a 3% likelihood of verbally dissenting after transcript publication began. This is a very significant drop. When we conduct a similar exercise for voting Bank presidents, we observe that they would have a 17% likelihood of dissenting before 1993 and a 13% likelihood of dissenting after transcript publication began. This is a smaller but still significant reduction in the probability of dissent.[18]

Meade and Stasavage conclude from their investigation "that while there may be clear benefits to establishing greater transparency in government, advocates and institutional designers should also take into account the possibility that openness can entail important costs."[19] This conclusion fits the concern of Chambers that not all publicity has beneficial effects.

Robert J. MacCoun gives an informative overview of the psychological literature on the effects of publicity. He begins his essay in

---

[17] Ellen Meade and David Stasavage, "Two Effects of Transparency on the Quality of Deliberation," *Swiss Political Science Review* 12 (2006), 123.

[18] Meade and Stasavage, "Two Effects of Transparency," 130.

[19] Meade and Stasavage, "Two Effects of Transparency," 131.

the following way: "In a democratic society, the desirability of openness and transparency in government decision making would seem
nearly self-evident."[20] He then shows that "some attempts to achieve
transparency may have unintended and undesirable consequences."[21]
MacCoun relies heavily on experimentation with college students, and
he is very much aware of the limits of such experiments for real life in
politics: "These studies provide strong causal inferences about cognitive mechanisms, but weak external validity. Importantly, these experiments inevitably exclude organizational structure, historical context,
and most of the tactical and dramatic elements that characterize the
'rough and tumble' of real-world politics. Thus, the ideas presented
here should be considered hypotheses for further consideration rather
than firm conclusions about political systems."[22] Being aware of the
limited validity of experiments with students for political decision-
making, MacCoun still claims that "a basic finding in social psychology is that public commitment to a position makes people more
resistant to moderating their views in light of subsequent argument."[23]
Should this finding indeed apply to politics, we would have to conclude that a key deliberative element is hurt by publicity since actors
would be less willing to change their positions based on the force of the
better argument. The summary conclusion of MacCoun with regard
to the effects of publicity is mixed: "Efforts to increase transparency
can and probably do eliminate many decisions from the worst end of
the continuum, but it is conceivable that they do so at the expense of
impairing high quality decisions at the other extreme."[24] Here again,
empirical data show that it is problematic to consider publicity as an
unquestionable virtue in the deliberative model. Daniel Naurin arrives
at the same conclusion based on interviews with business lobbyists in
Sweden and the EU. Contrary to his expectation, these lobbyists were
more civilized behind closed doors than in public.[25]

---

[20] Robert J. MacCoun, "Psychological Constraints on Transparency in Legal and
    Government Decision Making," *Swiss Political Science Review* 12 (2006), 112.
[21] MacCoun, "Psychological Constraints on Transparency," 113.
[22] MacCoun, "Psychological Constraints on Transparency," 113.
[23] MacCoun, "Psychological Constraints on Transparency," 116.
[24] MacCoun, "Psychological Constraints on Transparency," 121.
[25] Daniel Naurin, *Deliberation Behind Closed Doors* (Colchester: ECPR Press,
    2007).

(c) Normative implications of empirical results

Although not much empirical research is available on the effect of public openness on deliberation, the research that I could present still allows having some doubts on whether public openness is always good for deliberation, as claimed by many theorists, or whether there are situations where deliberation profits from confidentiality. The question then is when, in the interest of good deliberation, it is advisable to keep a discussion out of the public eye. We need to think here in terms of different phases of a political decision process, as Goodin has suggested.[26] We have seen earlier in the chapter that he has presented interesting ideas about phases in which deliberation is particularly important and phases where it has less importance. I now attempt to elaborate on Goodin's ideas with regard to the specific aspect of public openness. I find it important that the early phase of a decision process takes place away from the public eye. This is the phase where new creative ideas should be discussed. As the psychological research of MacCoun has shown, a non-public environment makes it more likely that actors do not stick to their old positions but are willing to consider new ideas. Politicians are always in danger of being considered unprincipled and wishy-washy if they change their positions, so in public they have a tendency to stick to their positions. Behind closed doors, however, they have the luxury of time and privacy to speculate about new ideas. Therefore, I agree with Goodin that it may be better if political parties work out new positions behind closed doors. In this way, they can play with new ideas without immediately being criticized by other parties. Informal brainstorming groups may be helpful in this respect.

In an earlier research project, I studied such a brainstorming group by participant observation in the Free Democratic Party of the Bern Canton in Switzerland.[27] For two years, I was able to attend all party meetings, a total of 111 meetings. Among these meetings was a regular working luncheon of the party president, the party secretary, and

[26] Robert E. Goodin, "Sequencing Deliberative Moments," *Acta Politica* 40 (2005), 182–96.

[27] Jürg Steiner and Robert H. Dorff, *A Theory of Political Decision Making: Intraparty Decision Making in Switzerland* (Chapel Hill: University of North Carolina Press, 1980).

the two Free Democratic cabinet members of the cantonal executive. At the beginning of these working luncheons, my silent observer status was somewhat awkward, but after a while the four top party leaders got accustomed to my presence so that their discussion could take their normal path. I assured them that no details of these luncheon meetings would ever be revealed and that I was only interested to establish causal relations among various characteristics of the observed meetings. Comparing these luncheon meetings with more formal party meetings, I was struck by the highly deliberative nature of the luncheon meetings. There was no fixed agenda. The conversation usually began with non-political issues like sport events, and in these initial conversations I also took part, which made my role as observer less awkward. Slowly, the discussion then turned to political issues. No formal decisions were ever made since these informal luncheon meetings had no authority to do so. The purpose was to hear new ideas about future policy positions of the party. When stating new ideas, the four leaders often emphasized that these ideas were not yet carefully thought out and possibly would lead nowhere. In a quick interactive give-and-take, the discussion was usually spirited with the leaders carefully listening to each other. In sum, the level of deliberation tended to be high. It was clear that the confidential nature of these working luncheons behind closed doors helped with their deliberative nature.

In recent public debate not only in Switzerland but in many other countries as well, such informal party discussions get a bad rap as backroom politics. In my view, however, political parties are well served if they prepare their long-term positions in such informal non-public brainstorming meetings. Such meetings, of course, should involve not only top party leaders but also lower-level party leaders, and most importantly, ordinary party members and supporters also. Here the idea of mini-publics, as discussed in Chapter 1, can be implemented. Randomly selected groups of party members and supporters would get the task to come up with new ideas for the party program.

With political parties having established their policy positions in a broad-based internal process, at election time, as Goodin puts it, they can submit their positions "to the maximally expansive deliberative body, the public at large."[28] Here then, a high degree of public

---

[28] Goodin, "Sequencing Deliberative Moments," 193.

openness is given. In other respects, however, the level of deliberation is low in election campaigns. This is particularly true for the willingness to yield to the force of the better argument. When party leaders debate their respective election platforms on television, one should not expect that they be convinced by arguments of the other side. And this is a good thing. Otherwise, the election campaign would have a fluidity that would make it hard for voters to make up their minds, since they would be unsure where the individual parties really stand. On the basis of some of the data presented in Section (b), one has also to expect that in the heat of the election campaign some of the rhetoric may be low on mutual respect. There seems to be a trade-off between public openness and other deliberative elements. If public visibility is low, other deliberative elements flourish, and when public visibility is high, other deliberative elements suffer.

When the election is over, a cabinet has to be put together. In parliamentary systems, this usually means putting together a coalition of two or more parties. If a single party is strong enough to form the cabinet alone, intraparty negotiations are still necessary. Negotiations to put a cabinet together are also necessary in presidential systems. As we have seen in Section (a), according to Goodin, in all these cases "party leaders convene a probably only semi-public session to cut deals." Empirically, this is probably true, and some of these negotiations may even take place behind closed doors. Normatively, however, I think that negotiations to put together a cabinet should be in full public view. Voters, after all, should be allowed to see how the policy positions of the various actors are put together into a cabinet program. Voters should be suspicious of deals where, for example, support for the cabinet is bought with appointments of unqualified people to governmental positions or wasteful governmental subsidies. Therefore, party leaders should make explicit to the public which criteria are used to put together the cabinet program, and they have to explain why some electoral policy programs are included and others dropped. Cabinet formation should be more than deal-making, where each group attempts to maximize its own position. In my view, in cabinet formation the level of deliberation should be at a high level. Negotiations should be in full public view, arguments should be justified in an elaborate way and in terms of the common good, the policy positions of all negotiating partners should be considered with respect, and negotiators should be willing to yield to the force of the better argument. Under these conditions, there is hope for a coherent cabinet program.

When a cabinet and its policy program have been established, the next phase is the preparation of enabling legislation. For this phase, public openness should be at a minimum. To prepare good legislation, much creative detailed work is necessary. The government bureaucracy, often helped by outside advisory committees, should be able to focus in a concentrated way on this work, without constantly being questioned by journalists and lobbied by interest groups. The cabinet members in charge and the cabinet at large also have great responsibilities in preparing draft legislation. For this task, they should also be shielded from constant public scrutiny. In my view, cabinet meetings should be kept confidential. Leaks to the media hurt the free and creative exchange of ideas among cabinet members. With the same argument, minutes of cabinet meetings should not be verbatim but should register only cabinet decisions. Later in the decision process, cabinet members will be highly exposed to public view. But when they prepare draft legislation they should be able to do this among themselves in a confidential way, which should help with the coherence of what they decide upon.

Draft legislation then passes to parliamentary committees. Sometimes, parliamentary committees take it upon themselves to draft legislation. Whatever path is chosen, it is controversial whether parliamentary committees should be open to the public or not. In most countries, parliamentary committees meet behind closed doors. Landwehr, however, as we have seen earlier in the chapter, advocates that doors to parliamentary committees should stay "ajar," allowing access to researchers and journalists. From a deliberative perspective, trade-offs are involved. As we have seen earlier in the chapter, meetings behind closed doors help parliamentary committees to reach a high level of reciprocity compared with public plenary sessions. Opening the doors to parliamentary committees may remove this advantage, which would be detrimental to interactive give-and-take in discussing draft legislation. A possible solution may be to give access only to a single so-called "pool" journalist. This method is sometimes chosen in delicate situations where giving access to all journalists would be disruptive. A trusted member of the journalistic corps is then chosen to report for all. For parliamentary committees, limits could be set for such a "pool" journalist in the sense that he or she could report only on the arguments discussed but not on who makes the arguments. In this way, the public could begin to make up its mind on the merits of the various arguments. At the same time, committee members could still feel free to have a spirited exchange of views without immediately being exposed to public criticism. In the current media situation, such a proposal may seem naive but it is still worth trying.

When draft legislation reaches the plenary sessions of parliament, there is agreement among theorists that the debates must be in full public view. This is indeed the time when the public learns in a final way what the arguments are and who supports the various positions. From a deliberative perspective, there is a different trade-off than in the committees: the glare of publicity encourages parliamentarians to justify their arguments in an elaborate way and to refer often to the public good; at the same time, however, there is less mutual respect shown during plenary sessions.

Having described the entire decision process with regard to public openness, the question is where exactly ordinary citizens fit in. In which decision phases do they have the best opportunities to take an active part in the decision process? When political parties develop their policy positions behind closed doors, as I suggested above, ordinary party members and supporters should also be involved, in the form of randomly chosen mini-publics. The discussions could take place face-to-face, or, often more conveniently, online. For a practical example of how this can be done, I will discuss in Chapter 8 the research of Raphaël Kies on the Radical Party in Italy.

When political parties present their policy positions in election campaigns, this is the time for all citizens to become heavily involved. Citizens should deliberate with each other about the policy positions of the various parties. In this context, Bruce Ackerman and James S. Fishkin have presented the idea of a Deliberation Day before presidential elections in the US:

Deliberation Day would begin with a nationally televised debate between the presidential candidates, conducted in the traditional way. But then citizens would deliberate in small groups of 15, and later in larger plenary assemblies. The small groups would begin where the televised debate left off. Each group would spend an hour defining questions that the candidates had left unanswered. Everybody would then proceed to a 500-citizen assembly to hear their questions answered by local party representatives. After lunch, participants would repeat the morning procedure. By the end of the day, citizens would have moved far beyond the top-down debate of the morning. Through a deliberative process of question and answer, they would have achieved a bottom-up understanding of the choices confronting the nation.[29]

I support this idea of a Deliberative Day, although in praxis it may be organized only by some local communities and not nationally. The crucial point in the present context is that citizens do not merely listen to the election campaign in a passive way but get actively involved in discussing the policy positions of the various parties with other citizens.

When it comes to the preparation of draft legislation, ordinary citizens can be involved with randomly drawn mini-publics. This involvement can be done in a formal way. Just as experts are consulted in order to prepare legislation, randomly chosen mini-publics of ordinary citizens can be consulted as well. I agree with the following statement of Maija Setälä, who also wishes to make mini-publics part of the formal decision process: "The impact of mini-publics could be strengthened by the institutionalization of their use and by developing ways in which their recommendations are dealt with in representative institutions."[30] When parliamentary debates begin, usually first in committees and then in plenary sessions, the views of ordinary citizens tend to come into play only through survey data. It is a key message of this book that opinions of ordinary citizens should not simply be asked in a raw form from the top of their heads. Citizens should first deliberate their opinions with other citizens so that their opinions are more reflective. Here, randomly chosen mini-publics can again be of crucial importance. During parliamentary debates, mini-publics should be organized around the country, and in this phase of the decision process their discussions should be widely publicized with the help of newspapers, radio, and television. It is also important that moderators of mini-publics steer the discussions in such a way that they arrive at clear positions with regard to the issues debated in parliament. If mini-publics represent a random sample of the entire citizenship, their

---

[29] Bruce Ackerman and James S. Fishkin, "For a Smarter Public: Deliberation Day," *The American Prospect*, January 1, 2004.

[30] Maija Setälä, "Designing Issue-Focused Forms of Citizen Participation," paper presented at the Conference on Democracy: A Citizen Perspective, Åbo, May 25–27, 2010, p. 15.

policy positions will have a significant influence on the outcome of parliamentary debates.

Ordinary citizens have an even greater say if parliamentary decisions are submitted to a referendum, as is regularly the case in Switzerland.[31] Other countries increasingly use the referendum. Even the UK, the classical case of a pure parliamentary system, submitted the reform of its electoral system to a national referendum in May 2011. From the perspective of deliberative democracy, I support an increased usage of the referendum because referendum campaigns give citizens good opportunities to deliberate policy issues. For Swiss referenda, Hanspeter Kriesi found "evidence that Swiss voters are less minimalist than generally expected," and that "argument-based voting" is quite frequent. Of great importance is his finding "that the quality of the deliberation of individual voters crucially depends on the quality of the arguments exchanged among members of the political elites in the course of the debate preceding the vote."[32] This finding suggests the possibility of a positive feedback loop between political leaders and voters. If the leaders discuss at a high deliberative level, this stimulates good deliberation at the citizen level, which may send a signal to the leaders to further increase the quality of their discourse since they become aware of how reflective citizens have become. Randomly chosen mini-publics should play an important role in such positive feedback processes. I agree with Yves Sintomer that a combination of referenda and mini-publics offers an "interesting path" for democratic renewal.[33] This path was chosen in British Colombia where, for the discussion of a new electoral law, a "Citizens' Assembly" chosen by lot was coupled with a referendum of the citizens at large.[34] All in all, I am optimistic about the potential of referenda combined with mini-publics to increase the level of deliberation in a country. The caveat is, however, that referenda needs to be used over a long period to be a useful vehicle to increase the quality of deliberation. The one-shot

---

[31] Markus M.L. Crepaz and Jürg Steiner, *European Democracies*, 7th edn. (New York: Longman, 2010), pp. 124–8.

[32] Hanspeter Kriesi, "Argument-Based Strategies in Direct-Democratic Votes: The Swiss Experience," *Acta Politica* 40 (2005), 299.

[33] Yves Sintomer, "Random Selection, Republican Self-Government, and Deliberative Democracy," *Constellations* 17 (2010), 484.

[34] Mark E. Warren and Hilary Pearse, *Designing Deliberative Democracy: The British Colombian Citizens' Assembly* (Cambridge University Press, 2008).

referendum, as in the Netherlands on the EU Constitution, may even be detrimental to good deliberation.[35]

This chapter has suggested that public openness is certainly an important deliberative element but it cannot have the same importance in all phases of a political decision process. From a systemic level, the crucial point is that overall public openness is good enough if ordinary citizens have sufficient access points to see what is going on at critical junctures and how they can make their influence felt. For a deliberative system it is not necessary and not even desirable that all phases of a political decision process are open to the public. A certain confidentiality in some phases is quite compatible with the requirements of a deliberative system.

[35] Crepaz and Steiner, *European Democracies*, p. 303.

6 | *Force of better argument in deliberation*

(a) Normative controversies in the literature

When Jürgen Habermas postulates "the unforced force of the better argument,"[1] he goes to the very core of the deliberative model. The essence of the statement is that political decisions should be based on good arguments. What constitutes a good argument is not a priori given but must be found out in mutual discussion where everyone has an equal voice. As John S. Dryzek puts it, "no individuals may possess authority on the basis of anything other than a good argument."[2] The controversy concerns the question of to what extent reasonable people can agree what the best arguments are and therefore what the probability of consensus is. Habermas expresses hope that consensus is possible when he writes that "consensus brought about through argument must rest on identical reasons that are able to convince parties in the same way."[3] Joshua A. Cohen also emphasizes that "ideal deliberation aims to arrive at a rationally motivated consensus."[4] Note that neither Habermas nor Cohen argue that deliberation will always lead to consensus; they merely express hope that this may be the case. In a pragmatic way, they also accept that sometimes consensus may be based on different reasons. Michael A. Neblo goes a step further in pointing out that in the interest of pluralism it may sometimes even be better if actors offer different reasons for a specific policy because this may lead to a more lively

---

[1] Jürgen Habermas, *Between Facts and Norms: Contributions to a Discourse Theory of Law and Democracy* (Cambridge, MA: MIT Press, 1996), p. 305.

[2] John S. Dryzek, *Discursive Democracy: Politics, Policy, and Political Science* (Cambridge University Press, 1990), p. 41.

[3] Habermas, *Between Facts and Norms*, p. 166.

[4] Joshua A. Cohen, "Deliberation and Democratic Legitimacy," in Alan Hamlin and Philip Pettit (eds.), *The Good Polity: Normative Analysis of the State* (Oxford: Blackwell, 1989), p. 23.

debate.[5] As an illustration he mentions that a coalition to eliminate agricultural subsidies for growing corn may mix those who support the measure primarily on grounds of economic efficiency and those who support it primarily out of environmental concerns. For Neblo there is nothing wrong from a deliberative perspective if such a coalition forms.

There are deliberative theorists like Robert E. Goodin, who warns that "reasonable disagreement is a fact of life in complex societies … public deliberation can help us to see others as 'reasonable', albeit, in our view, still wrong."[6] In the same vein, James Bohman and Henry S. Richardson doubt that there are always reasons that all can accept: "On account of having different conceptions of what counts as a reason, different people will be unable to accept different things as being reasons."[7] They argue "that the idea of deliberative democracy cannot solve the problem of pluralism by offering up the idea of reasons that all can accept as a specification of what it means for diverse people to give reasons to one another."[8] Bohman and Richardson illustrate their position with the following example: "Some may refuse to recognize the fact that the Bible says one ought not to engage in certain behavior as a reason we ought not to allow it, while others may believe that this is a paradigmatic reason for action."[9] Luigi Pellizzoni writes in the very title of his paper of "the myth of the best argument";[10] he argues that "sometimes conflicts are deep-lying, principles and factual descriptions are profoundly different, and uncertainty is radical. The best argument cannot be found."[11] Pellizzoni still expects, however, that deliberation can lead to non-strategic agreements. For him, "the purpose of deliberation is not to reach agreement on the reasons for a choice, but to reach non-strategic agreement."[12] He postulates "a dialogue in which

---

[5] Michael A. Neblo, *Common Voices: Between the Theory and Practice of Deliberative Democracy* (unpublished book manuscript), see especially ch. 4.

[6] Robert E. Goodin, "Talking Politics: Perils and Promise," *European Journal of Political Research* 45 (2006), 254–5.

[7] James Bohman and Henry S. Richardson, "Liberalism, Deliberative Democracy, and Reasons That All Can Accept," *Journal of Political Philosophy* 17 (2009), 254.

[8] Bohman and Richardson, "Liberalism, Deliberative Democracy," 253.

[9] Bohman and Richardson, "Liberalism, Deliberative Democracy," 254.

[10] Luigi Pellizzoni, "The Myth of the Best Argument: Power, Deliberation and Reason," *British Journal of Sociology* 52 (2001), 59.

[11] Pellizzoni, "The Myth of the Best Argument," 59.

[12] Pellizzoni, "The Myth of the Best Argument," 81.

the argumentation is cautious and non-categorical, and which looks for similarities and isomorphisms between events and practice."[13] If consensus is not achieved and a vote has to be taken, Anne Elizabeth Stie considers it crucial that the losing minority feels fairly treated: "If an issue has been properly treated in a fair process, the likelihood is that those who were opposed to the outcome will nevertheless respect it as a legitimate constraint on their behaviour despite the fact that their position was rejected in the final decision-making moment."[14]

Some theorists even see a danger if the emphasis is put on consensus. Thus, Kasper M. Hansen warns that consensus may not always be desirable since "it can elude some arguments from the discussion as some participants might be reluctant to voice views that are in conflict with the emerging consensus ... an *a priori* restriction on consensus being the outcome of deliberation would violate the very idea of a pluralistic society."[15] From the perspective of critical theory, Christian F. Rostbøll goes a step further in postulating that sometimes deliberation has the task of breaking up consensus: "Under certain conditions, I shall argue, deliberation should aim not at creating consensus but at breaking an existing consensus, at least as an initial step."[16] What are these conditions that Rostbøll refers to? He mentions domination of any kind, in particular workers under capitalism, women in patriarchal societies, and minority cultures. Under such conditions, the very core of deliberative democracy must be

a concern with the possibility of criticizing ideologies, biases, conventions, and the like ... if agreement is the product of ideological domination, then the aim of deliberation is to show that the agreement is only apparent, or that it is not the product of free deliberation. To see this, deliberative democrats should not forget their roots in critical theory and the importance of the critique of ideology.[17]

For Rostbøll, "a common misunderstanding of deliberative democracy is that it sees any agreement reached on the basis of talk as good. But

---

[13] Pellizzoni, "The Myth of the Best Argument," 80–1.
[14] Anne Elizabeth Stie, *Democratic Decision-Making in the EU: Or Technocracy in Disguise?* (unpublished book manuscript), ch. 2.
[15] Kasper M. Hansen, *Deliberative Democracy and Opinion Formation* (Odense: University Press of Southern Denmark, 2004), p. 103.
[16] Christian F. Rostbøll, *Deliberative Freedom: Deliberative Democracy as Critical Theory* (Albany: State University of New York Press, 2008), p. 23.
[17] Rostbøll, *Deliberative Freedom*, pp. 25, 149.

clearly language is not only a medium of reaching free agreements; it also can be used as means of domination, exclusion, and social power."[18] Rostbøll is not in principle against consensus, but agreement must be based on personal autonomy, which means "to be continually open to learning, to revise one's views in light of new evidence."[19]

Henrik Friberg-Fernros and Johan Karlsson Schaffer speculate on a possible paradox with regard to the role of consensus in deliberative theory.[20] They ask the question, "if deliberation aims to reach a rationally grounded consensual agreement, what happens to deliberation after that aim has been attained?"[21] They fear that "reaching a massive consensus results in a homogeneous opinion environment, where the conditions for deliberating are worse than in an environment with greater dissent and heterogeneity in opinions. If dissent fuels political debate, replacing it with consensus will likely cause deliberative activities to stagnate." Normatively, Friberg-Fernros and Schaffer conclude from their argument that it "might point in the direction of those normative models of deliberative democracy that put less emphasis on the search for consensual agreement and play up the agonistic quality of public deliberation, recognizing reasoned disagreements as a valid outcome."[22] In the same vein, Stefan Rummens postulates "that we resist the urge to insist on reaching actual agreements in the real world because this might lead to the premature closure of deliberation."[23] Giovan Francesco Lanzara warns that participants may censor themselves, not daring to express divergent opinions.[24]

---

[18] Rostbøll, *Deliberative Freedom*, pp. 148–9.
[19] Rostbøll, *Deliberative Freedom*, p. 87.
[20] Henrik Friberg-Fernros and Johan Karlsson Schaffer, "The Consensus Paradox: Why Deliberative Agreement Impedes Rational Discourse," paper presented at the Oslo–Paris International Workshop on Democracy, Paris, October 18–20, 2010.
[21] Friberg-Fernros and Schaffer, "The Consensus Paradox," p. 2.
[22] Friberg-Fernros and Schaffer, "The Consensus Paradox," p. 11.
[23] Stefan Rummens, "Staging Deliberation: The Role of Representative Institutions in the Deliberative Democratic Process," paper presented at the Workshop on the Frontiers of Deliberation, ECPR Joint Sessions, St. Gallen, April 12–17, 2011, p. 11.
[24] Giovan Francesco Lanzara, "La deliberazione come indagine publicca," in Luigi Pellizzoni (ed.), *La deliberazione publica* (Rome: Meltemi editore, 2005), p. 70: "La pressione alla costruzione del consenso ... può avvenire addirittura attraverso l'auto-censura."

In conclusion, one can say that theorists agree on the importance of arguments but differ widely on the role of consensus in the deliberative model and on how much preferences should change as a result of deliberation. Theorists disagree whether the goal of deliberation is merely to clarify positions or to bring positions together.

(b) Empirical results

Literature review

There are very few empirical studies in the literature about the force of the better argument, and from the existing studies it is difficult to establish whether positions are indeed changed by the force of the better argument or for strategic reasons. In our previous research on parliamentary debates in Germany, Switzerland, the UK, and the US we distinguish between plenary sessions and committee meetings.[25] In plenary sessions, in 2.2 percent of the speech acts the speaker explicitly indicated a change in position, in committee meetings there were 4.5 percent such speech acts. It is hard to say to what extent such willingness to change position is caused by the force of the better argument. It is also possible that actors move from their initial position based on strategic bargaining in order to reach a compromise acceptable to all sides. We have to recognize that in this crucial aspect of the deliberative model, empirical research can only go so far. Why actors yield from their initial position is hard to determine and may not even be fully known to the actors themselves. There are probably many intermediate cases where arguments play a role but where strategic bargaining is also important. That changes of positions are more frequent in committees than in plenary sessions is no surprise. Perhaps it is more surprising that there were any changes in positions in the formal and public setting of plenary sessions.

We also studied under what conditions parliamentary debates ended with a consensus. We were particularly interested in whether a high level of deliberation helped to reach consensus. As we have seen in the analyses above and in previous chapters, the level of deliberation in

---

[25] Jürg Steiner, André Bächtiger, Markus Spörndli, and Marco R. Steenbergen, *Deliberative Politics in Action: Analysing Parliamentary Discourse* (Cambridge University Press, 2005), pp. 178–9.

parliamentary debates is quite low, so we do not have enough variation to explain the occurrence of consensus. Therefore, we looked for a parliamentary setting particularly favorable for deliberation, and we found it in the German Mediation Committee (*Vermittlungsausschuss*).[26] This committee has the task to mediate disagreements between the two chambers of the German parliament, and has an equal number of members from both chambers. It meets behind closed doors, and its minutes are kept secret for a certain number of years. The committee can solicit expert testimony and hear from representatives of the government. The proposals that the committee works out have to go back to the two parliamentary chambers for acceptance. Proposals that do not have wide support in the committee are likely to fail in the further parliamentary process, so there is considerable incentive for the committee to adhere to deliberative methods. For the selection of the decision cases, we had to go sufficiently far back in time to access minutes of the Mediation Committee that were no longer kept secret. We also wanted no change in the government composition to keep this important institutional variable under control. We settled on the years of the coalition of Social Democrats and Free Democrats from 1969 to 1982. We selected 20 decision cases, for which we coded all speech acts with our Discourse Quality Index (DQI). The overall level of deliberation was indeed quite high, allowing us to identify ten cases with a substantial level of deliberation. We could then compare these ten cases with the other ten cases where the level of deliberation was sufficiently low that we had enough variation in our explanatory variable. Thus, we could investigate whether the level of deliberation in a decision process had an influence on whether the committee reached consensus. This was indeed the case in the sense that a high level of deliberation significantly increased the likelihood of a consensus outcome. In the ten cases with high discourse quality, consensus was reached in nine cases; in the ten cases with low discourse quality, only two cases. This difference is statistically highly significant.[27] Consensus was also helped when the initial positions were evenly divided, when the issue under discussion was not very polarizing, and when the actors were relatively young. Introducing these three aspects as control variables

---

[26] Steiner *et al.*, *Deliberative Politics in Action*, pp. 138–64.

[27] Steiner *et al.*, *Deliberative Politics in Action*, pp. 145, 150. There it is also described that the definition of consensus allows a few dissenting votes.

into the logistic regression analysis did not wash out the effect of the level of discourse quality. The overall conclusion of our investigation is that under favorable institutional conditions such as the German Mediating Committee the level of deliberation may be quite high, which, in turn, helps to reach consensus decisions.

The research of Elzbieta Wesolowska on Polish parents discussing sex education in school, mentioned in previous chapters, also has interesting findings with regard to the consensus aspect. Consensus was easier when the discussion groups consisted only of women who shared, in the term of Habermas, a common *Lebenswelt* (life world) of motherhood and sexuality.[28] The research of Wesolowska is also relevant to the statement of Habermas quoted above that "consensus brought about through argument must rest on identical reasons." There were indeed some cases where Polish parents reached consensus on this Habermasian basis. But there were other cases where common solutions were found "despite their justifications through differing rationales ... for example, in one of the groups, parents agreed that the school should discourage the use of chemical contraception and justified it with very different rationales. Some parents indicated the health risk of using chemicals while others pointed to a contradiction with the teachings of the Catholic Church."[29] This example does not fulfill the Habermasian demand for a true consensus, whereas for other theorists like Goodin the example is quite compatible with good deliberation.[30]

Claudia Landwehr and Katharina Holzinger in a German study addressed how much preferences change as a result of deliberation at the level of both parliamentarians and ordinary citizens.[31] They compared the discussion on embryonic stem cells in the Bundestag and a citizens' conference.[32] In the Bundestag, 460 members had signed one of three motions before the debate, while 138 members had not done so. Of those who had signed a motion, only a single member changed

---

[28] Elzbieta Wesolowska, "Social Processes of Antagonism and Synergy in Deliberating Groups," *Swiss Political Science Review* 13 (2007), 677.

[29] Wesolowska, "Social Processes of Antagonism," 677.

[30] Goodin, "Talking Politics," *passim*.

[31] Claudia Landwehr and Katharina Holzinger, "Institutional Determinants of Deliberative Interaction," *European Political Science Review* 2 (2010), 373–400.

[32] For the research design for the citizens' conference, see Section (b) of Chapter 9.

his position, voting in the first ballot for his initial motion, changing in the second ballot to another motion, but returning in the third ballot to his initial motion. Landwehr and Holzinger give three possible reasons for these changes: in the second ballot he may have accidentally ticked the wrong box, he was convinced in informal conversations between the ballots, or he changed on the basis of the debate.[33] They are unsure which of these alternative explanations is the most plausible. Whether any of the 138 members who had not signed a motion before the debate changed preferences during the debate was difficult to determine. Landwehr and Holzinger attempted to investigate this problem by sending questionnaires to these members. Only 26 sent back the questionnaires. As Landwehr and Holzinger concede, "the small number of respondents does not allow us to draw far-reaching conclusions from the survey."[34] Analyzing the 26 survey responses, they find "only a single case of manifest preference transformation in the sample: one respondent indicates that, originally a supporter of a complete ban, she was persuaded to vote for a compromise motion."[35] Landwehr and Holzinger conclude that "the number of MPs who did change their preferences seems to be extremely small."[36] One has to be careful, however, not to generalize this finding too much. It is not only in committee meetings but also in plenary sessions of parliament that occasionally preferences are changed, as I have shown above with our investigation of parliamentary debates in Germany, Switzerland, the UK, and the US. A particularly dramatic case happened in the US Senate during a debate on the Confederate flag when Carol Moseley Braun, the chamber's only black member, made an emotional plea that the patent for the flag should not be renewed. "Her radical challenge stimulated a reflective and highly respectful debate that changed senators' minds, or at least their position."[37] Another well-illustrated

---

[33] Landwehr and Holzinger, "Institutional Determinants of Deliberative Interaction," 394.

[34] Landwehr and Holzinger, "Institutional Determinants of Deliberative Interaction," 395.

[35] Landwehr and Holzinger, "Institutional Determinants of Deliberative Interaction," 395.

[36] Landwehr and Holzinger, "Institutional Determinants of Deliberative Interaction," 395.

[37] André Bächtiger, "On Perfecting the Deliberative Process: Agonistic Inquiry as a Key Deliberative Technique," paper presented at the annual meeting of the American Political Science Association, Washington, DC, September 2–5, 2010.

case in this context is a debate in the Swiss parliament about a linguistic amendment to the constitution where some positions were changed.[38]

To come back to the study of Landwehr and Holzinger: for ordinary citizens they organized a group discussion on embryonic stem cells, held over three weekends. They also had a control group without a discussion. In this control group, there were no significant changes over the three weeks; in the discussion group, however, there were significant changes in the sense that participants became more critical with regard to stem-cell technology. This is strongly persuasive that the dialogical nature of the meetings led to many transformations of preferences. We should also note, however, that Landwehr and Holzinger do not code whether there were any cases where, during the discussion, participants explicitly changed position and acknowledged that this happened by the force of the better argument of other participants. As we will see next, this is precisely the aspect that we investigated in our experiments.

New data on deliberative experiments[39]

In *Colombia* we distinguished with regard to the force of the better argument four categories:

1. The speaker indicates a change of position. Gives as reason for change arguments heard during the experiment.
2. The speaker indicates a change of position. Does not refer to arguments heard during the group discussion.
3. The speaker does not indicate a change in position. Does acknowledge the value of other positions heard during the group discussion.
4. The speaker does not indicate a change in position. Does not acknowledge the value of other positions heard during the group discussion.

---

[38] André Bächtiger, Seraina Pedrini, and Mirjam Ryser, "Prozessanalyse politischer Entscheidungen: Deliberative Standards, Diskurstypen und Sequenzialisierung," in Joachim Behnke, Thomas Bräuninger, and Susumu Shikano (eds.), *Jahrbuch für Handlungs- und Entscheidungstheorie*, vol. VI (Wiesbaden: VS Verlag, 2010).

[39] For the research designs, see Introduction, Section (b).

With these categories, we do not capture changes in position from the pre-experiment to the post-experiment questionnaires. We will further explore this aspect in Chapter 9. In the context of the present chapter, we are interested in whether participants explicitly acknowledge a change in position based on the force of the better argument or at least acknowledge the value of other positions. None of the speech acts of the ex-combatants could be coded according to the first two categories. The fact that nobody acknowledged having changed his or her position does not look deliberative. We have already seen in previous chapters that ex-combatants behaved in a very cautious way during discussions; this applies here, too. These cagey attitudes were understandable in the experiments, since the participants had just been demobilized from a bloody armed conflict. We should also remember that parliamentarians hardly ever change positions during a debate. From this perspective, the data for the ex-combatants in Colombia are not too far from the data for parliamentarians in mature democracies. Of the speech acts of the ex-combatants, 5 percent could be coded according to the third category. Here the speakers acknowledged that other opinions also have their value, although they were not ready to change their own positions. Here is an example voiced by a 25-year-old ex-guerrilla: "Well, what you say is fine. But let me ask you a question. What about jobs and all of the rest?"[40] The speaker acknowledges that the other has a point but wishes to change the topic to jobs. The interactive nature of such statements can help to build trust in the sense that the speaker acknowledges that the other side also has certain rationality, and this gives the other side a human face, which is particularly important in countries emerging from an internal armed conflict. If we look not at the speech acts but at the participants as the units of analysis, the picture brightens: 16 percent of the ex-combatants uttered in at least one of their speech acts that they acknowledged the value of other positions. Who were these 16 percent? Here again the pattern with regard to education continues. We have already seen in previous chapters that ex-combatants with a low level of education were often as deliberative as those with a high level of education. Now we see that acknowledgment of the value of other opinions is even

---

[40] "Bueno, está bien lo que tú dices, pero yo te hago una pregunta: ¿Y el trabajo y lo demás?"

somewhat higher for those with a low level of education. For gender and age there are no clear differences.

In *Srebrenica* in *Bosnia–Herzegovina*, like in Colombia, there was not a single speech act in which a Serb or a Bosnjak expressed a change in position. There was not even a speech act where a speaker explicitly acknowledged the value of other positions. Does this mean that in this regard deliberation was at an extremely low level? Not necessarily. One has to consider, as we have seen in Chapter 3, that the ordinary Serbs and Bosnjaks participating in the experiments shared very hostile attitudes toward the local authorities, who were seen as corrupt and incompetent. Therefore, a certain solidarity developed in the experimental groups so that it was quite easy to agree on issues that the authorities should deal with. These issues were not articulated in any detail so there were hardly any real disagreements. Participants focused on putting together a long list of non-controversial demands. It was proposed, for example, that a dog shelter should be built, but it was not discussed where it should be located, in a Serb or Bosnjak neighborhood. Or, it was suggested that the local spa should be opened again, but nothing was said about whether it should be run by the municipality or by private initiative. At this general level it was easy to agree, so the deliberative element of being convinced by the force of the better argument had little relevance. Perhaps the participants were wise enough not to formulate their suggestions in any detail, thus avoiding controversies across the deep ethnic divide. In this way, a common "life world" was beginning to be established, preparing the ground for more developed deliberation in the future where one could also tentatively address controversial matters. In the experiments in *Stolac* with Croats and Bosnjaks, the atmosphere was also very cautious with hardly any explicit disagreements expressed. Here, too, hostility was articulated against the authorities, while the discussion among the participants remained at an abstract and non-controversial level. Therefore, like in Srebrenica, the discussion did not evolve in such a way that changes of position were called for.

In *Belgium*, of the 1,664 speech acts uttered by ordinary citizens, a minuscule 22 indicated a change in position; of these 22 speech acts it was acknowledged in only 12 that the changes occurred because of arguments heard during the discussion. Thus, a mere 0.7 percent of the speech acts correspond to the Habermasian ideal where an actor acknowledges that the force of the better argument changed his or her opinion. The Belgian situation looks better with regard to the acknowledgment of the value of other positions; in 42 percent of the speech acts it was recognized that other positions had value, although such acknowledgments did not lead to a change in one's own position. Breaking down the results, there is no difference between the mixed groups of Flemish and Walloons and the linguistically homogeneous groups, which contrasts with what we found in previous chapters where the Belgian mixed groups tended to have a higher deliberative level. But it is still remarkable that when Flemish and Walloons met, the value of other positions was as often acknowledged as when the two language groups met among themselves. Theoretically, we had expected that in homogeneous groups the social pressure would have been greater than in mixed groups to acknowledge the value of other positions. Binary analysis by gender, age, and education reveals no differences between men and women, and a greater acknowledgment of the value of other positions for highly educated and younger age groups.

For *Europolis* and *Finland*, we did not code whether positions were changed by the force of the better argument. Pre-coding indicated that the pattern of Colombia, Bosnia–Herzegovina, and Belgium continued, in that there were hardly any cases where actors indicated that arguments heard during the discussion made them change position. Since our coding scheme was very long, this was a good place to cut and to simplify the coding process.

(c) Normative implications of empirical results

With regard to the force of the better argument, the empirical results show that the real world of politics is far away from the regulative ideal of deliberation as postulated in the Habermasian version. In all the studies reviewed in the previous section, at both the elite level and the level of ordinary citizens, it happens rarely or not at all that actors explicitly acknowledge that they have learned from each other and correspondingly change their positions. If consensus occurs, it is hardly ever based on reasons shared by all actors. Actors most often have different reasons to accept a common solution, and it often remains unclear what the reasons really are. Consensus solutions are to a large extent compromises reached by bargaining. Normatively, the question is what we do with this empirical finding. Should we keep the Habermasian concept of the force of the better argument as a regulative ideal, or should we rather follow theorists who relax many aspects of this element of the deliberative model? I take the position that large parts of the Habermasian version should be relaxed. In my view, the crucial point should be that participants in a political debate acknowledge that others also have reasonable arguments. In difficult political situations like in deeply divided societies it is already a great achievement if people consider the other side not as enemies but as adversaries. If this is accomplished, the other side is humanized. One may never agree with the other, but one may recognize that the other side also has a point. Using this relaxed standard as sufficiently deliberative, the empirical data look more optimistic from my normative perspective. Even in Colombia, 16 percent of ex-combatants acknowledged that other arguments also had value, although no changes in position ever occurred. I consider this as sufficiently deliberative, especially in deeply divided societies. If ex-combatants are able to acknowledge that others also have valuable positions, they may be less likely to shoot at each other because they see each other as worthwhile human beings, perhaps still as adversaries but no longer as enemies. Even in countries without an internal armed conflict, much is already accomplished if each side acknowledges that the other side also has a point. Unfortunately, I see much anecdotal evidence that in the two countries where I spend most of my time, Switzerland and the US, even this relaxed standard of deliberation is often not attained. In Switzerland, many representatives of the Social Democrats and the Greens, on the one hand, and the Swiss People's Party on the other hand, are no longer willing to grant that the other side has valuable arguments, in particular concerning how to treat immigrants;[41] the same holds true for many Democrats and Republicans in the US, especially with regard to taxes and social programs. Thus, even mature democracies like Switzerland and the US are far from the Habermasian ideal of yielding to the force of the better argument and even of acknowledging that the other side also has reasonable arguments.

As we have seen earlier in the chapter, Hansen and Rostbøll argue that pressure for consensus may suppress arguments since some participants may be reluctant to voice views that are in conflict with an

---

[41] Markus M.L. Crepaz and Jürg Steiner, *European Democracies* (New York: Longman, 2010), pp. 89–93.

emerging consensus. David Austin-Smith and Timothy J. Feddersen are also suspicious of unanimity rule when they argue in a theoretical model that veto power and unanimous voting rules create incentives for some actors to conceal information, which makes information from all discourse participants suspect. Consequently, the deliberative process tends to break down under unanimity rule.[42] It seems to me, however, that these authors have a one-sided view in *not* considering that majority vote may also suppress arguments and allow deliberation to break down. When a majority vote is taken, each side wants to win, and bringing additional arguments into play may muddle the situation making the outcome less predictable. Therefore, members of each side are encouraged to stick to their guns and to support the arguments offered by their leaders. In sum, both consensus and majority rule have a role to play in deliberative democracy. Consensus requirements enhance coordinative pressures, which are important for preference transformation. Majority rule tends to reduce transaction costs. In my view, it depends on the specific situation whether consensus or majority vote is preferable. There should certainly not be social pressure for consensus as the only deliberative way. If all minority positions are duly considered and a decision needs to be made urgently there is nothing wrong from a deliberative perspective with taking a majority vote. In a recent paper, Hélène Landemore and Scott E. Page enrich the literature on consensus versus majority voting from a deliberative perspective. They argue that consensus is more appropriate for problem-solving, for example what to do about high unemployment, whereas majority rule fits better when predictions have to be made, for example, how unemployment will develop in the coming 12 months.[43]

---

[42] David Austin-Smith and Timothy J. Feddersen, "Deliberation, Preference Uncertainty, and Voting Rules," *American Political Science Review* 100 (2006), 209–18.

[43] Hélène Landemore and Scott E. Page, "Deliberation and Disagreement: Problem-Solving, Prediction, and Positive Dissensus," paper presented at the Conference on Epistemic Democracy in Practice, Yale University, New Haven, CT, October 20–22, 2011.

7 | Truthfulness in deliberation

(a) Normative controversies in the literature

In the Habermasian version of deliberative theory, truthfulness (*Wahrhaftigkeit*) is a key element. Other theorists, however, give less weight to truthfulness or, under certain conditions, even allow some "white lies." In an early work, Jürgen Habermas postulates that "each person may only assert what he believes himself."[1] He sticks with this assertion in a more recent work where he writes that in deliberation participants must abstain from deceptive behavior (*ohne Täuschung*).[2] Habermas claims that in most social situations it is routine praxis to assume that others are truthful; otherwise one would not engage in any conversation at all. If this assumption is violated, deliberation breaks down. For Habermas, without truthfulness no real deliberation can take place. For him, truthfulness is a necessary condition of deliberation in a constitutive sense. Habermas explicitly bases his theory on Immanuel Kant, so it is relevant to explore what Kant means by truthfulness.[3] Like Habermas, Kant used the concept of *Wahrhaftigkeit*, which for him had a much deeper connotation than the English translation of truthfulness.[4] The concept *Wahrhaftigkeit* for Kant certainly includes not telling lies, but it is much broader in its meaning. To be *wahrhaftig* means to be true to one's inner self, to find one's innermost identity. For Kant, to be *wahrhaftig* is to find one's human dignity. He went as far as to write that not to be *wahrhaftig* is a crime because one destroys one's human dignity.[5] Without human dignity,

---

[1] Jürgen Habermas, *Moralbewusstsein und kommunikatives Handeln* (Frankfurt a.M.: Suhrkamp, 1983), p. 98. "Jeder Sprecher darf nur behaupten, was er selber glaubt."
[2] Jürgen Habermas, *Ach, Europa* (Frankfurt a.M.: Suhrkamp, 2008), p. 148.
[3] Jürgen Habermas, *Vorstudien und Ergänzungen zur Theorie des kommunikativen Handeln* (Frankfurt a.M.: Suhrkamp, 1984).
[4] Sincerity is another possible, but also not quite satisfactory, translation.
[5] Immanuel Kant, *Metaphysik der Sitten* (Hamburg: F. Meiner, 1986).

we become mere "speech machines" (*Sprachmaschinen*). For Kant it is a duty (*Pflicht*) to oneself and to others to be *wahrhaftig*. If we are not *wahrhaftig* with others, we do not respect their human dignity, and we do not act according to our own dignity.

The argument against the Habermasian position with regard to truthfulness runs as follows: motives for deliberative behavior do not count for much. What really counts is behavior itself. If a participant in a discussion expresses a high level of respect toward another participant, only this utterance matters, whether it is meant truthfully or not. Dennis F. Thompson presents this argument in a forceful way. In his view, the key is that deliberators present all possible arguments in terms that are accessible to the relevant audience, respond to reasonable arguments presented by opponents, and manifest an inclination to change their views. This requires no special window into the motives or inner life of actors. According to Thompson, "empirical researchers therefore should not worry, as some evidently do, about formulating an independent test for sincerity or truthfulness."[6] In the same vein, Mark E. Warren argues that "deliberative institutions should not depend upon, or be defined by, the deliberative intentions of participants."[7] Let me illustrate this argument against the Habermasian position with a speech act in the British House of Commons. In a December 5, 1997 debate, Conservative MP Richard Ottaway addressed Estelle Morris, Labour Under-Secretary of State for Education and Employment, in the following way: "I am pleased to hear that the Minister's commitment to special education needs is being developed through the Green Paper. I am also pleased at the tone of her speech."[8] The argument against Habermas would be that this utterance of respect may or may not have been truthful, but that this would be irrelevant. The only relevant issue would be whether the utterance of Ottaway contributed to a good outcome with regard to special education.

---

[6] Dennis F. Thompson, "Deliberative Democratic Theory and Empirical Political Science," *Annual Review of Political Science* 11 (2008), 6.

[7] Mark E. Warren, "Institutionalizing Deliberative Democracy," in Shawn W. Rosenberg (ed.), *Deliberation, Participation and Democracy* (London: Palgrave Macmillan, 2007), p. 278.

[8] Jürg Steiner, André Bächtiger, Markus Spörndli, and Marco R. Steenbergen, *Deliberative Politics in Action: Analysing Parliamentary Discourse* (Cambridge University Press, 2005), pp. 176–7.

Warren even goes further in arguing that under certain conditions "white lies" are justified. He stresses, however, that he is "not, of course, advocating insincerity" as a general rule, but only under very specific circumstances, namely when there are "histories of distrust, mutual ignorance, suspicion, and status inequality." Under these conditions, absolute sincerity would be detrimental to deliberation, since it "will cause injury, will be a conversation stopper, and so amounts to a choice against deliberation."[9] In such situations, Warren calls for manners, and manners not in a conventional snobbish way, but as deliberative diplomacy "which may require expressive insincerity to be preferred when issues are at their most sensitive, and conditions of discourse are less than ideal."[10] For Warren, "well-mannered people self-censor and tell little white lies," if absolute sincerity and honesty would have unfavorable consequences.[11] He believes that sometimes "the civilizing hypocrisies of good manners" may help deliberation.[12] Robert E. Goodin is another prominent theorist who argues "that, politically, some things are better left unsaid."[13] He agrees with Warren, that sometimes "sensitivities are good grounds for taking certain topics off the agenda … Merely raising the topic can sometimes profoundly offend certain segments of the community."[14]

The position of theorists like Thompson, Warren, and Goodin is controversial in the current philosophical literature. Thus, Patti Tamara Lenard wrote a critical reply to Warren, in which she insists that Habermas has the right "intuition" when he postulates as a criterion for good deliberation "mutual trust in subjective sincerity."[15] Lenard postulates that "we must believe that others do not intend to deceive us in some way and that they are sincerely advocating the position they put forward, and that they are genuinely committed to

---

9 Mark E. Warren, "Deliberation under Nonideal Conditions: A Reply to Lenard and Adler," *Journal of Social Philosophy* 39 (2008), 658–60.
10 Mark E. Warren, "What Should and Should Not Be Said: Deliberating Sensitive Issues," *Journal of Social Philosophy* 37 (2006), 164.
11 Warren, "What Should and Should Not Be Said," 177.
12 Warren, "What Should and Should Not Be Said," 179.
13 Robert E. Goodin, *Innovating Democracy* (Oxford University Press, 2009), p. 64.
14 Goodin, *Innovating Democracy*, pp. 75–6.
15 Patti Tamara Lenard, "Deliberating Sincerely: A Reply to Warren," *Journal of Social Philosophy* 39 (2008), 629.

the reasons with which they support their position."[16] She addresses specifically sensitive situations that Warren worries about and takes a counter-position:

In situations of intense vulnerability, such as the kind Warren describes, deliberators will need to have confidence precisely in the sincerity of the views expressed by others. There is considerable debate in the confidence-building literature about the mechanisms by which deliberators should be protected from the insincerities of others; this debate is predicated on the view that conflict resolution or transformation can emerge only under conditions in which sincerity is the norm.[17]

Lenard concludes that in situations of intense hostility, the advice of Warren "may be a dangerous rather than a productive strategy for those involved in negotiations."[18] There are many other theorists, besides Lenard, who stick with the Habermasian position that truthfulness must be considered a key element in the deliberative model. Ian O'Flynn, for example, states: "Truthfulness is important to the ethos of democracy. We would never deliberate with others unless we thought that they were, in the main, truthful. We respect people if and because we think that they are truthful."[19] In the same vein, James Bohman and Henry S. Richardson make the point that deliberation requires "a level of sincerity and mutual recognition."[20] Michael A. Neblo goes in the same direction when he writes: "It is difficult to see how being coerced on the basis of polite lies shows any deep kind of respect to those who come out in the minority. Thus, without a sincerity constraint, deliberation may lose much of both its epistemic values, and its respect expressing function."[21] For Simon Niemeyer, "truthfulness should be aspired to, even if it is ugly," and he defends this position with the argument "that as soon as you admit untruthfulness

[16] Lenard, "Deliberating Sincerely," 629.
[17] Lenard, "Deliberating Sincerely," 633.
[18] Lenard, "Deliberating Sincerely," 633.
[19] Personal communication, January 15, 2009.
[20] James Bohman and Henry S. Richardson, "Liberalism, Deliberative Democracy, and Reasons That All Can Accept," *Journal of Political Philosophy* 17 (2009), 270.
[21] Michael A. Neblo, "Family Disputes: Diversity in Defining and Measuring Deliberation," *Swiss Political Science Review* 13 (2007), 541. See also his paper, "Motive Matters: Liberalism and Insincerity," online at: http://polisci.osu.edu/faculty/mneblo.

you open the door back to strategic manipulation."[22] Jane Mansbridge wants participants in deliberation to "speak truthfully." For her, "lying is a form of coercive power."[23]

Mathilde Cohen looks at truthfulness from the perspective of how political decisions are justified to the general public once they have been made.[24] She argues that at this point the motives of decision-makers are irrelevant. Reasons must be given that are plausible and convincing to the general public. These reasons may not necessarily correspond to why the decisions were made in the first place. In such cases, there is a lack of truthfulness in how decisions are justified. For Cohen this is not a problem; as she puts it, "the law is not interested in individual preferences."[25] As an illustration, she gives the decision of a French préfet on stricter animal protection and assumes that he or she was motivated by the belief that animals have a soul. According to Cohen, the préfet would not need to refer to this motif but could refer, for instance, to public health concerns. Such insincerity would be unethical in private but not in public life.

This section has shown that theorists differ widely on the role of truthfulness in the deliberative model. Whatever weight is given to truthfulness, the focus is on truthfulness of motives. Rudy Andeweg brings to my attention that there is another important aspect of truthfulness that is neglected in the theoretical literature, namely whether *facts* are presented in a truthful way. As an example he mentions "political leaders who knowingly overstated the intelligence on weapons of mass destruction in Iraq in order to convince others that military intervention against Saddam was justified. These leaders were truthful about their own motives and goals, but they deceived others by presenting 'untruthful' factual information."[26] This example shows, indeed, that truthfulness may refer to both motives and facts, and that the two aspects may not necessarily go hand in hand. André Bächtiger

---

[22] Personal communication, September 8, 2009.
[23] Jane Mansbridge with James Bohman, Simone Chambers, David Estlund, Andreas Follesdal, Archon Fung, Christina Lafont, Bernard Manin, and José Luis Marti, "The Place of Self-Interest and the Role of Power in Deliberative Democracy," *Journal of Political Philosophy* 18 (2010), 66, 81.
[24] Mathilde Cohen, "La sincérité peut-elle être une norme juridique?," *Archives de philosophie du droit* 54 (2011), 243–59.
[25] Cohen, "La sincérité peut-elle être une norme juridique?," 258: "le droit ne s'intéresse pas aux préférences individuelles."
[26] Personal communication, January 14, 2010.

also puts emphasis on the factual aspect of truthfulness.[27] According to him, "it may be futile to get hold of the inner motives of participants during a decision process."[28] He wants to "reverse an intention-based approach to truthfulness by viewing truthfulness as an element that can emerge out of a critical and thorough process of agonistic inquiry."[29] In Chapter 4, I have already mentioned that Bächtiger considers critical questioning, disputing, and insisting as core deliberative values. On this basis, deliberation should come closer to the factual truth by using methods "similar to cross-examination in court" and "investigative news media."[30] In this way, it may be possible to "unravel relevant information that otherwise would be withheld."[31] With this argument, Bächtiger is in agreement with Gary Mucciaroni and Paul J. Quirk whose work I discussed in Chapter 2.[32] They argue that a decision process must be rational also in the sense that actors check the accuracy of information by consulting the best available research evidence.

In sum, while there is controversy on the importance of truthfulness as a motive of deliberators, it is accepted as self-evident that the factual basis of deliberation must be truthful, although this latter aspect is often neglected.

(b) Empirical results

Literature review

The normative-philosophical controversies on truthfulness reveal hypotheses that cry out for empirical testing. The big question is whether absolute and unconditional truthfulness helps or hurts deliberation. This raises the challenge for empirical scholars to measure in a reliable and valid way to what extent participants in a political

---

[27] André Bächtiger, "On Perfecting the Deliberative Process: Questioning, Disputing, and Insisting as Core Deliberative Values," paper presented at the annual meeting of the American Political Science Association, Washington, DC, September 2–5, 2010.

[28] Bächtiger, "On Perfecting the Deliberative Process," p. 13.

[29] Bächtiger, "On Perfecting the Deliberative Process," p. 13.

[30] Bächtiger, "On Perfecting the Deliberative Process," p. 13.

[31] Bächtiger, "On Perfecting the Deliberative Process," p. 13.

[32] Gary Mucciaroni and Paul J. Quirk, "Rhetoric and Reality: Going Beyond Discourse Ethics in Assessing Legislative Deliberation," *Legisprudence: International Journal for the Study of Legislation* 4 (2010), 35–52.

discussion are truthful. How can we investigate whether politicians, or, for that matter, ordinary citizens, mean what they say when they discuss political issues? Some rational-choice theorists have developed models where truthfulness and lying play an important role. These models, however, remain at a theoretical level and have not been empirically tested. Let me give two examples of papers that have the concept of deliberation in the title and are therefore relevant in the present context. David Austin-Smith and Timothy J. Feddersen ask in a mathematical model whether in a jury lying or truthfulness is more likely under majority or unanimity rule.[33] But they undertake no effort to empirically test their hypotheses, nor do they show what such tests could look like. In a similar vein, Dimitri Landa and Adam Meirowitz present game-theoretical ideas about institutional settings that make lying least likely, but again without any hints of how their ideas could empirically be tested.[34]

I, for my part, have come to the conclusion that *Wahrhaftigkeit* in the Habermasian sense eludes *direct* empirical measurement. Neblo points out the problem of measuring truthfulness in the deliberative context: "Sincerity is a notoriously difficult concept to get a handle on empirically. The fear is that there is simply no scientifically serviceable way to operationalize the concept for most purposes of deliberative research."[35] Let me justify why, in my view, a direct measurement of *Wahrhaftigkeit* is impossible or at least highly problematic. As stated earlier in the chapter, to be *wahrhaftig* in the Kantian and Habermasian sense means to be true to one's inner self, which raises the question of how we can know what our most inner self is. How do we know whether we are true to this self? I assume that our most inner self is not something fixed that we can discover if only we dig deep enough. I rather assume that the inner self is something malleable and elusive that, despite all our inner searching, we can never quite know. Such a view of the inner self is compatible with deliberative theory, which predicts that we are open to changing our preferences based on the force of better arguments. Such openness would not exist if we were sure what

---

[33] David Austin-Smith and Timothy J. Feddersen, "Deliberation, Preference Uncertainty, and Voting Rules," *American Political Science Review* 100 (2006), 209–18.

[34] Dimitri Landa and Adam Meirowitz, "Game Theory, Information, and Deliberation," *American Journal of Political Science* 53 (2009), 427–44.

[35] Neblo, "Family Disputes," 540.

exactly our inner self is, so we would have no reason to listen to others in order to be *wahrhaftig*. We would simply do whatever our inner self tells us. According to deliberative theory, talking with others will help us in the search for our inner self. Thus, good deliberation can be instrumental to better understand our own deeper identity, but we will never be quite sure what this identity really is. This is a very Kantian position; Kant stated that we can never know our true inner self, but we should always search for it, and in this search we can be helped by our friends, which he practiced in his own life.[36]

This elusive and changing nature of our inner self means that we never quite know whether we are *wahrhaftig* in a particular situation. If a politician or an ordinary citizen supports a specific position, he or she can never be quite sure whether this position is fully compatible with his or her inner self. Outside observers will be all the more uncertain about the *Wahrhaftigkeit* of the taken position. All this means that it seems to be impossible to measure the level of *Wahrhaftigkeit* with a sufficient level of reliability and validity. This does not mean, of course, that we are not able to detect crude lies in a political discussion, especially when not motives but facts are involved. But it is a much more subtle issue whether someone is being truthful, for example, in referring to the common good or showing respect to other actors. Not being truthful in such situations is much more difficult to detect than it is to discover crude lies about factual matters. The elusive character of one's most inner motives is also stressed by Goodin:

> The point is not just one about veracity in reporting one's own motives. The fear is not so much that the agent will lie, but that without any reality check neither he nor we will have any way of telling what the truth of the matter really is. Nor is the worry that he will necessarily cook the books in his own favour, attributing to himself nobler motives than he in fact harbours. He may do just the opposite, engaging in moral self-debasement and attributing to himself less noble motives than are really at work.[37]

Although, in my view, truthfulness in a political debate cannot be measured in a systematic way, we know that participants in a discussion are usually interested in whether other participants are truthful or not. As Goodin puts it: "Coming to understand a person's motives for acting

---

[36] Manfred Kuehn, *Kant: A Biography* (Cambridge University Press, 2001).
[37] Robert E. Goodin, "Do Motives Matter?," *Canadian Journal of Philosophy* 19 (1989), 411.

as he did enables us to explain his past behavior, and to do so in such a way that allows us to predict his future behavior."[38] Of course, perceived truthfulness may not correspond to the actual reality of truthfulness. But if most participants feel that people express what is truly on their minds, this perception is an important social reality. Perhaps there are some participants who are untruthful, but if they hide their untruthfulness in such a way that nobody notices, such untruthfulness has no significance for the group, although it has significance for the internal dignity and identity of the untruthful persons. On the other hand, if most participants do not trust the other participants, this perception is also an important social reality. Perhaps they are not being truthful themselves, so they project their behavior onto other participants. If everyone expresses the view that much untruthfulness occurs with regard to both motives and factual information, this reveals a very different group atmosphere than if the perception is one of mutual truthfulness. Thus, the perception of truthfulness is an important social reality that can be empirically measured. This we tried to do in our experiments.

New data on deliberative experiments[39]

In *Colombia*, immediately after the experiments participants had to take a position on two items intended to measure the perception of truthfulness:

Overall, I feel that people expressed what was truly on their mind.

Strongly agree	27%
Agree	50%
Neutral or do not know	17%
Disagree	4%
Strongly disagree	2%

I cannot escape the feeling that many participants were hiding their true beliefs from the discussion.

Strongly agree	10%
Agree	32%
Neutral or do not know	28%
Disagree	21%
Strongly disagree	9%

---

[38] Goodin, "Do Motives Matter?," 415.
[39] For the research designs, see Introduction, Section (b).

The answers depend on the formulation of the items, revealing the well-known phenomenon that people have the tendency to answer in the positive. This tendency was probably even stronger among ex-combatants because they were particularly cagey about not choosing the wrong words, as we have already seen in previous chapters. Some 77 percent agreed that the other participants were truthful when they spoke up, which is an impressive figure for traumatized ex-combatants, although there was most likely social pressure to answer in the positive. When, in the second item, the question of truthfulness was formulated in a negative way, there were still 30 percent who explicitly said that they disagreed that the other participants were hiding their true beliefs. And with 42 percent it was not even a majority who expressed suspicion that the others were not truthful. All in all, it seems that the perception of truthfulness was not at a worryingly low level given the background of the participants. This augurs well for future progress in the discourse quality. If one is not constantly worried that others are not telling the truth, one is more likely to search for common solutions in the interest of all. In the breakdown of the Colombian data by gender, age, and education, no statistically significant big differences emerged.

In *Bosnia–Herzegovina* in the experiments both in Srebrenica with Serbs and Bosnjaks and in Stolac with Croats and Bosnjaks the results are similar to Colombia, showing reasonable level of trust given the recent history of civil war. Again, the pattern continues, with trust being much lower when the question is formulated in a negative way.

In *Belgium*, perceptions of truthfulness were much stronger than in Colombia and Bosnia–Herzegovina. An overwhelming 96 percent expressed the feeling that other participants in the experiments said what was truly on their minds. When the item was formulated in a negative way, still only 7 percent expressed the view that other participants were hiding their true beliefs. The overwhelming trust in what other participants said existed not only in the linguistically homogeneous groups but also in the mixed groups of Flemish and Walloons. This is remarkable at a time when Belgian political leaders trusted each other so little that for more than a year they were unable to put together a cabinet. Citizens on both sides of the linguistic divide seem to trust each other much more than politicians do. Thereby, one has to consider that the participants in the experiments had to arrive at a decision on the tricky language issue, seemingly all the more reason to be critical of each other. That citizens in Belgium trust each other more than do ex-combatants in Colombia and survivors of the civil war in Bosnia–Herzegovina is no surprise because political violence has a strong tendency to create mistrust.

For *Europolis*, there were so many other items in the questionnaire that only the first of the two items asked in Colombia and Bosnia–Herzegovina could be included. As is the custom for Deliberative Polling, the answers had to be given on a scale from 0 (completely disagree) to 10 (completely agree). As in Belgium, the 348 randomly chosen EU citizens showed overwhelming trust in the other participants. Only 3 percent chose the lowest three categories expressing strong disagreement that people said what was truly on their mind. By contrast, 80 percent selected the three top categories of agreement with this item. Trust in other participants was particularly high among women, the older participants, and the highly educated. To evaluate the results for Europolis one has to consider that moderators encouraged deliberation and that the discussions were free-floating with no decision point at the end. These two factors may very well have influenced the answers in the direction of more trust in other participants. It probably would be a different matter if participants of all EU countries were to one day be involved in a real-life decision process and have to make hard decisions, for example, on financial support for member countries in trouble. In *Finland* no items on perception of truthfulness were included in the questionnaire filled out by the participants after the experiments.

(c) Normative implications of empirical results

How does the previous section help us to sort out the normative issues raised in the first section of the chapter? It seems to me that with regard to the deliberative element of truthfulness, empirical data are only of limited value to draw normative implications for the controversies found in the philosophical literature. As I have argued in the previous section, it is impossible or certainly highly problematic to measure the truthfulness of motives in political discussions. This does not mean, however, that we should eliminate the element of truthfulness as a normative part of deliberative theory. As Ian O'Flynn puts it, "just because something is not objectively visible does not mean that that thing is morally or politically irrelevant."[40] What is the relevance of truthfulness in the deliberative model of democracy? As I wrote in the Introduction, as an engaged citizen I will take a stand with regard not only to empirical but also to normative issues. For this particular issue, I must do it without much help from empirical data. It is my position that truthfulness has a value per se. From a moral or deontological perspective, truthfulness is an important value, although I would not go as far as Kant by disallowing any untruthfulness. I acknowledge that there are situations, for example a committee on national security, where it may sometimes be justified not to be altogether truthful in reporting the results to the outside world. I also agree with Warren that rules of good manners may sometimes require telling "white lies," for example not to say that a meeting was boring when indeed this is what one felt.[41] I also agree with Christian F. Rostbøll that for reasons of privacy the deliberative model does not require that participants reveal all their innermost desires and interests in order to justify arguments.[42] As a general norm, however, participants in a political discussion should strive for truthfulness when they use a deliberative vocabulary. With the argument that motives are relevant, I get help from David Hume, who writes: "We must look within to find the moral quality ... A virtuous motive is requisite to render an action virtuous."[43] Following Hume, I would like to keep truthfulness as a normative regulative element of deliberation. Perhaps truthfulness is helped if actors have to express their preferences in public; as Jon Elster states, "even a strategic actor may be embarrassed to 'lie in public' by expressing preferences that everybody knows she does not hold."[44]

---

[40] Personal communication, January 15, 2009.

[41] Mark E. Warren, "What Should and Should Not Be Said: Deliberating Sensitive Issues," *Journal of Social Philosophy* 37 (2006), 163–81.

[42] Christian F. Rostbøll, *Deliberative Freedom: Deliberative Democracy as Critical Theory* (Albany: State University of New York Press, 2008), pp. 178, 220.

[43] David Hume, *A Treatise of Human Nature*, ed. David Fate Norton and Mary J. Norton (Oxford: Clarendon Press, 2007), p. 307.

[44] Jon Elster, "Deliberation, Cycles, and Misrepresentations," paper presented at the Conference on Epistemic Democracy in Practice, Yale University, October 20–22, 2011, p. 14.

To keep truthfulness as a normative element in the deliberative model is particularly important if we think of how we should teach our students about deliberation. Without the element of truthfulness, it is easy to see deliberation as a shrewd tactic to further one's personal interests. Even in good deliberation, strategic actions will never be completely absent. It is only in the unreachable ideal type of deliberation that political actors consider only the common good and express respect without any ulterior motives. Real-life discussions are always characterized by mixed motives. Some actors will always be to some extent untruthful in a political debate. But it seems to me desirable that we postulate as a general regulative rule that truthfulness be a normative goal. In this way, deliberation has a moral value in itself and is not only valuable because it may have good consequences. This is what we should teach students. Although much lying, cheating, and corruption may go on in the political arena, students should internalize the norm that this is not inevitable and that the goal should be politics with more truthfulness and sincerity.

Although I have no data for the level of truthfulness of political discussions, I was able to present in the previous section some data on the *perception* of truthfulness. In Colombia and Bosnia–Herzegovina, participants never called each other liars during the experiments, but in the questionnaire completed after the experiments there were quite a few complaints that other participants were not being truthful when they spoke up. According to Kant and Habermas, in order to be truthful, participants should have articulated these complaints during the discussion itself. But this is a situation where I side with Warren that telling other participants face-to-face that they are liars would have endangered any signs of emerging deliberation. So it was a sign of appropriate prudence that complaints about untruthfulness were expressed only in the questionnaire after the experiments.

In Belgium and the Europolis project, the situation was different in the sense that very few participants complained in the questionnaires that there was untruthfulness during the experiments. Here, for the sake of truthfulness, it may perhaps have been appropriate that such complaints would have been expressed during the experiment itself. This probably would not have endangered deliberation but may have had a liberating effect for the few participants who perceived other participants as untruthful. This comparison between Colombia and Bosnia–Herzegovina on the one hand and Belgium and Europolis on the other hand shows again the complexity of how to handle truthfulness in a deliberative spirit. It depends on the specific context whether the requirement of truthfulness can be somewhat relaxed so that future deliberation is not endangered.

8 | Deliberation in the media and the Internet

(a) Normative controversies in the literature

Jürgen Habermas has always been strongly interested in the media, and as a public intellectual he often intervenes in the media. For him, the media play a crucial role in the deliberative model. He summarizes his position once again in a recent paper entitled "Political Communication in Media Society."[1] For him, "mediated political communication in the public sphere can facilitate deliberative legitimation processes in complex societies only if self-regarding media systems gain independence from their social environment, and if anonymous audiences grant feedback between an informed elite discourse and a responsive civil society."[2] Habermas acknowledges the great influence of the media when he writes that "the dynamics of mass communication are driven by the power of the media to select and shape the presentation of messages and by the strategic use of political and social power to influence the agendas as well as the triggering and framing of public issues."[3] Given this great influence of the media, it is all the more important for Habermas that

first, a self-regulating media system must maintain its independence vis-à-vis its environments while linking political communication in the public sphere with both civil society and the political center; second, an inclusive civil society must empower citizens to participate in and respond to a public discourse that, in turn, must not degenerate into a colonizing mode of communication.[4]

In linking an active citizenship in civil society with the political authorities and doing this in an independent way and in both directions, the

---

[1] Jürgen Habermas, "Political Communication in Media Society: Does Democracy Still Enjoy an Epistemic Dimension? The Impact of Normative Theory on Empirical Research," *Communication Theory* 16 (2006), 411–26.
[2] Habermas, "Political Communication in Media Society," 411–12.
[3] Habermas, "Political Communication in Media Society," 415.
[4] Habermas, "Political Communication in Media Society," 420.

media play a great role in the Habermasian deliberative model. "To put it in a nutshell, the deliberative model expects the political public sphere to ensure the formation of a plurality of considered public opinions."[5] In contrast to most other aspects of the deliberative model, with regard to the media there is hardly any controversy among deliberative theorists. Virtually all stress the importance of the independence of the media and their role in opening mutual channels of communication between the political center and citizens. The concern of deliberative theorists is that the media reality deviates too much from the ideal articulated by Habermas. He himself has great concerns in this respect: "In the final analysis, we are nevertheless confronted with the prima facie evidence that the kind of political communication we know from our so-called media society goes against the grain of the normative requirements of deliberative politics."[6] Habermas fears that new developments in the media "would rob us of the centerpiece of deliberative politics."[7] He forcefully expresses this concern in his latest book *Ach, Europa*.[8]

(b) Empirical results

A pioneer in empirical research on the level of deliberation in the media was Jürgen Gerhards.[9] He investigated to what extent two German high-quality newspapers were deliberative in their contributions to the abortion debate. Gerhard used three indicators: the degree of respect toward other positions, the extent of justification of one's position, and the degree of rationality defined as expressing conflicting values. Gerhards concluded that the discourse quality in the two newspapers is "far away"[10] from the ideal speech situation of Habermas. Dennis Pilon arrives at equally negative findings about the discourse quality of newspapers in the Canadian province of Ontario.[11] The topic was

---

[5] Habermas, "Political Communication in Media Society," 416.
[6] Habermas, "Political Communication in Media Society," 420.
[7] Habermas, "Political Communication in Media Society," 423.
[8] Jürgen Habermas, *Ach, Europa* (Frankfurt a.M.: Suhrkamp, 2008), p. 163.
[9] Jürgen Gerhards, "Diskursive versus liberale Öffentlichkeit: Eine empirische Auseinandersetzung mit Jürgen Habermas," *Kölner Zeitschrift für Soziologie und Sozialpsychologie* 49 (1997), 1–34.
[10] Gerhards, "Diskursive versus liberale Öffentlichkeit," 27.
[11] Dennis Pilon, "Investigating Media as a Deliberative Space: Newspapers Opinions about Voting Systems in the 2007 Ontario Provincial Referendum," *Canadian Political Science Review* 3 (2009), 1–23.

a possible change of the election system from single-member plurality to proportional representation. In order to investigate the issue, the provincial government had chosen a Citizens' Assembly of 107 randomly chosen ordinary citizens. The discussions in this assembly were highly deliberative. According to Pilon, "members made decisions based on a systematic appraisal of competing expert knowledge and the evidence brought to bear about the working of different voting systems."[12] The assembly "received rave reviews from both their participants and their academic observers."[13] Based on their discussions, the Citizens' Assembly proposed a change to proportional representation. The question was then how well the regional newspapers could make the link between this mini-public of randomly selected citizens and the citizenship at large. How well were the newspapers willing and able to create a deliberative space in view of the popular referendum? In measuring the discourse quality of the debate in the media, Pilon uses the Discourse Quality Index (DQI) of our research group. "In attempting to operationalize how to assess the deliberative quality of the media treatment of Ontario's voting system referendum, I have decided to follow Steiner et al. (2004)."[14] This means, in particular, that Pilon measured to what extent the media were characterized "by broad inclusion and equality in terms of participation and an interactive dynamic where the assumptions or facts under-girding the decision could be called into question."[15] Pilon summarizes his findings as follows:

The results tend to confirm previous negative assessments of media's deliberative performance in referendum contexts ... Ontario's print media failed to create an effective deliberative space where citizens could gain a critical appreciation of the choices they faced. In fact, the results show that the media failed on all the key themes Habermas highlights as crucial to an effective deliberative process, specifically inclusion and balance, a willingness to deal with and answer questions of fact, honesty in presenting one's own position, and a desire to engage in dialogue ... All this suggests that Ontario's newspapers were not really sincere in their claim they would create an environment where all sides on the referendum issue could be deliberated over.[16]

---

[12] Pilon, "Investigating Media as a Deliberative Space," 2.
[13] Pilon, "Investigating Media as a Deliberative Space," 2.
[14] Pilon, "Investigating Media as a Deliberative Space," 6.
[15] Pilon, "Investigating Media as a Deliberative Space," 6.
[16] Pilon, "Investigating Media as a Deliberative Space," 3, 17.

Pilon almost despairs of how the media missed the opportunity to make the link between mini-publics of ordinary citizens and the broader public:

The evidence assembled here suggests that the scale problem – translating the benefits of deliberative democracy in small-scale settings like citizens' assemblies to genuinely mass democratic ones like referendums – is real and abiding. If the link is to be media – and government and most commentators have explicitly expected that media would be the link in the recent cases of British Colombia and Ontario – then the evidence provided here challenges whether the proposed link can or will do the job. If deliberative democracy is to be more than just talk, then new thinking will need to be applied to the problem of media failures as a deliberative space.[17]

In this empirical section, I also come back to Habermas. We have seen in the first section that prima facie evidence causes him concern that the current reality of the media is far away from how he sees the role of the media in the deliberative model. What prima facie evidence does he have in mind? His foremost case is Silvio Berlusconi, whom he considers "an infamous example." According to Habermas, Berlusconi

first exploited the legal opportunities for political self-promotion and, then, after taking over the reins of government, used his media empire to back dubious legislation in support of the consolidation of his private fortunes and political assets. In the course of this adventure, Berlusconi even succeeded in changing the media culture of his country, shifting it from a predominance of political education to an emphasis on marketing of depoliticized entertainment.[18]

Habermas also mentions Rupert Murdoch as an infamous example of a "media tycoon" and speaks generally of "pathologies of political communication."[19]

With the Internet, a new medium has emerged. Is this medium able to serve as a better link between citizens and the political authorities? Habermas is critical:

The internet has certainly reactivated the grassroots of an egalitarian public of writers and readers. However, computer-mediated communication in the

---

[17] Pilon, "Investigating Media as a Deliberative Space," 17.
[18] Habermas, "Political Communication in Media Society," 421.
[19] Habermas, "Political Communication in Media Society," 420–1.

web can claim unequivocal *democratic* merits only for a special context: It can undermine the censorship of authoritarian regimes that try to control and repress public opinion. In the context of liberal regimes, the rise of millions of fragmented chat rooms across the world tend instead to lead to the fragmentation of large but politically focused mass audiences into a huge number of isolated issue publics.[20]

While Habermas bases his judgment on anecdotal evidence, there are already systematic investigations about the deliberative level of online discussions. In Chapter 2, I have presented the results of two such studies of online discussions: one of New York citizens on how to rebuild the World Trade Center site, the other of Pittsburgh residents discussing problems of the city's public schools. The main finding of both studies was that personal stories may help good deliberation but may also distract from the topic under discussion.

A member of our research group, Raphaël Kies, in a Ph.D. dissertation at the European University Institute in Florence, undertook to investigate the "promises and limits of the web-site deliberation," the very title of his thesis.[21] The objective of his research "was to evaluate whether the increasing success of the online political debates could favorize the emergence of a more deliberative democratic process or, on the opposite, whether this phenomenon has no impact or a negative impact on the deliberativeness of our democracies."[22] Kies investigated such discussions in the Radical Party in Italy and the French town of Issy-les-Moulineaux. Founded in 1955, the Italian Radical Party (*Partito Radicale*) is an anti-clerical and anti-communist party with an emphasis on greater social, religious, political, economic, and sexual freedom. The party was a pioneer in using the Internet. Already by the mid 1980s, it began to host one of the very first virtual communities in Europe, and in 2000 it was the first party worldwide to organize online binding elections, this for one-third of its executive board. When the party implemented an online forum called "radical community," it rapidly became one of the most successful forums with a great number of people registering and participating. Kies got access to the

---

[20] Habermas, "Political Communication in Media Society," 423.
[21] Raphaël Kies, "Promises and Limits of the Web-site Deliberation," Ph.D. dissertation, European University Institute, 2008. I served on the dissertation committee. The dissertation was published under the same title in 2010 by Palgrave Macmillan.
[22] Kies, "Promises and Limits of the Web-site Deliberation," p. 202.

contents of this forum and also interviewed a sample of participants. With regard to the discourse quality of the Internet forum the results are mixed. A large number of messages were exchanges, and they were frequently read by the leaders of the party, in particular by Marco Pannella, the charismatic leader of the party. Thus, the Internet helped to open a channel between regular party members and the leadership of the party.[23] Participation, however, was one-sided. The highly educated and males participated most. Among those who had registered, the frequency with which they sent messages was uneven:

Sent messages every day	9%
Send messages every week	19%
Sent messages every month	21%
Sent messages more rarely	51%

There were more party members who *read* messages, but here, too, distribution was uneven:

Read messages every day	39%
Read messages every week	34%
Read messages every month	15%
Read messages more rarely	12%

Despite unequal participation, a great plurality of opinions was expressed. Indeed, in the survey, 59 percent applauded the fact that the atmosphere of the forum encouraged a high or very high propensity to voice alternative proposals. Only 21 percent considered this propensity as low or very low, while 20 percent took an intermediate position. These results speak to the issue raised in the normative literature of whether it is more important that everyone speaks up or that all alternatives are heard. The online forum of the Italian Radical Party corresponds to the latter position in the sense that a large number of messages came from a small minority of registered persons but that nevertheless a great plurality of views entered the debate. With regard to respect, the results are mixed: 38 percent considered the level of respect as high or very high, 34 percent as low or very low, while 28 percent took no position. When looking at the transcripts, Kies registered a certain rudeness in the debate.

[23] The forum was also open to non-party members, and a small number of them registered.

Issy-les-Moulineaux, where Kies studied another online debate, is a town of 63,000 inhabitants which is close to Paris. The town implemented an ambitious project putting the election campaigns of the 16 district councilors online. There are four districts in the town, and each district could elect four councilors. Their task is mostly consultative, bringing local grievances to the attention of town authorities. There were 53 candidates running for the 16 seats. With regard to the voters, less than 3 percent registered. This low percentage may have been due to the unfamiliar and relatively complicated registration process and the fact that many voters had no access to the Internet. Such voters had the option to go to the polling station but very few did so. The election of district councilors has little political importance. In the survey, the online experiment was evaluated unevenly. A positive response was that "the debate seemed to me to be well thought out and relatively realistic in terms of wishes expressed and possibilities for action." A negative response was that "I don't think the blog particularly favors serious reflection, as some will type at great speed and in two lines … It is not necessarily an environment conducive to a high standard of democratic debate."[24] The most deliberative aspect was that in Issy-les-Moulineaux respect was much higher than in the Italian Radical Party. Only about 10 percent of the messages were considered as disrespectful in the sense of being rude and unfriendly or involving personal attacks. With regard to equal participation, however, Issy-les-Moulineaux was even less deliberative than the Italian Radical Party. Counting the number of messages, Kies found that about as many stemmed from candidates as from voters. A voter joked that one gets the impression "that there are more councilors than residents in Issy-les-Moulineaux."[25] The conclusion of Kies of his two studies and the survey of other studies on Internet discussions is as follows:

The users of the online political forum are an elite composed by a majority of highly educated men who are relatively young and strongly interested in politics … The numerous examples we came across reveal that, generally, the opinions expressed in the forums are justified even if not in an elaborate way, that the debates do generally not lead to polarization of opinions, that the debates are generally not completely invaded by unrespectful behaviors, that the online debates can contribute to enlighten the opinions

[24] Kies, "Promises and Limits of the Web-site Deliberation," p. 191.
[25] Kies, "Promises and Limits of the Web-site Deliberation," p. 170.

of its active and passive users and that some of them have concrete political outcomes.[26]

For Kies, "the real question is not so much whether the online debates are deliberative in general but under which circumstances the online debates foster deliberative forms of debates." His main hypothesis is

> that if participants at an online forum believe that what they write will be widely read and have an impact on the decision making process, they will be more motivated to participate and to adopt a deliberative attitude. This means they will be more motivated to be reciprocal, respectful, sincere, reflective to reach a common agreement and to justify their opinions.[27]

This conclusion indicates that the Internet can only be an effective link between citizens and political authorities if the latter are willing to listen to and take seriously the messages posted on the Internet.

In a large-scale Internet project in the UK, Corinne Wales *et al.* arrive at the conclusion that their analyses "neither confirm the utopian impulse that the online world is the hotbed of deliberative democracy or the dystopian impulse that it is a world where the loudest and brashest are heard. Our findings are more mixed."[28] In 2009, two randomized groups of about 1,000 citizens each discussed online the following questions: "Should we have more activities for young people or better policing? Do faith schools have a role to play in bringing neighbourhoods together or do they create more divisions?" With regard to participation, this project is in line with the research of Kies that many participate little or not at all. "Just under half of those invited to join in the deliberation chose to take no part in it."[29] Of those who logged on, about half did not post any message. This means that only about one-quarter did take an active part in the discussion. Also in line with the research of Kies, the most active participants were highly educated and politically interested. But in contrast to the findings of Kies, women and older persons were more active

---

[26] Kies, "Promises and Limits of the Web-site Deliberation," pp. 202, 205.
[27] Kies, "Promises and Limits of the Web-site Deliberation," pp. 205–6.
[28] Corinne Wales, Sarah Cotterill, and Graham Smith, "Do Citizens Deliberate in On-line Discussion Forums? Preliminary Findings from an Internet Experiment," paper presented at the Participatory and Democracy Specialist Group of the Political Studies Association Conference, Edinburgh, March 29–April 1, 2010, p. 30.
[29] Wales *et al.*, "Do Citizens Deliberate in On-line Discussions Forums?," p. 15.

participants than men and younger people. With regard to justification, the authors find the results "problematic from the perspective
of deliberative democracy ... the majority of contributions on both
threads offered no form of justification: they were simple assertions of
opinion."[30] If justifications were given, they were mainly based on personal experiences. With regard to reciprocity, "only around 20 percent
of participants ... offered any reliable evidence of reciprocity at all:
generally simple statements of agreement or disagreement ... from a
deliberative perspective this general failure to acknowledge the contributions of others is problematic."[31] With regard to mutual respect, the
findings come closer to the deliberative ideal: "The fears of those who
believe that internet discussion forums by their nature will degenerate
into flaming on controversial topics are not confirmed: posts generally remained within the rules of discussion established for the forum
and the contributions that we defined as disrespectful were far from
overly offensive."[32] There were also many references to the common
good, and the authors speculate that the two virtues of mutual respect
and common-good orientation "may be self-reinforcing."[33] With these
overall mixed results, the authors conclude that "the deliberative cup
is half full – or half empty."[34]

Blogging has generally a bad reputation for its lack of deliberative
quality. In an opinion piece in the *Wall Street Journal*, Joseph Rago
summarizes the popular negative position on the quality of political
blogs: "We rarely encounter sustained or systematic blog thought;
instead, panics and maniacs, endless rehearsing of arguments put forward elsewhere; and a tendency to substitute ideology for cognition."[35]
To test the validity of such claims, John W. Robertson and Elizabeth
McLaughlin investigated 12 blogs in the UK, using an expanded version of our DQI.[36] Six blogs were from newspapers like the *Guardian*,
six from independent sources like Guido Fawkes of the Libertarian

---

[30] Wales *et al.*, "Do Citizens Deliberate in On-line Discussion Forums?," p. 22.
[31] Wales *et al.*, "Do Citizens Deliberate in On-line Discussion Forums?," pp.
    25–6.
[32] Wales *et al.*, "Do Citizens Deliberate in On-line Discussion Forums?," p. 30.
[33] Wales *et al.*, "Do Citizens Deliberate in On-line Discussion Forums?." p. 31.
[34] Wales *et al.*, "Do Citizens Deliberate in On-line Discussion Forums?," p. 32.
[35] Quoted in John W. Robertson and Elizabeth McLaughlin, "The Quality of
    Discussion on the Economy in UK Political Blogs in 2008," *Parliamentary
    Affairs* 64 (2011), 109.
[36] Robertson and McLaughlin, "The Quality of Discussion," 106–28.

right. All 12 blogs had to do with the economic crisis at the end of 2008. Analyzing these posts, Robertson and McLaughlin arrive at the following conclusion:

There does seem scope for optimism in the light of the evidence from this study ... the debate in many of these sampled blogs had much to commend it in terms of civilized behaviour, range of economic models, the use of reason and evidence ... The high level of interactivity in many of these blogs does seem a positive phenomenon and is perhaps suggestive of the kind of openness Habermas sought ... negative framing was rare.[37]

These positive results are perhaps due to the choice of issues covered by the blogs, namely taxes and spending in an economic crisis. These topics may lend themselves better to a high quality of deliberation than more emotional issues like abortion or homosexuality.

Thomas Häussler and Marianne Fraefel, two other members of our research group, undertook a systematic comparison of the level of deliberation on TV/radio on the one hand, and on the Internet on the other hand.[38] They investigated the discussions in Switzerland prior to a 2005 referendum on bilateral treaties with the EU. For TV and radio, they looked at both public and private stations. For the Internet, they chose online discussions run by Google and media companies. With regard to the interactive aspect, it was equally low on TV/radio and online. Only 19 percent of the statements on TV/radio and 20 percent online made references to messages of other participants. As Fraefel and Häussler conclude, "a 'real' exchange of ideas is not what takes place much of the time."[39] For the level of justification, TV and radio were more deliberative than the web forums. Participants on TV/radio justified their claims in 32 percent of the cases, online in 20 percent. For the respect category, TV and radio were also more deliberative than the web forums, although participants on both media were highly respectful. Disrespectful utterances were made in only 16 percent of the statements online and only 6 percent on TV/radio. Despite the

---

[37] Robertson and McLaughlin, "The Quality of Discussion," 124–5.
[38] Marianne Fraefel and Thomas Häussler, "Deliberation and Opinion Formation in Dialogic Formats," paper presented at the Conference on Mediated Citizenship: Political Information and Participation in Europe, University of Leeds, September 17–18, 2009.
[39] Fraefel and Häussler, "Deliberation and Opinion Formation in Dialogic Formats," p. 10.

generally lower level of deliberation online, Fraefel and Häussler state that it must also be considered that the web gives much more opportunities for ordinary citizens to participate in political discussions; "as a consequence web fora conform more closely than radio or television to the ideal of a discourse where everyone is free to participate."[40] The overall conclusion of Fraefel and Häussler is that they are less pessimistic than Habermas about the deliberative potential of web forums, "hence, it would be a precipitate conclusion to dismiss online debates as unimportant or even disruptive for public deliberation as they allow citizens to articulate themselves and test the reflexivity of their positions."[41]

In his Ph.D. dissertation, Thomas Häussler looked at British newspapers from a deliberative perspective.[42] For his analysis, he chose the following six issues for specific years going back to the 1960s:

1. nuclear disarmament (1960)
2. Commonwealth immigration (1965)
3. union picketing rights (1980)
4. Northern Ireland secretariat (1985)
5. fuel issue (2000)
6. anti-terror legislation (2005).

He included five newspapers in his investigation: *The Times, The Guardian,* the *Daily Telegraph, The Independent, The Sun.* To determine the level of deliberation, he used our DQI adapted to the media world. With regard to justification, in 45 percent of all articles no justification is offered, in 40 percent a single justification, and in 15 percent two justifications or more. These data do not mean that the actors on which the newspapers reported justified their position to such a low degree. It only means that there were a large number of positions where no justifications were reported in the newspapers. Journalists often take shortcuts by reporting positions without giving the corresponding justifications. Is the glass half full or half empty with regard

---

[40] Fraefel und Häussler, "Deliberation and Opinion Formation in Dialogic Formats," p. 13.
[41] Fraefel and Häussler, "Deliberation and Opinion Formation in Dialogic Formats," p. 14.
[42] Thomas Häussler, "Contest, Conflict, and Consensus: An Empirical Study of the Discursive Transformation of the British Public Sphere (1960–2005)," Ph.D. dissertation, University of Bern, 2011.

to justifications reported in the newspapers? One has also to consider that many validity claims are undisputed or repetitive, so it looks not too bad from a deliberative perspective that, after all, 55 percent of all articles contained some justification. With regard to the content of justification, Häussler is at first puzzled that the common good is rarely mentioned explicitly as reported in the newspapers. An interpretation could be that journalists do not tend to consider references to the common good as newsworthy, so they often omit such references. They focus rather on the actions to be taken, irrespective of the motivation for the proposed actions. Häussler also points out that, initially, it was not clear to many actors what the common good was in their particular situation and that it was precisely the process of discussion that should find out the contours of the common good. Sometimes this could be done successfully, but very often not.

Häussler also codes the dimension of *reciprocity* across articles and finds that in 68 percent of the articles no explicit reference is made to other articles, in 24 percent a reference is made but not in a substantive way, in 4 percent the reference is substantive but not in any detail, and in another 4 percent details are included and the arguments in other articles are evaluated. Thus, reciprocity is low. To the extent that references are made to other articles, the political and administrative authorities are very much at the center. It is not only that actors in civil society often refer to political and administrative authorities, but it is also the case that actors in the political and administrative authorities often refer to each other. Häussler can also show, however, that there are conditions under which reciprocity between the political and administrative authorities and civil society becomes quite frequent, with actors of civil society taking a more active role, for example in the discussion of the fuel issue. But there are also marginal groups who are hardly included in the discussion: a stark example is the bill on Commonwealth immigration where those directly affected had virtually no voice. In summary, there are certainly articles in British newspapers that attain a high standard of deliberation, but such articles are relatively rare. An interesting finding of Häussler is that deliberation in the newspapers is helped if political conflicts are clearly articulated rather than glossed over. This corresponds to the argument of André Bächtiger in Chapter 4 that a spirited discussion with questioning, disputing, and insisting helps deliberation. After all, when there are no visible conflicts there is nothing to be deliberated about.

The importance of clearly articulated conflicts for good deliberation in general is also stressed by Giovan Francesco Lanzara, who argues that an increased level of conflict may bring forward arguments and points of view that participants had not thought about before.[43]

(c) Normative implications of empirical results

In this chapter I have had the most difficulty in drawing meaningful normative implications from the empirical data. In the philosophical literature, there is no controversy over how the media should appear to be deliberative; there is consensus that ideally the media should offer a platform for a respectful and sophisticated dialogue with all policy positions being included on an equal level. Yet, the real media world tends to be so far removed from this ideal that it looks frustrating from a deliberative perspective. I agree with Habermas, quoted in the first section of the chapter, that new developments in the media "would rob us of the centerpiece of deliberative politics." It is particularly disheartening to come to grips with the negative role of the media in Ontario, as reported earlier in the chapter. After a highly deliberative discussion by the Citizens' Assembly on a change to the election system, the citizenship at large had to vote in a referendum on the proposed change. The media were the crucial linkage between the Citizens' Assembly and the referendum. As we recall, Dennis Pilon, the author of the study, concludes "that the media failed on all the key themes Habermas highlights as crucial to an effective deliberative process."

The frequent failure of the media from a deliberative perspective, as illustrated by the Ontario case, cannot be attributed primarily to individual journalists. Many of my former students both in the US and in Switzerland went into journalism with good deliberative intentions but succumbed to the competitive pressure of the media system. This pressure means to present politics as an entertainment game with

---

[43] Giovan Francesco Lanzara, "La deliberazione come indagine publicca," in Luigi Pellizzoni (ed.), *La deliberazione publicca* (Rome: Meltemi editore, 2005), p. 60: "Il caso che un processo deliberativo si risolva in un accresciuto livello di conflitto, ma che da esso emergano al tempo stesso, forse proprio per effetto della radicalizzazione, ragioni, argomentazioni, punti di vista ... che I partecipanti non avenano mai avuto modo di esprimere pubblicamente prima di allora."

winners and losers. Let me illustrate this with the main political discussion forum on German Swiss television, called *Arena*. In the opening credit sequence of the show, one sees the popular Swiss version
of a wrestling match where one wrestler wins, putting the other on
his back.[44] This scene sets the tone for the ensuing discussion. Who is
smart and clever enough to put others, figuratively speaking, on their
backs? Together with a former student, who works in a prominent
role for Swiss television, we submitted a plan that when federal referenda are discussed on *Arena* not politicians but a random sample
of ordinary citizens should be the participants. The rationale for our
plan was that during the parliamentary debates and before, politicians had enough opportunities to present their positions, therefore
when it was the turn of citizens to express their positions in the referendum, *Arena* should be reserved for citizens. The hope was that
Arena would not look like a wrestling match, but as a serious deliberation of the issues to be considered in the referendum. Our plan
had no chance. Politicians were not willing to give up their opportunities to show what good wrestlers they are when it comes to political
debates. This episode also reveals that it is not only the media but
also politicians who want to have politics represented in the media
as entertainment battles with winners and losers. What about citizens
themselves? They often complain about the lack of deliberation in
the media; as consumers of the media, however, they may very well
enjoy the entertainment character of competitive political discussions.
Perhaps watching ordinary citizens discussing a forthcoming referendum on *Arena* would not be entertaining enough, so Swiss television,
given the competitive nature of the media market, had good reasons
to keep *Arena* as it is. This brings me full circle back to how media
have to operate in order to survive in an increasingly competitive
market with all the new technological possibilities. Full-fledged civilized deliberation does not fit well into this market.

However, I do not give up the effort to make the media more deliberative. In this effort, one may have to refer to market forces as well.
What I have in mind is that university institutes specializing in deliberative research will regularly publish reports about the deliberative
quality of various media outlets, using something like our DQI. Such

---

[44] Called *Schwingen* in Swiss German.

reports would also cover online debates on the Internet. As we have seen earlier in the chapter, there is great variation in the deliberative quality of such online debates. Published reports on the deliberative quality of online debates may help to direct interested persons to find forums to their liking. In contrast to newspapers, radio, and television, online debates with high deliberative quality do not need a large public. Twenty or so people may discuss on a regular basis a political topic of common interest like education, national defense, or global warming. To ensure good deliberative quality, participants would have to register with their full names. If such a group were to get high marks for their deliberative quality, other like-minded people might be eager to join. Online discussion groups may be organized at the local level but also globally. Perhaps globally organized groups would have a particularly great appeal, as indicated to me by many of my students. Discussing, for example, poverty in the world with participants from Sweden, Peru, China, South Africa, and so on, seems very attractive to deliberatively oriented people. Many others, to be sure, will never be interested in such online discussions. They may just be interested in exchanging jokes, trivial stories, and such like.

In sum, it seems to me that the Internet offers opportunities for deliberative niches. Published reports on such niches will help interested people to find them. By contrast, I am not optimistic that the main media outlets of newspapers, radio, and television will become more deliberative any time soon, although here, too, there are opportunities for deliberative niches, for example *All Things Considered* on National Public Radio in the US or *Echo der Zeit* on Swiss Public Radio. The media are currently the most problematic link for the development of deliberative democracy, and we have to make all our efforts to remedy the situation, because, as I quoted from Habermas at the beginning of the chapter, the "deliberative model expects the political public sphere to ensure the formation of a plurality of considered public opinions." Taking up this point, Charles Girard shows how ideally the media could contribute to more deliberation at the societal level. The key aspect would be that all positions would be equally and fairly presented in the media, which would allow ordinary citizens to deliberate individually what should be done politically. Girard acknowledges that we are far away from this situation, but that there are no absolute obstacles to make progress in this direction.[45] For me this is also the only hope to arrive at more deliberation in society at large. As I will show in the last chapter, deliberative education in schools and deliberative praxis in mini-publics will be important steps in this direction.

---

[45] Charles Girard, "La délibération médiatisée: Démocracie et communication de masse," *Archives de philosophie du droit* 54 (2011), 207–24.

9 | *Favorable conditions for deliberation*

(a) Normative controversies in the literature

Establishing favorable conditions for deliberation is not a straightforward task because, empirically, deliberation is a multidimensional phenomenon. This was not fully recognized for a long time in the philosophical literature. In the Habermasian ideal speech situation, all deliberative elements have high values. Habermas acknowledges that this ideal speech situation hardly ever occurs and is as rare as "islands in the ocean in everyday praxis."[1] Therefore, particular speech acts in the real world are always more or less distant from the ideal speech situation. Most theorists do not pay sufficient attention to the possibility that for a particular speech act some deliberative elements may be closer to the ideal speech situation than others. The prevailing assumption is that for a given speech act all deliberative elements have more or less the same distance to the ideal speech situation. If, for example, actors justify their claims in a rational way, they also show respect toward the claims of others. If, on the other hand, the level of justification is low, the level of respect is also low. In this way, deliberation is seen as a one-dimensional phenomenon. All elements cluster together in a single dimension, and if one element goes up or down, all other elements do the same. Also, not enough attention is paid by many theorists to the possibility that during a decision process the level of deliberation may fluctuate over time.

Robert E. Goodin was the first theorist to systematically investigate the multidimensional and sequential aspects of deliberation.[2] We

---

[1] "Inseln im Meer der alltäglichen Praxis." Jürgen Habermas, *Die Einbeziehung des Anderen: Studien zur politischen Theorie* (Frankfurt a.M.: Suhrkamp, 1996), p. 323.

[2] Robert E. Goodin, "Sequencing Deliberative Moments," *Acta Politica* 40 (2005), 182–96. Goodin developed the sequencing argument further in his *Innovating Democracy* (Oxford University Press, 2008), ch. 9.

have already encountered part of his argument in Chapter 5. There, we have seen that for Goodin it is not necessary that all phases of a decision process are open to the public. His larger point is that deliberation has to be seen in sequences of a decision process and that not all deliberative elements need to be present in all sequences. What counts for Goodin is "having all of the deliberative virtues on display at *some* point or another in the decision process."[3] He emphasizes the multidimensional and sequential character of deliberation when he postulates "deliberative virtues coming in the right combination and the right order," and he acknowledges that there may be "interactions between different deliberative virtues."[4] Using our Discourse Quality Index (DQI), Goodin reflects on the importance of the different deliberative elements in the various sequences of a decision process. In a stylized way, he distinguishes the following four sequences of a decision process:

First, let us suppose, there is the "caucus room" deliberation where all the MPs of a single party get together to formulate their own program. Second, let us suppose, there is the "parliamentary debate," when MPs from all parties publicly present arguments for their preferred position and against other positions. Third, let us suppose, there is an "election campaign," in which parliamentary candidates compete for office based on the policy positions their parties have taken. Fourth, let us suppose, there is "post-election arguing and bargaining," in which party leaders negotiate policy deals with one another based on the number of representatives they elect.[5]

Goodin is aware that his four sequences of a decision process are a great simplification and that "there is much more that goes on within representative democracy," but the "four stages will suffice to illustrate the point."[6] He then shows which deliberative elements are, in his view, most crucial for each sequence. For the party caucus rooms, authenticity is most important in the sense that actors express their preferences without deception. In parliamentary debates, particular attention should be given to rational justifications of one's validity claims and respect toward counter-arguments. In election campaigns it is key that every competent individual be free to take part in the

[3] Goodin, "Sequencing Deliberative Moments," 193.
[4] Goodin, "Sequencing Deliberative Moments," 193.
[5] Goodin, "Sequencing Deliberative Moments," 189.
[6] Goodin, "Sequencing Deliberative Moments," 188.

discourse and that participants show a sense of empathy for the well-being of others and the community at large. Finally, in post-election arguing and bargaining it matters that participants show respect for counter-arguments and aim at a rationally motivated consensus.[7] In focusing on the most important deliberative elements in each sequence of a decision process, Goodin does not imply that other deliberative elements can be neglected, but they are less important for particular sequences in the process. In the same vein as Goodin, Michael A. Neblo argues:

> one might judge that, ceteris paribus, it is relatively more important for criteria linked to the respect-expressive aspects of deliberation to be emphasized in judicial deliberation than, say, those tracking substantive outcomes. Conversely, we might tolerate somewhat more distributive horse-trading in legislatures, without really holding their deliberations to the strict standards of sincerity that may be more important in private deliberations. In order to be a bit more systematic in our evaluations, it is necessary to characterize the main moments and sites of the deliberative system and how they relate to each other.[8]

With this innovative approach, theorists like Goodin and Neblo move the theoretical discussion forward from simply asking how important or unimportant deliberation is. Deliberation is now conceptualized as a multidimensional and sequential phenomenon allowing a much more differentiated discussion of the various elements of deliberation and their antecedents. One can ask how the individual elements interact with each other, how they evolve over time, and how all of this can be explained. This approach is also taken by Claudia Landwehr, who "advocates a sequential model of deliberative democracy, which sticks to the central importance of deliberation while acknowledging the essential functions of non-deliberative modes of interaction."[9] Kasper M. Hansen goes a step further in warning that some deliberative elements are damaged if others are improved. He expects this to be the case in particular for the element of equality among all participants. A

---

[7] Goodin, "Sequencing Deliberative Moments," 190.
[8] Michael A. Neblo, *Common Voices: Between the Theory and Practice of Deliberative Democracy* (unpublished book manuscript, ch.2).
[9] Claudia Landwehr, "Discourse and Coordination: Modes of Interaction and Their Roles in Political Decision-Making," *Journal of Political Philosophy* 18 (2010), 102.

deliberative culture emphasizing rational justifications in terms of the common good, according to Hansen,

disadvantages people not used to express their opinions in terms of the common good. People inexperienced with meetings, less educated and shy people are easily sidetracked and, consequently, individuals with strong rhetorical skills and demagogues are in a more advantageous position when justifying their interests ... This challenge to the theory is also accentuated by the fact that such participants are already overrepresented in the political system ... participants who are unable to abstract from their social roles are excluded from the deliberation, thus violating political equality not to mention liberty of speech and causing certain experiences to be lost in the deliberative process.[10]

Hansen also sees problems for other deliberative elements if the criterion of publicity is stressed too much. For Hansen,

paradoxically, opinion change and publicity do not go hand in hand. On the contrary, they are often contradictory as publicity can be a barrier to opinion change ... If participants change opinions in public, they might lose face, credibility and be presented as self-contradictory, which would disadvantage them in future deliberation. Therefore, participants may decide to stick to their already expressed views, even if new knowledge or better arguments are voiced.[11]

Thus, there would be great tension between a high level of publicity and the willingness to yield to the force of the better argument. Also looking at deliberative systems at large, Jane Mansbridge sees the possibility that non-deliberative elements in some forums may actually help deliberation in other forums. She argues "that a good deliberative system might and perhaps must include certain highly non-deliberative spaces."[12] As an example she mentions "angry moments" that may help to include "perspectives that can be accessed only through anger ... Anger distorts cognition but, like many other emotions, also motivates thought."[13]

---

[10] Kasper M. Hansen, *Deliberative Democracy and Opinion Formation* (Odensee: University Press of Southern Denmark, 2004), pp. 119–20.
[11] Hansen, *Deliberative Democracy and Opinion Formation*, pp. 124–5.
[12] Jane Mansbridge, "Everyday Talk Goes Viral," paper presented at the annual meeting of the American Political Science Association, Washington, DC, September 2–5, 2010.
[13] Mansbridge, "Everyday Talk Goes Viral."

Considering deliberation not only at the level of individual speech acts or particular group discussions but at the level of entire political systems, the theoretical discussion has moved into high complexity where it is difficult to determine when deliberation is appropriate and when not. Donatella della Porta contributes to this discussion when she reflects on various ways to define democracy at large. She argues that deliberation can be only one element among others, like bargaining and aggregation, and postulates that one needs to experiment with how the various elements can best be integrated.[14] She claims that it is not possible to maximize all elements at the same time.

To explain variation in such complex deliberative systems is a great challenge. For Claudia Landwehr, to take up this challenge is of high importance: "Exploring the context conditions for successful and democratic deliberation thus remains the most important challenge for deliberative theory and deliberative politics."[15] At a very abstract level, Habermas has argued that a common *Lebenswelt* (life world) helps deliberation. By a common *Lebenswelt*, he understands the sharing of traditions, texts, art work, theories, objects of material culture, institutions, social systems, and personality structures.[16] Although it seems plausible that the sharing of such a common *Lebenswelt* facilitates deliberation, as an empirically testable hypothesis the formulation is too abstract. Also at an abstract level, Mark Warren argues that deliberation requires that people feel secure, trust each other, and feel recognized.[17] In sum, the philosophical literature has not much to say about favorable conditions for deliberation. Its interest was always more on favorable *consequences* of deliberation, to which we will turn in the next chapter. With regard to favorable conditions of deliberation, there are hardly any great controversies among theorists; for this, their reflections are on too abstract a level.

---

[14] Donatella della Porta, "Democrazia: sfide e opportunità," *Rivista Italiana de Scienza Politica* 40 (2010), 190. "Il dibattito sulla democrazia comporta spesso la sperimentazione di soluzioni intermedie, integrando diversi."

[15] Claudia Landwehr, "Discourse and Coordination: Modes of Interaction and Their Roles in Political Decision-Making," *Journal of Political Philosophy* 18 (2010), 120.

[16] Jürgen Habermas, *Theorie des kommunikativen Handelns*, vol. I (Frankfurt a.M.: Suhrkamp, 1981), p. 159. "Texte, Überlieferungen, Dokumente, Kunstwerke, Theorien, Gegenstände der materiellen Kultur, Güter, Techniken … Institutionen, gesellschaftliche Systeme und Persönlichkeitsstrukturen."

[17] Personal communication, May 5, 2010.

(b) Empirical results

Literature review

Although the normative literature has not much to say about favorable conditions for deliberation, there is already a rich empirical literature on factors that contribute to deliberation. There are some theorists who take a double role, also launching themselves into empirical work. One of them is John S. Dryzek, who summarizes the empirical literature and identifies the following favorable conditions for deliberation:[18]

- literacy and education;
- a shared language;
- a preferential voting system allowing the expression of more than one preference.

As unfavorable conditions, he mentions:

- religious fundamentalism;
- ideological conformity;
- segmental autonomy.

For political culture, Dryzek, together with Jensen Sass, makes a special claim that more research needs to be done in this respect.[19] They review anthropological research on places like Botswana and Madagascar and find great differences in the respective cultures that are relevant for deliberation. In Botswana, "public officials are compelled to face the public and engage in open-ended processes of justification," a culture favorable for deliberation.[20] In Madagascar, by contrast, the culture requires "strict practices of politeness," which is an unfavorable condition for deliberation because it makes it difficult to engage political leaders in real discussions.[21] Dryzek and Sass conclude from

---

[18] John S. Dryzek, "Democratization as Deliberative Capacity Building," *Comparative Political Studies* 42 (2009), 1394–9.

[19] Jensen Sass and John S. Dryzek, "Deliberative Cultures," paper presented at the Workshop on Frontiers of Deliberation, ECPR Joint Sessions, St. Gallen, April 12–17, 2011.

[20] Sass and Dryzek, "Deliberative Cultures," p. 7.

[21] Sass and Dryzek, "Deliberative Cultures," p. 8.

this review of anthropological studies that different cultures can shape "the communication texture of everyday life."[22]

In our earlier research on parliamentary debates in Germany, Switzerland, the UK, and the US, we encountered the multidimensionality of deliberation, which I have discussed in earlier chapters.[23] The implication is that we cannot limit ourselves to explaining antecedents of deliberation at large, but we also need to look for explanations of specific deliberative elements. We found, in particular, that rational justifications of one's claims, references to the common good, and respect for the claims of others do not tightly cluster together, and therefore are not located on a single dimension. Behind closed doors in committee meetings, justifications of arguments are less elaborate and references to the common good less frequent than in plenary sessions, but respect is higher in committee meetings than in plenary sessions. Given this multidimensionality it is not possible to increase all deliberative elements at the same time. This multidimensionality, however, does not mean that the individual deliberative elements do not somehow hang together. Level of justification, references to the common good and respect for groups to be helped are the three elements for which we have sufficient variation and data for all speech acts; the average polychoric correlation coefficients among these three elements is 0.794, a relatively high value. The only clear outlier is respect shown toward the demands of other participants, where the correlations with the other elements are even negative.[24]

André Bächtiger *et al.* address the dynamic aspect of deliberation and inquire how its various elements evolve over time. A good illustration for their approach is the debate about a language issue in a committee meeting of the Swiss National Council, the first chamber of parliament. The committee took eight sessions to discuss the issue. The most striking development was that at first many actors told personal stories and that this storytelling greatly diminished in later sessions. It is noteworthy that references to the common good and rational

---

[22] Sass and Dryzek, "Deliberative Cultures," p. 8.
[23] Jürg Steiner, André Bächtiger, Markus Spörndli, and Marco R. Steenbergen, *Deliberative Politics in Action: Analysing Parliamentary Discourse* (Cambridge University Press, 2005).
[24] Marco R. Steenbergen, André Bächtiger, Markus Spörndli, and Jürg Steiner, "Measuring Political Deliberation: A Discourse Quality Index," *Comparative European Politics* 1 (2003), 40.

justifications also decreased over time. Bächtiger *et al.* are more ambitious than to merely register such temporal developments over the eight sessions. Based on the combinations among the individual deliberative elements, they construct the following five types of discourses and study how these five types evolve over the eight sessions.[25]

Proto-discourse is everyday talk with the goal of providing information and social comfort. Of the various deliberative elements, only storytelling is at a high level. Common-good orientation and respect are at a middle level. Equality, rational justification, interactivity, constructivity, and bargaining are all at a low level.

Conventional discourse consists of a list of loosely associated demands and narratives. Again, storytelling is the only deliberative element at a high level. At a middle level are equality, rational justification, common-good orientation, respect, constructivity, and bargaining. At a low level is interactivity.

Competitive discourse – here Bächtiger *et al.* quote Michael Walzer, for whom such a discourse "is very often a contest between verbal athletes with the object to win the debate. The means are the exercise of rhetorical skill, the mustering of favorable evidence (and the suppression of unfavorable evidence), and the discrediting of the other debaters."[26] Using Walzer's definition, Bächtiger *et al.* characterize competitive discourse as high on bargaining and common-good orientation (at least rhetorically) and low on respect and constructivity. At a middle level are equality, rational justification, interactivity, and storytelling.

Cooperative discourse has the aim of constructing a shared understanding of the problem and how it is addressed. Storytelling and bargaining are at a middle level, all other deliberative elements are at a high level: equality, rational justification, common-good orientation, respect, interactivity, and constructivity.

---

[25] André Bächtiger, Shawn Rosenberg, Seraina Pedrini, Mirjam Ryser, and Marco R. Steenbergen, "Discourse Quality Index 2: An Updated Measurement Instrument for Deliberative Processes," paper presented at the 5th ECPR General Conference, Potsdam, September 10–12, 2009. The discourse types are a further development of Shawn W. Rosenberg, "Types of Discourse and the Democracy of Deliberation," in Shawn W. Rosenberg (ed.), *Deliberation, Participation and Democracy: Can the People Govern?* (London: Palgrave Macmillan, 2007), pp. 130–58.

[26] Michael Walzer, "Deliberation, and What Else?," in Stephen Macedo (ed.), *Deliberative Politics* (Oxford University Press, 1999), p. 171.

Rational discourse is the most complex and demanding form. Here, Bächtiger *et al.* introduce the category "very high," which is given to common-good orientation, respect, interactivity, and constructivity. Equality and rational justifications are high, while storytelling and bargaining are low or non-existent.

Having distinguished five discourse types, Bächtiger *et al.* apply them to the eight sessions of the committee of the Swiss National Council discussing a language issue. The first session was characterized by a cooperative discourse, the second session by a rational discourse, the third and fourth sessions again by a cooperative discourse, the last four sessions by a conventional discourse. With such classification, Bächtiger *et al.* bring a dynamic dimension to the analysis. The dynamic of a discussion can also be studied in a qualitative way. This is what Maria Clara Jaramillo of our research group does for the experiments with ex-combatants in Colombia. Her main theoretical concept is *transformative moment*, either in the direction of more deliberation or in the direction of less deliberation. In Chapter 2, we have seen that a personal story by one of the ex-combatants led to a transformative moment increasing the level of deliberation.

Thomas Flynn and John Parkinson also look at the dynamic aspect of deliberation, based on a test of an experimental economics methodology in the UK.[27] Specifically, they are interested in whether during deliberation participants shift from "I" to "we" reasoning; the latter they call team reasoning. Over four weekly sessions in 2009, participants discussed whether health authorities should be allowed to store and share private data of patients. The first session was devoted to information and learning, the second session to questioning and clarification, the third session to discussing and debating, the last session to debating and decision-making. Tests after the first session revealed a sharp increase in team reasoning. As the decision-making point approached in the third session, team reasoning tended to stabilize or even to decrease. Emerging differences "reduced the salience of any social identity that had been built up among some individuals in the earlier deliberative phases, raising the salience of personal

---

[27] Thomas Flynn and John Parkinson, "Deliberation, Team Reasoning, and Idealized Interlocutor: Why It May Be Better to Debate with Imagined Others," paper presented at the Workshop on Frontiers of Deliberation, ECPR Joint Sessions, St. Gallen, April 12–17, 2011.

identity."[28] If confirmed, this is an important finding for deliberative theory; thinking in terms of "we" rather than "I" is easier in earlier "learning" phases than in the later "decision-making" phases. This is what we have already seen in Chapter 1, in discussing the research of Simone Chambers on the referendum of Québec independence. Flynn and Parkinson have an interesting twist to their findings. When the interlocutor was not someone in the experimental group itself, but an imagined idealized interlocutor, team reasoning also increased during the process of decision-making. For Flynn and Parkinson, the interpretation is that "the stereotype of the idealized deliberator was never challenged by reality [in the group] and thus maintained its prescriptive character and power."[29] As a general conclusion, they state "that in some circumstances, people could be more likely to team reason when confronted with *ideal* co-deliberators than with *actual* ones."[30] They leave open what this means for the construction of deliberative institutions.

In our own investigation of parliamentary debates, we focused on institutional factors to explain variation in the level of deliberation in its various elements.[31] One such factor concerns the difference between committee meetings and plenary sessions. In earlier chapters, I have already shown the results for this institutional factor. We have seen that one cannot simply say that deliberation is higher in committees or higher in plenary sessions. The causality is more complex. Respect for the arguments of other participants is higher in committees, but rational justifications and references to the common good are higher in plenary sessions. Another institutional factor concerns the question of whether a debate takes place in the first or second chamber of parliament. It is commonly assumed that second chambers are more deliberative bodies. For this analysis, we omitted the UK since the House of Lords has little power. If we look at the results for Germany, Switzerland, and the US, the speech acts in the second chambers indeed reveal more respect and are more constructive in the

---

[28] Flynn and Parkinson, "Deliberation, Team Reasoning, and Idealized Interlocutor," p. 17.
[29] Flynn and Parkinson, "Deliberation, Team Reasoning, and Idealized Interlocutor," p. 17.
[30] Flynn and Parkinson, "Deliberation, Team Reasoning, and Idealized Interlocutor," p. 1.
[31] Steiner *et al.*, *Deliberative Politics in Action*, ch. 5.

sense that the actors stick less to their initial positions. For the level of justification, however, there was no statistically significant difference. Thus, here, too, it is necessary to differentiate the effect for the individual deliberative elements.

For the differences between parliamentary and presidential systems, we contrasted Germany and the UK with the US, while omitting Switzerland, which does not clearly fit into one of the two categories. We expected that the level of deliberation would be higher in presidential systems since the legislature has a strongly independent role so that coordination between president and legislature is necessary. But once again, we do not register a uniform effect on deliberation. The US as a presidential system shows more respect but is lower on rational justifications and constructive politics than Germany and the UK as parliamentary systems. If a political system has strong veto players like powerful interest groups and a strongly independent national bank, one would expect that there would be pressure to deliberate since otherwise each of the players with veto power could block a decision. Our results are, once again, mixed for this hypothesis. Respect is indeed higher in parliamentary contexts with strong veto players. Levels of justification and of constructive politics, on the other hand, show no statistically significant differences. Finally, we were interested to see whether consensus or competitive political systems are more conducive to deliberation. We compared the UK and Switzerland, the two archetypical cases of the two institutional settings. Switzerland practices executive power-sharing and cooperative federalism, while the UK usually has one-party governments and is strongly centralized. In order to have a good comparative basis, we looked at an issue that was discussed at the same time in both countries. The chosen issue was the minimum wage. Here, the results are clearly in a uniform direction in the sense that Switzerland was at a higher level for all deliberative elements than the UK. Jessica Bogas confirms the finding that deliberation is more frequent in consensus institutional settings. Using our DQI, in her study she finds a higher level of deliberation in parliamentary debates in the Netherlands as a consensus system than in the UK.[32] A last result from our investigation of parliamentary

[32] Jessica Bogas, "Captivated or Complacent Audiences? Assessing Deliberative Quality in Competitive and Consensus Democracies," unpublished thesis, University of Leiden, 2009.

debates is that deliberation is more difficult to achieve when the issue under discussion polarizes the participants. This may not seem surprising but theoretically one could not totally exclude the idea that a polarizing situation would be perceived as so disruptive for the group that attempts would be made to use deliberative means in order to calm the situation.

Also using our DQI, Laura McLauchlan *et al.* investigated a parliamentary debate in New Zealand with a surprisingly high level of deliberation, allowing them to come up with some interesting explanations for this outlier case.[33] The debate dealt with a bill on Human Assisted Reproductive Technology. The authors show that in other countries, for example in the UK, parliamentary debates on reproductive legislation are usually of a low deliberative level. The authors also state that "the New Zealand Parliament is noted for robust and often boisterous debate."[34] By contrast, they characterize the debate on the reproductive bill as deliberative: "These debates were relatively calm and respectful ... marked by parliamentarians' consideration of and respect for the values of other speakers ... their emphasis on the goal of public benefit ... high degree of harmony ... a great degree of empathy."[35] Parliamentarians were themselves surprised by the deliberative tone of the debate, as one member put it: "Look at us tonight – quiet as lambs."[36] What was so special about the conditions of this debate that allowed a high quality of deliberation? McLauchlan *et al.* see as one reason that the party whip was suspended so that the issue could cut across party lines: "Such splitting within parties and agreement across parties may offer a partial explanation of the low levels of contention within the debates. It may be that members have toned down their attacks on other parties because of their awareness of the existence of similar viewpoints within their own parties."[37] Second, the authors argue that there was "learning from other nations' debates on similar matters," making

---

[33] Laura McLauchlan, Jessica MacCormick, and Julie Park, "Quiet as Lambs: Communicative Action in the New Zealand Parliamentary Debates on Human Assisted Reproductive Technology," *Sites: A Journal of Social Anthropology and Cultural Studies* 7 (2010), 1–21.

[34] McLauchlan *et al.*, "Quiet as Lambs," 1.

[35] McLauchlan *et al.*, "Quiet as Lambs," 1–3, 13, 19.

[36] McLauchlan *et al.*, "Quiet as Lambs," 10.

[37] McLauchlan *et al.*, "Quiet as Lambs," 8.

parliamentarians in New Zealand careful, avoiding the discussion "of irresolvable questions such as those surrounding foetal person-hood [there was] only limited discussion of embryos."[38] A member of parliament explicitly stated: "We have learnt from overseas experiences ... I was actually in England and Australia when they were debating their legislation on this issue, and the debate was very heated."[39] Third, there were "attempts to allude to values assumed to be shared, particularly those of care for humans and desire to lessen suffering."[40] It was easy, for example, to agree against "human cloning for reproductive purposes [or] the implantation of a human embryo into an animal and vice versa."[41] Such appeals to common values "also appeared to contribute to the temperateness of the discourse."[42] Among these explanations, I find particularly interesting that countries can learn from failed deliberation in other countries.

Looking at still another institutional variation, also using our DQI, in the Netherlands Jan Willem Rozier compared debates in plenary sessions of parliament and the cabinet (Council of Ministers).[43] Such an investigation was possible because in the Netherlands the minutes of cabinet meetings are made public after 20 years. The most striking result was that in cabinet meetings arguments were less thoroughly justified and respect levels were lower, indicating a lower discourse quality than in parliament. With regard to justification, this finding corresponds to our own finding that the level of justification is lower behind closed doors because actors are likely to take shortcuts more often when they are not in the public eye (see comparison above between plenary parliamentary sessions and committee meetings). That respect levels in the Dutch cabinet are lower than in parliament may be due to the fact that the cabinet is highly politicized. As Rozier puts it, the real game in the Netherlands is not between coalition parties and opposition parties in parliament but among the usually many coalition parties in the cabinet.

---

[38] McLauchlan *et al.*, "Quiet as Lambs," 9.
[39] McLauchlan *et al.*, "Quiet as Lambs," 10.
[40] McLauchlan *et al.*, "Quiet as Lambs," 11.
[41] McLauchlan *et al.*, "Quiet as Lambs," 10.
[42] McLauchlan *et al.*, "Quiet as Lambs," 19.
[43] Jan Willem Rozier, "The Effect of Audience: Deliberation Quality in the Dutch Council of Ministers and the Second Chamber," unpublished thesis, University of Leiden, 2009.

Claudia Landwehr and Katharina Holzinger investigated for Germany whether it makes a difference for the level of deliberation if the same topic is discussed in a plenary session of parliament or a citizens' conference.[44] (I have referred to this study already in Chapter 6 in context of the force of the better argument.) The topic for discussion was whether embryonic stem cells should be allowed to be imported to Germany. On January 30, 2002, the Bundestag discussed the issue in plenum. "The debate was celebrated as one of the parliament's finest hours, and the quality and atmosphere of argumentation were widely appreciated. The procedure chosen differed from normal legislation in that the requirement to vote according to party policy (the whip) was officially suspended, allowing and demanding MPs to vote according to their conscience."[45] Despite these favorable conditions, only 16 percent of the speech acts had a dialogical character. Landwehr and Holzinger explain this low number as follows:

Apparently, the underlying logics of interaction and procedural requirements in this setting effectively prevented dialogue. Speaking time in the Bundestag is assigned according to the number of signatures of a motion, and the list of speakers determined in advance. This creates a division of the forum into speakers and listeners, for whom it is almost impossible to become speakers themselves – if not by means of interruption. Speakers have their contributions prepared in advance, and limited speaking times are rigorously enforced.[46]

After the embryonic stem-cell debate in the Bundestag, the same topic was discussed in a citizens' conference, described by Landwehr and Holzinger as follows:

14,000 persons living in the cities of Berlin, Bernau, and Nauen were selected randomly from a telephone register and contacted by mail with information about the topic and goals of the conference and asked to reply if they were interested in participation. From the 400 or so people who replied two groups of 20 people were drawn according to socio-demographic criteria

---

[44] Claudia Landwehr and Katharina Holzinger, "Institutional Determinants of Deliberative Interaction," *European Political Science Review* 2 (2010), 373–400.

[45] Landwehr and Holzinger, "Institutional Determinants of Deliberative Interaction," 382.

[46] Landwehr and Holzinger, "Institutional Determinants of Deliberative Interaction," 389.

such as age, gender, and occupation. One group was the actual citizen group, the other a control group for evaluation. Among the citizens selected, 17 turned up for the first weekend meeting, of which five dropped out before the second meeting ... Despite the sophisticated selection procedure, both the actual citizen group and the similarly composed control group thus suffered from a lack of representativeness due to process of self-selection.[47]

The citizens' conference met over three weekends. Landwehr and Holzinger investigated an afternoon session during the second weekend. With regard to the dialogical nature of the discussion, the citizens' conference had a much higher level than the Bundestag: of the speech acts in the citizens' conference, 56 percent had a dialogical character, much higher than the 16 percent for the Bundestag. Landwehr and Holzinger explain the difference as follows: "The dialogical quality [in the citizens' conference] was enabled by the comparatively small size of the forum and encouraged by the moderators. The clear intention in procedural rules and the set-up of the forum was that each of the citizens should be at liberty to speak whenever they wanted to."[48] It would be interesting to see what the dialogical quality in the citizens' conference would be were it the same size as the Bundestag and had no encouragement by the moderator for dialogical behavior. It is only in this way that the deliberative behavior of parliamentarians and ordinary citizens could be compared in a controlled way.

In their investigation of citizens' conferences on climate change in the French region of Poitou-Charentes, Julien Talpin and Laurence Monnoyer-Smith also look at institutional variation in distinguishing between face-to-face and online discussions.[49] They found that online discussions were more interactive in the sense that participants referred more often "to other participants to back up an argument." Online discussions were also "more informed" and "more precise" than face-to-face discussions.[50] Talpin and Monnoyer-Smith acknowledge that

---

[47] Landwehr and Holzinger, "Institutional Determinants of Deliberative Interaction," 383.
[48] Landwehr and Holzinger, "Institutional Determinants of Deliberative Interaction," 389.
[49] Julien Talpin and Laurence Monnoyer-Smith, "Talking with the Wind? Discussion on the Quality of Deliberation in the Ideal-EU Project," paper presented at the IPSA International Conference, Luxembourg, March 18–20, 2010.
[50] Talpin and Monnoyer-Smith, "Talking with the Wind?," p. 20.

their findings "partly contradict the results of some previous research that stressed the monological aspect of online discussions in comparisons to face-to-face ones."[51] In a later research project, Laurence Monnoyer-Smith, this time collaborating with Stéphanie Wojcik, came to a finding that conflicted with her previous research with Talpin. This time, the topic of the discussion concerned the possible replacement of an old waste-treatment facility in the Parisian agglomeration with a modern methanization unit. Again, the discussion was partly face-to-face, partly online, but now "for almost all the [deliberative] criteria, the on-line discussions were of a superior quality to the offline discussions."[52] Thus, it is still an open question whether institutionally it matters for the level of deliberation whether a discussion takes place online or face-to-face.

Julien Talpin conducted another interesting study relevant in the current context.[53] As we have already seen in Chapter 4, Talpin studied the involvement of ordinary citizens in the budgeting process at the local level in Morsang-sur-Orge in the Paris banlieue, the eleventh district in Rome, and Seville in Spain. Within an upper limit, citizens had the power to allocate money to various community programs. Talpin identified four institutional features that helped deliberation in these budget discussions. First, a small number of participants makes deliberation more likely. As an illustration for this hypothesis, Talpin mentions that in Rome the first two meetings of a group had more than 30 participants, which "resulted in a discursive messiness, people not listening to each other, speaking over the other, moving from one topic to another. At the third meeting, participants decided to divide in three working groups ... Discussion dynamics thus changed drastically. I followed one of the working groups where discussion was calm and constructive."[54] As a second institutional factor that helped deliberation, Talpin mentions the "spatial organization of the meetings ... everyone

---

[51] Talpin and Monnoyer-Smith, "Talking with the Wind?," p. 20.
[52] Based on a modified version of the DQI: Laurence Monnoyer-Smith and Stéphanie Wojcik, "Technology and the Quality of Public Deliberation: A Comparison Between On and Off-line Participation," paper presented at the 61st Conference of the International Communication Association, Boston, May 26–30, 2011, p. 25.
[53] Julien Talpin, *Schools of Democracy: How Ordinary Citizens (Sometimes) Become Competent in Participatory Budgeting Institutions* (Colchester: ECPR Press, 2011).
[54] Talpin, *Schools of Democracy*, p. 303.

should be able to see each other when talking. People need to see and hear each other properly to answer each other and be fully responsive."[55] Third, turn-taking seems to help deliberation, which Talpin justifies in the following way:

While in general, the floor is captured by a few speakers, the discussion takes a different shape when everyone has to give his or her opinion. While people with few oral skills lack confidence to speak up spontaneously, they take the chance offered to them to express themselves. This again can increase the pool of expressed arguments, and therefore favour the emergence of disagreement and the breaking off of monological sequences.[56]

Finally, according to the research of Talpin, deliberation tends to be at a higher level when detailed minutes are distributed from meeting to meeting.

In sum, we can say that, based on the existing literature, institutions matter as causal factors to explain variation in the level of deliberation. As Michael E. Morrell rightly insists, however, in addition to institutions, we also have to consider psychological factors in order to explain variation in deliberation.[57] He undertook a broad survey of psychological experiments relevant for deliberation. His starting point is the finding "that actors tend to attribute their successful behaviors to their own dispositions and their unsuccessful behaviors to situational factors," whereas they tend to see the behaviors of others exactly in reverse, attributing successful behaviors to situational factors, unsuccessful behaviors to their own dispositions.[58] Morrell illustrates this finding of psychological experiments as follows:

A wealthy lawyer will likely view her own economic success arising from her own dispositions, such as hard work and intelligence, while she will likely view the economic failure of others as being due to their dispositions, such as lack of effort or ability. In contrast, a poor laborer will likely attribute his lack of economic success to situations, such as having attended poor schools or facing overwhelming problems in life, while he will likely

---

[55] Talpin, *Schools of Democracy*, p. 302.
[56] Talpin, *Schools of Democracy*, p. 305.
[57] Michael E. Morrell, *Empathy and Democracy: Feeling, Thinking, and Deliberation* (University Park: Pennsylvania State University Press, 2010).
[58] Morrell, *Empathy and Democracy*, p. 103.

attribute the success of the wealthy to their life situations, as coming from a wealthy family or getting the lucky breaks in life that eluded him.[59]

Morrell concludes from these attribution biases for the chances of success of deliberation:

> If interlocutors do not view the basic reasons for their respective behaviors similarly, if they tend to judge those who are least like them by stronger moral standards than they judge themselves or those closest to them, and if they attribute unethical and strategic motives to those with whom they disagree, one can hardly imagine how it would be possible for them to give each other equal consideration, reach any sort of mutual understanding, or be able to reciprocally address validity claims.[60]

After reviewing these pessimistic psychological findings for the success chances of deliberation, Morrell presents "good evidence that instructing people to pay attention to others' feelings will decrease biases they have regarding others ... empathic process can help close this gap."[61] In these experiments subjects get instructions such as: "imagine a day in the life of this individual as if you were that person, looking at the world through his eyes and walking through the world in his shoes," while the subjects in a control group do not get these instructions.[62] These experiments indicate that instructing subjects to be empathic leads to characteristics favorable to deliberation. According to Morrell's survey:

> the empirical evidence supports the hypothesis that instructing people to be sensitive to others' thoughts and feelings will increase the probability that they will come to see others as more multifaceted and complex, and because of this, be less biased in their attributional judgments ... it appears highly likely that we need citizens to engage in the process of empathy if deliberation is to function properly. In order to decrease biases and polarization, and increase cooperation and reciprocity, deliberators must demonstrate predispositions to both perspective taking and empathy, and the deliberative system must somehow encourage citizens to act on these predispositions.[63]

---

[59] Morrell, *Empathy and Democracy*, p. 104.
[60] Morrell, *Empathy and Democracy*, p. 104.
[61] Morrell, *Empathy and Democracy*, pp. 106–7.
[62] Morrell, *Empathy and Democracy*, p. 110.
[63] Morrell, *Empathy and Democracy*, pp. 108, 114–15, 128.

Morrell does not deny that the right kinds of institution are important for deliberation, but he insists that "no matter how well structured
the procedures, the threat of impasse and breakdown looms large,"
if the element of empathy is missing. He also does not deny that the
cognitive aspect is important for deliberation since experimental psychological studies "support the multi-dimensional process model of
empathy by indicating that both affective and cognitive sensitivity to
others is what helps individuals overcome their biased perceptions of
others' motivations and behaviors."[64] How do we get more empathy in
a political system so that deliberation can flourish? Morrell makes two
suggestions. First, he states "that we ought to include empathy as part
of democratic education. In doing so we can aim at increasing citizens'
predisposition for empathy, specifically for perspective taking and
empathic concern, so that they will be more likely to take into account
the perspectives of their fellow deliberators."[65] Second, for Morrell, "it
is possible that through presentations in literature, film, and other arts
we can encourage citizens to be empathetically sensitive."[66]

Marli Huijer found in a Dutch study that ambiguity helps with
deliberation.[67] I have discussed this study in Chapter 2 in the context
of the role of storytelling for deliberation. As we recall, she studied the
political debate in the Netherlands about embryo selection for hereditary breast cancer (pre-implantation genetic diagnosis, PGD). The
Labor Party argued that such genetic diagnosis should henceforth be
permitted based on the principle of patient autonomy, so female carriers of a serious hereditary disease should have the option of PGD to
protect their children. This argument was opposed by the Reformed
Christian Party, who warned of a slippery slope: since we are all genetically at risk for something, in the end this diagnosis would be used
for all kinds of potential hereditary diseases. At the beginning of the
debate, the two positions were presented in stark contrast, not leaving
space for compromise. Then ordinary people with hereditary breast
cancer in their families began to tell their stories in the media, taking
positions on both sides of the issue. Huijer characterizes these stories

---

[64] Morrell, *Empathy and Democracy*, p. 107.
[65] Morrell, *Empathy and Democracy*, p. 127.
[66] Morrell, *Empathy and Democracy*, p. 127.
[67] Marli Huijer, "Storytelling to Enrich the Democratic Debate: The Dutch
Discussion on Embryo Selection for Hereditary Breast Cancer," *BioSocieties* 4
(2009), 223–38.

in the following way: "Rather than providing simple answers, [the stories] emphasized the moral complexity of the situation. A clear plot was often lacking. Moreover, their style of speaking was more emotional and less rhetorical; it was more aimed at reaching understanding than persuading others ... [the stories] were more ambiguous than those of the politicians."[68] Huijer's analysis identifies a strong effect of these stories on the debate among politicians:

> In sum, after listening to the ambiguous stories of women and men who directly experienced the anguish of living with hereditary breast cancer, the unambiguous and principled way the Labour Party and the Reformed Christian Party started the public discussion on PGD for hereditary breast cancer came across as disrespectful. The stories helped to transform the public sphere, where politicians and the public generally act and speak, into a realm where people were prepared to listen to each other and reach mutual understanding.[69]

This understanding involved a compromise solution with which both political parties could live: "each request for PGD was to be separately evaluated. Assisted by a multidisciplinary team of experts, in each case the patient and physician are to take into account the severity and nature of the disease, the treatment options, additional medical criteria, and psychological and moral factors."[70] Huijer concludes from her research that "more than any reasoned argument the stories of the carriers demonstrate the moral complexity of their situation. In a democracy, where most political leaders and private citizens prefer clear-cut positions to ambiguity, that is a huge accomplishment."[71]

As we have seen at the beginning of this section, Dryzek sees a shared language as a favorable condition for deliberation. Nicole Doerr presents data that conflicts with this hypothesis.[72] As we have seen in Chapter 2, she investigated the European Social Forums, first at the preparatory national level and then at the European level.

---

[68] Huijer, "Storytelling to Enrich the Democratic Debate," 234.
[69] Huijer, "Storytelling to Enrich the Democratic Debate," 236.
[70] Huijer, "Storytelling to Enrich the Democratic Debate," 235.
[71] Huijer, "Storytelling to Enrich the Democratic Debate," 237.
[72] Nicole Doerr, "Activists Beyond Language Borders? Multilingual Deliberative Democracy Experiments at the European Social Forums," paper presented at the ECPR General Conference, Potsdam, September 2009.

Surprisingly, she found a higher level of deliberation at the European than at the national level, although the language barrier was much higher at the European level. We remember that her explanation is that at the European level the contributions had to be translated, which required careful listening, which in turn helped deliberation. By contrast, at the national level, most participants spoke the same language, which meant that there were stereotypical expectations about what words mean, so that participants felt less need to listen carefully. In a more recent paper, Doerr sums up her investigation about the role of translation that "public discourse was more inclusionary and transparent at the European level than at the national level."[73]

With regard to individual characteristics, there is great research interest in whether women or men are more deliberative. Marco R. Steenbergen concludes that "the empirical record in gender effects ... is somewhat mixed."[74] Early on in the discussion, Jane Mansbridge speculated that women may be more adept at deliberation than men because the consultative, participatory style of deliberation suits women better."[75] In experimental studies, Christopher F. Karpowitz and Tali Mendelberg indeed found that a large share of female participants enhances deliberation.[76] Lawrence R. Jacobs *et al.*, however, found no gender effect when they studied a random sample of American citizens about political talk in everyday life.[77] Didier Caluwaerts *et al.*, in a voter survey in Belgium, also addressed the question of how much women and men talk in families and with friends and work colleagues

[73] Nicole Doerr, "Europe in Translation: How Multilingual Social Movements Innovate Deliberative Politics in the EU," paper presented at the ECPR General Conference, Reykjavik, August 25–27, 2011, p. 16.

[74] Marco R. Steenbergen, "Deliberative Politics in Switzerland," in Adrian Vatter, Frédéric Varone, and Fritz Sager (eds.), *Demokratie als Leidenschaft: Planung, Entscheidung und Vollzug in der Schweizerischen Demokratie* (Bern: Haupt, 2009), p. 291.

[75] Jane Mansbridge, "Reconstructing Democracy," in Nancy J. Hirschmann and Christine Di Stefano (eds.), *Revisioning the Political: Feminist Reconstruction of Traditional Concepts in Western Political Theory* (Boulder, CO: Westview, 1996).

[76] Christopher F. Karpowitz and Tali Mendelberg, "Groups and Deliberation," *Swiss Political Science Review* 13 (2007), 645–62.

[77] Lawrence R. Jacobs, Fay Lomax Cook, and Michael X. Delli Carpini, *Talking Together: Public Deliberation and Political Participation in America* (University of Chicago Press, 2009), p. 57.

about politics.[78] Controlling for education, social class, associational membership, political efficacy, political interest, and social trust, they found that men talk more about politics with friends and at the workplace, whereas there was no difference between men and women with regard to political talk within families. The authors comment on this finding with the argument that women have no problem talking about politics in the safe environment of their families, but are hesitant when political talk becomes more public in groups of friends or work colleagues. Caluwaerts *et al.* conclude that with regard to gender, normative democratic theory faces a dilemma between two of its core assumptions, publicity and inclusion: the more political talk is public, the less women participate, the less it is public, the more they do so.

How does gender play out in parliamentary debates? Rita Grünenfelder und André Bächtiger of our research team did further analysis for this question for Germany and Switzerland, looking at both plenary sessions and committee meetings.[79] They looked at gender at the individual level and with regard to group composition. For the former aspect, after introducing a large number of control variables, they conclude that "there is practically no evidence for gendered deliberation in the sense that women MPs would behave differently compared to their male colleagues. This is a clear rebuttal for feminist authors arguing that women are generally more inclined to deliberative processes."[80] With regard to group composition, however, gender matters: "the higher the share of female legislators in committees and plenary sessions, the higher the respect level."[81] Grünenfelder and Bächtiger comment on the effects of gender composition "that once the share of female politicians increases, politics might become a little more pleasant and a little less adversarial."[82] In their analysis of plenary debates in the European Parliament, Dionysia Tamvaki and

---

[78] D. Caluwaerts, S. Erzeel, and P. Meier, "Différences de sexe en discussions politiques et implications normatives pour la démocratie délibérative," in K. Deschouwer, P. Delwit, M. Hooghe, and S. Walgrave (eds.), *Les Voix du Peuple* (Brussels: Editions du ULB, forthcoming).

[79] Rita Grünenfelder and André Bächtiger, "Gendered Deliberation? How Men and Women Deliberate in Legislatures," paper presented at the ECPR Joint Sessions in Helsinki, May 2007. The focus of the study is on the respect element.

[80] Grünenfelder and Bächtiger, "Gendered Deliberation?," p. 18.

[81] Grünenfelder and Bächtiger, "Gendered Deliberation?," p. 18.

[82] Grünenfelder and Bächtiger, "Gendered Deliberation?," p. 19.

Christopher Lord also look at the gender effect, but only at the individual level and not with regard to group composition.[83] They confirm the findings of Grünenfelder and Bächtiger that at the individual level gender has no influence on the level of deliberation.

Education is another factor that is often mentioned as an antecedent for deliberation. On the one hand, an often-heard argument is that good education, with its emphasis on the development of cognitive skills, contributes to good deliberation. On the other hand, some theorists have warned of the danger that great inequalities in education will have the consequence that the highly educated dominate deliberation, violating in this way a key virtue of deliberation. Iris Marion Young, for example, states: "Under conditions of structural inequality, normal processes of deliberation often in practice restrict access to agents with greater resources, knowledge, or connections [and such agents] therefore are able to dominate the proceedings with their interests and perspectives."[84] Caluwaerts *et al.* demonstrate for Belgium that highly educated persons talk more about politics with family and friends, whereas for political talk at the workplace education has no effect.[85] For the US, Jacobs *et al.* register a general trend for people with higher levels of education to engage more in political talk in everyday life.[86]

Has age anything to do with deliberation? One may speculate that good deliberation presupposes a long learning process so that the level of deliberation would increase with age. A conflicting hypothesis would be that life experience often reveals politics as a power game, so older people become more cynical and therefore less deliberative. Jacobs *et al.* do not find any significant age effect for everyday talk in the US with the exception that the youngest use new technologies most often to engage in political talk.[87]

I now turn to deeply divided societies where deliberation is most needed but also most difficult. What is the potential for deliberation

---

[83] Dionysia Tamvaki and Christopher Lord, "The Content and Quality of Representation in the European Assembly: Towards Building an Updated Discourse Quality Index at the EU Level," paper presented at the IPSA International Conference, Luxembourg, March 18–20, 2010.

[84] Iris Marion Young, "Activist Challenges to Deliberative Democracy," *Political Theory* 29 (2001), 680.

[85] Caluwaerts *et al.*, "Différences de sexe en discussions politiques."

[86] Jacobs *et al.*, *Talking Together*, p. 62.

[87] Jacobs *et al.*, *Talking Together*, p. 57.

in such societies? If a society is deeply divided by criteria such as language, religion, race, ethnicity, history, and social class, there is a great risk of political instability and even civil war. Consociational theory has shown that with the right kind of institutional and cultural elements, it may still be possible to achieve some level of democratic stability, although the risks of failure remain high.[88] The institutions advocated for deeply divided societies are proportionality for parliamentary elections, power-sharing of all major parties in the executive, federalism, and strong veto points in the system. Culturally, a society should have what Arend Lijphart called a spirit of accommodation for his analysis of the Netherlands[89] and I labeled amicable agreement for my study of Switzerland.[90] When consociational theory moved from single-country case studies to comparative analyses of more than 30 countries, the cultural aspect was more and more neglected because it was difficult to measure.[91] Thus, the theory increasingly focused on institutional factors, which became problematic. In countries such as Iraq and Bosnia–Herzegovina, the institutional elements of consociational theory were applied, but democratic stability is most difficult to achieve. It is obvious that a culture of a spirit of accommodation or amicable agreement is missing. The challenge is to get an empirical handle on this cultural factor. I took up this challenge in linking consociational theory with deliberative theory and replacing spirit of accommodation and amicable agreement with deliberation.[92] My argument is that deeply divided societies need consociational institutions as a necessary but not sufficient condition. In addition, such societies also need a culture of deliberation. While it is relatively easy through political engineering to establish consociational institutions in the constitution, it is much more difficult to establish a culture of deliberation.

---

[88] Markus M.L. Crepaz and Jürg Steiner, *European Democracies*, 7th edn. (New York: Longman, 2010), ch. 13.

[89] Arend Lijphart, *Politics of Accommodation: Pluralism and Democracy in the Netherlands* (Berkeley: University of California Press, 1968).

[90] Jürg Steiner, *Amicable Agreement versus Majority Rule: Conflict Resolution in Switzerland* (Chapel Hill: University of North Carolina Press, 1974).

[91] Arend Lijphart, *Democracies: Patterns of Majoritarian and Consensus Government* (New Haven, CT: Yale University Press, 1984).

[92] In several personal conversations, Arend Lijphart acknowledges that the concept of deliberation captures what he meant by a spirit of accommodation.

Ian O'Flynn has given much thought to the potential for deliberation in deeply divided societies.[93] He acknowledges that "groups caught up in a civil war can certainly be described as lacking reasonableness; under such conditions, there may be little point in insisting that those groups advance and respond constructively to principled arguments."[94] He then continues on a more optimistic note and sees potential for deliberation in the process of reaching a peace agreement.

To be sure, most, if not all, peace agreements begin life as pragmatic bargains. However, if those bargains are to provide a platform for sustainable peace, they must also reflect a commitment to basic principles ... peace agreements are binding on citizens in general and hence, if they are considered democratically legitimate, must be justified on terms that everyone can broadly accept.[95]

Put in other words, according to O'Flynn, power and interests always play an important role in deeply divided societies, but they are not sufficient to reach enduring peaceful solutions. For this to happen, some level of deliberation is needed based on commonly accepted basic principles. O'Flynn argues that this is precisely what happened when, in Northern Ireland in April 1998, the Good Friday Agreement was reached:

At bottom, Irish nationalists endorsed it because it held out the promise of achieving a united Ireland, whereas British unionists endorsed it because it held out the best opportunity of reconciling nationalists to the union. The important point about the agreement, however, is that both sets of aspirations are underpinned by a shared commitment to principles of self-determination, democratic equality, tolerance and mutual respect. It is those principles that give the agreement legitimacy, in the eyes of both ordinary citizens and the international community, and that sustain the hope for enduring peace and stability.[96]

Nevin T. Aiken also looked at Northern Ireland, and he showed that efforts at the local level of intercommunity contacts have positive results.[97] He found

---

[93] Ian O'Flynn, "Divided Societies and Deliberative Democracy," *British Journal of Political Science* 37 (2007), 731–51; Ian O'Flynn, *Deliberative Democracy and Divided Societies* (Edinburgh University Press, 2006).

[94] O'Flynn, "Divided Societies and Deliberative Democracy," 741.

[95] O'Flynn, "Divided Societies and Deliberative Democracy," 741.

[96] O'Flynn, "Divided Societies and Deliberative Democracy," 741.

[97] Nevin T. Aiken, "Learning to Live Together: Transitional Justice and Intergroup Reconciliation in Northern Ireland," *International Journal of Transitional Justice* 4 (2010), 166–88.

substantial evidence to suggest that increasing levels of intercommunity contact through the integrated "community relations" approach has had a measurable causal effect in promoting more positive intergroup relations in Northern Ireland ... increased contact has been highly effective in helping to increase cross-community tolerance, trust, friendship, understanding and positive affect, while at the same time reducing negative perceptions of intergroup threat, anxiety, bias and prejudice.[98]

Alain Nöel agrees with O'Flynn and Aiken that "for more dramatically divided societies ... successful deliberation may still be achieved, even in contexts where power and interests have much weight."[99]

New data on deliberative experiments[100]

Having presented in previous chapters the individual deliberative elements, we now want to know how these elements hang together so that we can get a handle on the discourse quality at large in the sense of our DQI. For *Colombia*, we apply a factor analysis to the polychoric correlation matrix of the individual deliberative elements. We end up with a one-only factor solution, which has the following loading:

Participation length	0.817
Level of rational justification	0.870
Reference to own group	0.671
Reference to other groups	0.537
Reference to common good	0.570
Reference to abstract principles	0.529
Force of better argument	0.439

To measure the overall discourse quality, this factor makes sense from a theoretical perspective: it is high when actors speak at some length; justify their arguments with some level of rationality; do not often refer to benefits and costs of their own group but do so for other groups, the common good, and abstract principles; and is relatively high with regard to the force of the better argument. How can variation in the overall discourse quality be explained? A multivariate

---

[98] Aiken, "Learning to Live Together," 184.

[99] Alain Nöel, "Democratic Deliberation in a Multinational Federation," *Critical Review of International Social and Political Philosophy* 9 (2006), 432.

[100] For the research designs, see Introduction, Section (b).

regression analysis shows that two variables have a significant effect: the number of speech acts that an individual utters and a rightist political family background. The first of these variables means that the more frequently an ex-combatant intervened in the discussion, the higher were his or her DQI scores as measured by the factor described above. Thus, speaking up more often was not just repetitive, but allowed the participant to expand and elaborate on previous speech acts. A rightist family background had a negative impact on the DQI scores; the emphasis on hierarchies and order in such families may explain this finding.

If we do the multivariate regression analysis not for the additive DQI but for the individual deliberative elements, we get some additional interesting results. With regard to education, the findings are mixed. On the one hand, the better educated ex-combatants were more likely to speak up and to refer more often to abstract moral principles. On the other hand, those with little or no formal education were as deliberative in other aspects as the better educated. This latter finding is remarkable given that in most research more education contributes to more deliberation. With regard to age, the youngest participants were least likely to speak up, but for other deliberative elements age had no significant influence. For gender, men and women were at about the same level for all deliberative elements. A remarkable specific finding is that poor participants referred least often to their own group interests, which indicates how social class discriminates in a subtle way against those at the bottom of society in the sense that the poor are perhaps too humble to look after their own interests. A promising finding is that those ex-combatants longest demobilized spoke up the most, which shows that the program of reintegration apparently had some positive effect in making ex-combatants less shy about being vocal.

In the questionnaire after the experiments, participants were asked how they *perceived* the level of deliberation during the experiment. The only variable that shows a statistically significant effect is education, with the highly educated recalling the experiment in a more negative light. This finding is worrisome in the sense that it may indicate that cynicism about deliberation increases with more education.

We also tested the influence of institutional factors on the various deliberative elements. In half of the 28 experiments, participants were asked to decide on the content of a letter on the future of Colombia to be sent to the High Commissioner for Reintegration. In the other half of the experiments, no such decision had to be made, so the discussion was free-floating and without an end point. In the latter situation, participants more often used rational reasons to justify their arguments. In the 14 experiments where a decision on a letter had to be made, in seven it was by unanimity, in the other seven by majority vote. When unanimity was required, arguments were more often rationally justified than when a simple majority was sufficient. Since attendance at the experiments greatly varied, a further institutional factor was the size of the discussion group. When the group was small, participants spoke at greater length, referred less often to benefits and costs of their own group, and justified their arguments at a higher level of rationality; they acknowledged, however, the value of other positions less often.

In *Srebrenica* in Bosnia–Herzegovina, we controlled in the experiments for participation and non-participation in the NGO Nansen Dialogue Center. As we have described in the Introduction, for half of the experiments the participants were recruited from this NGO, for the other half by random walk. The hypothesis was that participation in the activities of the NGO would lead to a learning process and thus to a higher level of deliberation in the respective experimental groups. After all, the goal of the NGO was to contribute to inter-ethnic dialogue. The hypothesis was rejected in the sense that there were no significant differences between the two sets of groups, which is a disappointment for NGOs like the Nansen Dialogue Center. Simona Mameli, who led the experiments, has the impression that the activities of the Center led to some dialogue fatigue. In Stolac we arrived at the same results, with no significant effect of participation in the activities of the Nansen Dialogue Center. Thus, the program of reintegration in Colombia, as mentioned above, seems to have been more successful than the NGO in Bosnia-Herzegovina.

For *Belgium*, the factor analysis revealed two main factors; the first factor was much more important and refers to form of deliberation, the second one to substance of deliberation.

Factor referring to form of deliberation

Respect for counter-arguments	0.842
Respectful listening	0.770
Rational justification	0.680
Force of better argument	0.622
Respectful language	0.542

Factor referring to substance of deliberation

    Reference to common good   0.706
    Respect for other group   0.642
    Reference to abstract principle   0.604

The five items that load strongly on the first factor all refer more to the form in which actors presented their arguments and reacted to the arguments of other participants. The items loading strongly on the second factor refer more to the substance of the arguments. Thus, we have two separate dimensions of deliberation. We used the first factor to construct an additive DQI. To explain variation in the DQI, the research design controlled for two variables: decision modes and group composition. For the decision modes, we had to consider that in Belgian politics, the two-thirds majority rule plays an important role. Therefore, we were interested to investigate how this rule influences the level of deliberation. As we remember from the Introduction, participants had to discuss future relations between the language groups and to make recommendations on this issue. For these recommendations, in three of the nine experiments participants were required to make a decision by two-thirds majority, in three by simple majority, and in three by unanimity. The highest level of deliberation occurred when unanimity was required, the lowest with majority rule, with the two-thirds majority rule in between. This finding is in line with the Colombian data where deliberation was higher with the rule of unanimity than with majority rule. Theoretically, these results make sense: the more decision rules require reaching agreement, the more actors have an incentive to take account of the arguments of others. Decision rules also had an impact on how participants perceived the level of deliberation when they filled out a questionnaire after the experiment. One item read, for example, "I feel that I was needlessly interrupted during the discussion." In the groups with simple majority rule, 31 percent agreed with this item, whereas none did so in the groups with two-thirds majority and with unanimity rules. The perception concurs with what actually happened in the various groups based on our DQI, in the sense that interruptions were much higher in the groups with simple majority rule.

For group composition, we have already seen in previous chapters that in Belgium the linguistic composition of the experimental groups has an influence on most deliberative elements, with the linguistically mixed groups reaching the highest level of deliberation. Thus, it is no surprise that the mixed group scored highest also for the additive DQI. Thereby, it is remarkable that in the questionnaire filled out after the experiment participants in the linguistically mixed groups perceived the truthfulness in the discussion as high as did participants in the linguistically homogeneous groups. One could have expected that there would be more suspicion across the linguistic divide but this was not the case, which augurs well for the likelihood of sincere deliberation when ordinary Walloons and Flemish meet. Looking at individual characteristics of the participants, with regard to education, it was confirmed for the DQI as a whole what we have seen in previous chapters for individual deliberative elements, namely that the level of deliberation increases with higher levels of education. For gender and age there were no significant differences, confirming what we have seen for the individual deliberative elements.

Comparing the influence of decision mode and group composition, a multivariate regression analysis shows that the decision mode had a greater influence, particularly in the linguistically homogeneous groups. In the divided groups, the level of deliberation tended to be generally high, almost irrespective of the decision mode. This means that there were other forces than decision mode contributing to a high level of deliberation in the mixed groups. As already mentioned several times in previous chapters, the high level of deliberation in the mixed groups was a real surprise, repudiating our initial hypothesis that a linguistically homogeneous context would be more favorable for deliberation. What were the forces helping deliberation in the mixed groups? We get more insight into this question when we do the multivariate regression analysis for the individual deliberative elements also. Here, the data are particularly revealing for justification and force of the better argument. As we recall from Chapter 2, for justification we used the following coding categories: no justification, justification with illustration, reason given but no connection with opinion, reason given and connection with opinion, more than one reason given and connections with opinion. Comparing the latter two categories of highest justification for speech acts in the homogeneous and the divided groups, it is revealed that for 100 such speech acts in the homogeneous groups there were 538 such speech acts in the divided groups. This means that when Flemish and Walloons met, they made a great effort to justify their arguments to the other side. They did not make as many shortcuts in their argumentation as participants did in the homogeneous groups. Encountering people from the other side gave an incentive to elaborate on the reasons why one supported particular policies for the future of the country. For the force of the better argument, we looked at the number of speech acts that indicated a change of position or at least an acknowledgment of the value of other position. For 100 such speech acts in the homogeneous groups, there were 350 such speech acts in the mixed groups. Thus, it is clear that participants in the divided groups were not only willing to justify their positions to the other side, they were also willing to listen to the other side and to look at their positions with respect and empathy.

Overall, for Belgium an optimistic story emerges; deliberation among ordinary citizens seems possible across a deep linguistic cleavage. This finding is all the more remarkable because at the time of the experiments there was hardly any deliberation among Belgian politicians who, because of the thorny language issue, were unable for more than a year to put together a government. Could it be that, contrary to conventional consociational theory, ordinary citizens are more willing than the elites to reach across deep societal divisions?[101] A caveat is, however, in order: one has to consider that deliberation in the mixed groups may have been helped by the fact that the discussion was simultaneously translated. That translation may help deliberation, as we have already seen earlier in this section when discussing the research of Nicole Doerr on the European Social Forum. For Belgium, we have some empirical evidence that translation helps deliberation. For the mixed groups, we took a special look at bilingual participants and found that they interrupted others more often than did non-bilingual participants. This non-deliberative behavior of the bilingual participants seems to be due to the fact that they did not depend on the translation and thus could interrupt more spontaneously.

For the *Europolis* project, we investigated the dynamic aspect of whether the level of deliberation changes over the course of a discussion, as we found for parliamentary debates. At the citizen level of Europolis, we did not find any such dynamic aspect. During two sessions about immigration the level of deliberation did not change much. This lack of a dynamic aspect may be due to the research design

---

[101] Markus M.L. Crepaz and Jürg Steiner, *European Democracies*, 8th edn. (New York: Pearson, 2012), ch. 13.

of Europolis where moderators were trained to encourage a high level of deliberation. Since they intervened in this sense during the entire discussion time, this may account for the fact that the level of deliberation stayed at about the same level. We have also investigated to what extent the different deliberative elements hang together at the individual level. Thereby, we have used a *Bayesian Item Response Analysis*. We could determine that the response functions have a positive slope, which indicates that deliberative quality forms a latent variable. But the deliberative elements do not hang together so tightly that one can speak of uni-dimensionality. Few participants were able to reach all deliberative standards in one session; if some deliberative elements were high, others tended to be low. Storytelling in particular has only a weak relationship with the latent dimension. Because deliberative elements only loosely hang together, we did the multiple regression for the individual elements. Following the usual pattern of Deliberative Polling, Europolis did not use control variables to manipulate the conditions for the individual experimental groups. Conditions for all groups were the same. We can, however, still do analyses at the level of characteristics of the individual participants. For frequency and length of participation, we found lower levels for women, working class, less educated, and participants from new EU member states in Central and Eastern Europe. With regard to rational justification, the levels were lower for working class, less educated, and participants from the new EU member states but not for women. For references to the common good, the only significant difference is that participants from the new EU member states made such references less often. Disrespectful statements were more frequent for women, working class, less educated, and participants from the new EU member states. Explicit expressions of respect we found only for the highly educated. Storytelling, finally, was more frequent among men. This analysis at the individual level is surprising in that women are more disrespectful and are less frequent storytellers, which contradicts other empirical data that I report in Chapter 4.

In *Finland* the research design had two treatment groups; the decision at the end of the discussion had to be either by majority vote or by consensus. In contrast to the findings in Colombia and Belgium, there was no effect and the level of deliberation was about the same in the two treatment groups. With regard to the individual characteristics of the participants, multiple regression analysis revealed no influence for education and gender, but significant influence for age, with the young being more deliberative. Staffan Himmelroos interprets the age effect as follows: "Could it be that the increased confidence that comes with age and experience, while it encourages one to be active, decreases your need to motivate beliefs and gives you less reason to consider views at odds with your own?"[102]

Summing up

Given the complexity of the empirical results in this section, a summary may be helpful. Let me distinguish contextual and individual explanatory variables. For the contextual variables I distinguish among institutions, culture, and issues. With regard to *institutions*, parliamentary debates are generally more deliberative in second chambers and consensus systems, whereas the results are mixed for plenary sessions versus committee meetings, presidential versus parliamentary systems, and the importance of veto points. An institutional factor favorable for deliberation is an election system allowing the expression of more than one preference. With regard to the size of a discussion group there is good evidence from different empirical studies that a small number of participants helps deliberation. Whether face-to-face or online discussions are better for deliberation is still unclear. Free-floating discussions tend to be more deliberative than when a decision has to be made at the end of the discussion; in the latter cases a decision rule of unanimity is more amenable to deliberation than majority rule. For the specific organization of a discussion, deliberation is helped when participants face each other around a table, when there is turn-taking among all participants, and when minutes are taken and handed out before the next meeting.

For *culture* there are many calls for more empirical research of how culture effects deliberation, but few good empirical findings. At a general level, it is claimed that religious fundamentalism and ideological conformity are bad for deliberation, but more research is needed to put these hypotheses on firmer ground. An encouraging finding is that in deeply divided societies deliberation is certainly difficult but not

---

[102] Staffan Himmelroos, "Democratically Speaking: Can Citizen Deliberation Be Considered Fair and Equal?," paper presented at the Workshop on Frontiers of Deliberation, ECPR Joint Sessions, St. Gallen, April 12–17, 2011.

impossible, at least at some low level. It is also encouraging that there are cultures open to learning deliberation from failed experiences in other places.

There is even less systematic research on how the *issue* under discussion influences deliberation. It is unclear, for example, whether deliberation is easier to attain for tax issues or for social issues. The only clear finding is that polarizing issues make deliberation more difficult. In this context, there are also many calls to study how different issues are framed depending on the particular context and how such framing affects deliberation. How is, for example, the issue of immigrants framed in different contexts and how does such framing influence deliberation? There is hardly any empirical research in this respect.

For *individual* variables, I distinguish psychological and demographic ones. Psychologically, empathy and ambiguity seem to have a positive influence on deliberation. For demographic variables, I consider gender, age, and education, since all three variables can be a basis for discrimination in political discussions, namely discrimination against women, the very young and the very old, and the less educated. Higher education contributes to deliberation, although not in a uniform way. For gender there is no clear pattern at the individual level, but there is some evidence that groups with a high number of women are more deliberative. For age there is no clear pattern.

(c) Normative implications of empirical results

Empirical research clearly shows that institutions have an influence on the level of deliberation. As we have seen in the previous section, however, most institutions shape the various elements of deliberation in different ways. Therefore, normatively speaking, one should avoid undifferentiated statements of which institutions to use to help deliberation. In designing institutions, one has to consider trade-offs among the various deliberative elements, for example, whether more weight should be given to high levels of respect or to high levels of justification. It is often not possible to maximize both elements at the same time. Furthermore, when making normative statements with regard to desirable institutions for deliberation, one has to be aware that such institutions are only a necessary but not a sufficient condition for deliberation. One also needs the proper psychological and cultural preconditions. As we have also seen in the previous section, empirical research stresses two favorable psychological conditions for deliberation: sensitivity to others' thoughts and feelings and a certain ambiguity in approaching issues to be discussed. To postulate these two broad psychological factors is begging the question of what measures can be taken to contribute in a positive way to these two factors. The literature mentions, for example, teaching empathy in schools and various arts programs in the community. What such measures will look like concretely is often an open question in the literature.

Where does this discussion lead us? What are the normative implications? Are there specific recommendations for how the institutional, psychological, and cultural preconditions for the various deliberative elements can be improved? My key message is that we should shy away from sweeping generalizations. One cannot simply say at a general level that such and such institutional, psychological, and cultural measures should be taken to increase deliberation. One rather needs to look at the specific situation. It is quite a different matter to increase deliberation in Srebrenica, investigated by Simona Mameli of our research team, or the Italian town of Piombino discussed in the Introduction. If one wishes to give recommendations, one has to immerse oneself in the historical, cultural, social, economic, and political context to give meaningful advice. There is no crystal ball telling us at a general level what has to be done to increase the various deliberative elements. It is hard and detailed work to investigate in specific cases what can be done to increase the chances of good deliberation. Normative and empirical research reported in the literature can certainly help, but one also needs good pragmatic intuition to give useful advice in concrete cases. Furthermore, one should not forget to include the people to be advised. It is precisely in the deliberative spirit that advice should not simply come from the outside but that the people themselves should be involved in discussing measures to increase deliberation in their communities. Deliberative scholars should refrain from presenting themselves as the only knowledgeable people on deliberation. What Jane Mansbridge *et al.* point out in general terms applies here too, namely that in a deliberative system experts should not have a monopoly of knowledge.[103] I hope that positive feedback will

---

[103] Jane Mansbridge, James Bohman, Simone Chambers, Tom Christiano, Archon Fung, John Parkinson, Dennis Thompson, and Mark Warren, "A Systemic Approach to Deliberative Democracy," paper presented at the Workshop on the Frontiers of Deliberation, ECPR Joint Sessions, St. Gallen, April 12–17, 2011.

result in the sense that deliberation about increased deliberation will lead to a higher level of deliberation, which in turn will help deliberation about further increases in deliberation, and so on. But one needs also to acknowledge that a good democracy consists of other elements than just deliberation, and here, too, what is desirable cannot be determined at an abstract level but must be evaluated for specific historical cases. Some situations, for example, may require forceful public protests, while in other situations emphasis on deliberation may be more appropriate. Some of my former students are confronted with this dilemma when the World Economic Forum meets in Davos, Switzerland. Should they participate in the discussions in Davos or should they protest by blocking the trains going up to Davos? No deliberative scholars can give a firm answer to this dilemma, but they can try to engage these people in deliberation, which I sometimes do.

10 | Favorable consequences of deliberation

(a) Normative controversies in the literature

While theorists have paid little attention to the *conditions* that lead to good deliberation, they have always been very interested in speculating about the *consequences* of good deliberation. Generally speaking, the expectation among theorists is that deliberation has favorable consequences. Claudia Landwehr makes this argument at a general level:

The theory assumes that the exchange of reasons in communicative interaction forms and transforms political preferences, and that if the interaction is sufficiently deliberative, they are transformed to the better. Preferences evolving from deliberation are expected to be better informed and less self-interested: besides the own perspective, they take into account the knowledge, experiences and interests of others.[1]

For Jürgen Habermas, "deliberation causes a pressure for rationality that improves the quality of the decisions."[2] For John S. Dryzek, deliberation is "a means for joint resolution of social problems … a large public policy literature points to the effectiveness of deliberation on the part of those concerned with a common problem in generating solutions that are both effective and mutually acceptable and that can work when top-down solutions are resisted by those whose interests and arguments are overridden."[3] Giovan Francesco Lanzara postulates that deliberation opens opportunities for new and beneficial actions for the community.[4] Daniel Oliver-Lalana, a legal theorist, states with

[1] Claudia Landwehr, "Discourse and Coordination: Modes of Interaction and Their Roles in Political Decision-Making," *Journal of Political Philosophy* 18 (2010), 101.
[2] Jürgen Habermas, *Ach, Europa* (Frankfurt a.M.: Suhrkamp, 2008), p. 144. "Rationalisierungsdruck, der die Qualität der Entscheidungen verbessert."
[3] John S. Dryzek, "Democratization as Deliberative Capacity Building," *Comparative Political Studies* 42 (2009), 1390.
[4] Giovan Francesco Lanzara, "La deliberazione come indagine publicca," in Luigi Pellizzoni (ed.), *La deliberazione publicca* (Rome: Meltemi editore, 2005),

regard to the legislative process "that there exists a link between the quality of a law and that of its underlying reasoning: broadly speaking, the better is the legislative argumentation the better will be the law resulting from it."[5]

In what sense exactly are theorists expecting that deliberation helps with the quality of political outcomes? Most frequently, they expect that deliberation increases the legitimacy of political decisions. As Dryzek puts it, in order to secure legitimacy,

> in a democracy, an especially secure basis involves reflective acceptance of collective decisions by actors who have had a chance to participate in consequential deliberation. This claim is at the heart of deliberative theory, which began as an account of legitimacy … Deliberative legitimacy can either substitute for or supplement other sources of legitimacy, such as the consistency of a process with constitutional rules or traditional practices.[6]

For Habermas, deliberation has "the power to give rise to legitimacy."[7] For Diego Gambetta, deliberation "can generate decisions that are more legitimate," and importantly, he adds, "including for the minority."[8] For Luigi Pellizzoni, deliberation has the capacity "to increase the legitimacy of the decisions."[9] In the same vein, Jan Sieckmann argues that

> rational argumentation will help a political system to demonstrate its legitimacy and to find support of its citizens. By contrast, a political system that openly violates requirements of rational argumentation will hardly be able to make people believe in its legitimacy and will have difficulties to find the support of the citizens in order to make the system work smoothly.[10]

---

p. 51. "Opportunità d'azione che abbiano un valore cognitivo aggiunto per la comunità."

[5] Daniel Oliver-Lalana, "Towards a Theory of Legislative Argument," *Legisprudence: International Journal for the Study of Legislation* 4 (2010), 4.

[6] Dryzek, "Democratization as Deliberative Capacity Building," 1390.

[7] Habermas, *Ach, Europe*, p. 147: "legitimitätserzeugende Kraft."

[8] Diego Gambetta, "Claro!: An Essay on Discursive Machismo," in Jon Elster (ed.), *Deliberative Democracy* (Cambridge University Press, 1998), p. 24.

[9] Luigi Pellizzoni, "Introduzione: Cosa significa deliberare? Promesse e problemi della democrazia deliberativa," in Luigi Pellizzoni (ed.), *La deliberazione pubblica* (Roma: Meltemi, 2005), p. 23: "di incrementare la legittimità delle decisioni."

[10] Jan Sieckmann, "Legislative Argumentation and Democratic Legitimation," *Legisprudence: International Journal for the Study of Legislation* 4 (2010), 72–3.

Another favorable consequence of deliberation which is often mentioned is an increase in social justice. Gambetta, for example, states that deliberation "can make the outcomes fairer in terms of distributive justice by providing better protection for weaker parties."[11] Sharon Krause also expects that deliberation helps distributive justice, but she goes further in hoping that deliberation also helps to remedy unintended stigmatization of underprivileged societal groups when she "calls for the kinds of deliberative ... exchanges – and solidarity – that over time can dismantle the cultural background of bias that unintentionally disrupts the exercise of agency among marginalized groups and hinders freedom."[12]

Many theorists see still another favorable consequence of deliberation in that it helps to clarify what dimensions are involved in a conflict and on what points there is agreement and disagreement. In this way, the resolution of the conflict becomes tractable. This argument is made, for example, by Dryzek: "Deliberation can produce agreement on a single dimension on which preferences are arrayed, thus ruling out the introduction of other dimensions to confound collective choice on the part of clever strategists."[13] The same idea is expressed by Kasper M. Hansen when he writes that

in the process of deliberation, the participants are forced to articulate their views and listen to other views. Such an articulation may potentially clarify personal opinions and may even create a more consistent and coherent set of opinions ... if deliberation is able to increase the individuals' ability to rank the alternatives into coherent patterns and to exclude the alternatives which nobody likes the choice of decision rule becomes less complex.[14]

Anne Elizabeth Stie sees deliberation as "a mechanism to clarify differences and potential misunderstandings, to shed light on facts and elaborate in ethical and moral dilemmas."[15] Jon Elster adds the qualification that it is the "*publicity* of deliberation [that] can reduce the

[11] Gambetta, "Claro," p. 24.
[12] Sharon Krause, "Beyond Non-Domination: Agency, Inequality, and the Meaning of Freedom," paper presented at the Political Theory Colloquium, University of North Carolina, December 9, 2010, p. 29.
[13] Dryzek, "Democratization as Deliberative Capacity Building," 1392.
[14] Kasper M. Hansen, *Deliberative Democracy and Opinion Formation* (Odensee: University Press of Southern Denmark, 2004), pp. 100–1.
[15] Anne Elizabeth Stie, *Democratic Decision-Making in the EU: Or Technocracy in Disguise?* (unpublished book manuscript), ch. 2.

dimensionality of the options and hence reduce the likelihood of cycles."[16]

Many theorists argue that deliberation may also have positive consequences for the participating actors themselves. Gary Mucciaroni and Paul J. Quirk give a concise summary of this argument: "Participants may learn about diverse subjects, acquire skill in reasoning, receive intellectual stimulation, become more tolerant of differences, develop awareness of distant places, come to identify with wider circles of humanity, overcome rigidity, and so on."[17] Mucciaroni and Quirk continue to argue that deliberation may have positive consequences not only for the participants as individuals but also for the group in which they participate: "A deliberative process may affect or directly embody certain relationships or other collective attributes of a group. It may express or produce equality, harmony, affective ties, legitimacy, or a variety of other group characteristics."[18] Jane Mansbridge argues that initially the "epistemic value" of deliberation has not been sufficiently acknowledged and adds it to the important standards of good deliberation. In talking with others at a high level of deliberation, actors should be able to increase their knowledge of the world.[19] Luigi Pellizzoni summarizes the positive effects of deliberation as it "produces 'better' citizens: individuals who are more informed, active, responsible, open to the arguments of others, cooperative, fair, able to deal with problems, ready to alter their opinions."[20]

Although most theorists expect positive consequences of deliberation, there are some theorists who contest this view. They fear that deliberation hurts the lower and marginalized social classes since they do not have the necessary cognitive skills to participate at an equal level in rational discussions of political issues. For the disadvantaged

---

[16] Jon Elster, "Deliberation, Cycles, and Misrepresentations," paper presented at the Conference on Epistemic Democracy in Practice, Yale University, October 20–22, 2011, p. 1.

[17] Gary Mucciaroni and Paul J. Quirk, "Rhetoric and Reality: Going Beyond Discourse Ethics in Assessing Legislative Deliberation," *Legisprudence: International Journal for the Study of Legislation* 4 (2010), 38.

[18] Mucciaroni and Quirk, "Rhetoric and Reality," 38.

[19] Jane Mansbridge, "Recent Advances in Deliberative Theory," paper presented at the Max Weber Workshop on Deliberation in Politics, New York University, October 29, 2010.

[20] Luigi Pellizzoni, "The Myth of the Best Argument: Power, Deliberation and Reason," *British Journal of Sociology* 52 (2001), 66.

in society it would be better to protest in the streets for their rights. In a stark form, this position against deliberation is taken by Chantal Mouffe, who denies

that there ever could be a free and unconstrained public deliberation of all matters of common concern ... the prime task of democratic politics is not to eliminate passions nor to relegate them to the private sphere in order to render rational consensus possible, but to mobilise those passions towards the promotion of democratic designs. Far from jeopardizing democracy, agonistic confrontation is in fact its very condition of existence.[21]

Alice Le Goff is sympathetic to the position of Mouffe that agonistic confrontation is necessary to defend the interests of disadvantaged social groups, but she does not accept that agonistic confrontation necessarily excludes deliberation. On the contrary, good deliberation can help to unveil latent conflicts and to make disadvantaged groups conscious of their true interests. Therefore, Goff finds it sterile to distinguish in an absolute sense between agonistic and deliberative approaches to politics; agonistic confrontations may be the basis for later successful deliberation, and vice versa, deliberation may actualize latent conflicts leading then to agonistic confrontations. She sees a fruitful combination of the perspectives of critical theory and deliberation.[22]

Another worry has to do with polarization. We encountered this factor in the previous chapter as a possible negative *antecedent* for deliberation. Now some theorists argue that polarization can also be seen as a negative *consequence* of deliberation. This argument has most prominently been made by Cass R. Sunstein.[23] He writes of a "law of group polarization"; as an example he gives a group of moderately pro-feminist women who after internal discussion become more strongly pro-feminist. Bernard Manin expands on this argument.[24] His

---

[21] Chantal Mouffe, "Deliberative Democracy or Agonistic Pluralism," *Social Research* 3 (1999), 752, 755–6.

[22] Alice Le Goff, "Démocratie délibérative, contestation et mouvements sociaux," *Archives de Philosophie* 74 (2011), 255–6: (la délibération) "peut rendre les acteurs plus conscients de leur intérêts et permettre une exploration de ces derniers et des conflits qui peuvent exister entre eux."

[23] Cass R. Sunstein, "The Law of Group Polarization," *Journal of Political Philosophy* 10 (2002), 175–95.

[24] Bernard Manin, "Democratic Deliberation: Why We Should Promote Debate Rather Than Discussion," paper presented at the Program in Ethics and Public Affairs Seminar, Princeton University, October 13, 2005.

basic premise is that people have the tendency to selectively absorb information and to consider mostly the aspects of arguments that correspond to their own arguments. When the level of deliberation is high, this means that many arguments are articulated, and "people seem to respond to the sheer quantity of arguments. To be sure, cogency of arguments matters, but sheer numbers carry weight too."[25] The consequence is that the large number of arguments in deliberation tends to reinforce the existing arguments of the participants and thus to increase polarization. According to Manin, this consequence "should be particularly troublesome for theories of deliberation because … it is the very process of advancing reasons that is driving the shift to the extreme."[26] Hélène Landemore and Hugo Mercier take a critical look at the "law of group polarization" and emphasize that sometimes group discussions indeed lead to more polarization, but sometimes not.[27] Thus, the challenge is how to take account of such variation. For Landemore and Mercier, one needs to distinguish between deliberation properly defined and mere discussions. "It is only groups of individuals that fail to deliberate properly that are likely to polarize. Where the normal conditions of reasoning are satisfied, dialogical deliberation of the kind favored by most deliberative democrats is likely to have the predicted epistemic and transformative properties."[28] According to Landemore and Mercier, it is also possible for relatively homogeneous groups such as pro-feminist women to properly deliberate if only they are open to a wide range of arguments: "Not all groups of like minded people are doomed to polarize, provided they contain at least some dissenting individuals and make effort to take their arguments seriously, that is make an effort to reason as opposed to let their confirmation bias run unchecked and produce only arguments for the side they already favour."[29]

At a practical but not trivial level, Gambetta worries that deliberation may sometimes be too time-consuming, especially if a problem

[25] Manin, "Democratic Deliberation."
[26] Manin, "Democratic Deliberation."
[27] Hélène Landemore and Hugo Mercier, "Talking It Out: Deliberation with Others versus Deliberation Within," paper presented at the Annual Convention of the American Political Science Association, Washington, DC, September 2010.
[28] Landemore and Mercier, "Talking It Out."
[29] Landemore and Mercier, "Talking It Out."

needs urgently to be solved: "if the quality of outcomes declines rapidly with time, deliberation may simply waste precious time." He illustrates this argument with a personal story: "In the ski-mountaineering club I used to belong, the instructors always consulted about the best route, but in bad situations we had as a rule (on which we had previously deliberated) to defer the decision to the school director."[30]

(b) Empirical results

Literature review

There is a fair amount of empirical studies that shed light on consequences of deliberation. In our earlier investigation of parliamentary debates in Germany, Switzerland, the UK, and the US, we realized that it is not so easy to establish causality between the level of deliberation and policy outcomes.[31] We took social justice as a policy outcome; while many theorists expect that deliberation contributes to social justice, there is also the counter position, represented in the first section of this chapter by Mouffe's argument, that lower social classes have no real say in deliberation, so they suffer from this mode of decision-making. There are, of course, different ways to define social justice; we took the definition of John Rawls for our empirical investigation. For him, social justice means that a decision has to be "to the greatest benefit of the least advantaged," a definition that implies an egalitarian doctrine of social justice.[32] Rawls does not advocate absolute equality but tolerates some differences; these differences, however, should not put the weakest in society in a desperate situation.

To test the causal effect of deliberation on social justice, we needed a research design where we had enough variation in the level of deliberation and could hold other key variables constant. Decision-making in the German Mediation Committee (*Vermittlungsausschuss*) seemed suited for this purpose. Its task is to mediate between the two parliamentary chambers. Whatever the committee decides has to go back to

---

[30] Gambetta, "Claro," p. 21.
[31] Jürg Steiner, André Bächtiger, Markus Spörndli, and Marco R. Steenbergen, *Deliberative Politics in Action: Analysing Parliamentary Discourse* (Cambridge University Press, 2005), ch. 6.
[32] John Rawls, *A Theory of Social Justice* (Cambridge, MA: Harvard University Press, 1971), p. 83.

the two chambers for acceptance. Recommendations of the committee usually only have a chance of being accepted by both chambers if the recommendation has wide support in the committee. Therefore, there is pressure not simply to vote along party lines but to listen in a deliberative way to what the other side has to say. Such pressure may vary from issue to issue, so we expected to find the desired variation in the level of deliberation. This is indeed what we found in our investigation of the minutes of the committee. With regard to confounding variables, we controlled for country, limiting this part of the study to Germany. We also limited ourselves to a single committee. This particular committee also had the advantage that there was little change in its membership over the years. A further control was that we concentrated on social issues, the reason being that for such issues the definition of social justice by Rawls is most relevant. With regard to the political context, the investigation focused on the years from 1969 to 1982 when there was the same composition of the cabinet, namely of Social Democrats and Free Democrats. Other contextual variables changed, of course, over these 13 years, for example the economic situation with the two oil crises in the 1970s. But, overall, we managed to have quite a controlled quasi-experimental situation with variation in the level of deliberation and some key variables under control.

Given all the controls, we could analyze the debates about 20 decision cases in the German Mediation Committee. Taking a convenient cut-off point, we distinguished 11 cases with a high level of deliberation and 9 cases with a low level. Looking at the level of social justice in the two groups, we found no statistically significant difference. Only when we looked at the individual elements of our Discourse Quality Index (DQI) did we find some statistically significant differences. The level of social justice was high when egalitarian arguments were brought into the discussion and when they were presented with a high level of rationality. These findings mean that for these two aspects of our DQI, there was some positive effect on the level of social justice but not for the other elements of the index. This result gives some credence, although not strongly, to theorists who see deliberation as being helpful for social justice in the sense of Rawls. The result is interesting in that it shows that the controversies among theorists about the causality between deliberation and social justice are overblown. When it comes to the real world of politics, at least in the German Mediation Committee, deliberation neither greatly helps nor greatly hurts social justice.

Tracy Sulkin and Adam F. Simon addressed the question of social just-ice in a computer-based experiment.[33] In a provocative way, they title their paper "Habermas in the Lab." In their experiment, two actors play the "ultimatum game"; one is the proposer, the other the acceptor. At stake are 100 dollars. The proposer starts the game by proposing how the money should be divided between the two actors. If the acceptor accepts the proposal, this is how the money is divided. If the acceptor rejects the proposal, however, neither actor gets anything. There were two experimental situations: either the two actors could communicate with each other for 180 seconds on the computer or no communication was allowed. The result of the experiments was that "when players are allowed to deliberate with each other before a proposal is made, the allocations made by the proposer to the acceptor are significantly higher than in the other condition."[34] One could interpret this result as show-ing that deliberation leads to a more egalitarian outcome, which would correspond to Rawls' notion of social justice. My critique would be that it is exaggerated of Sulkin and Simon to say that they put Habermas in the lab, since communicating with each other for 180 seconds on the computer is not exactly what Habermas means by deliberation. Nevertheless, the experiment shows that some communication is better than no communication for a more egalitarian outcome.

Christopher Gibson and Michael Woolcock looked at the causality between deliberation and social justice in local politics in Indonesia.[35] In their quasi-experimental research design, in half of the localities facilitators made a deliberative intervention in encouraging partici-pants to deliberate with each other. The other half of the localities served as a control group with no such intervention. The result of the study is that the deliberative intervention helped marginalized groups to get more power, so these localities increased social justice in the sense of Rawls.

Manlio Cinalli and Ian O'Flynn want to know whether deliberation helps to integrate minorities, another important aspect of deliberative

[33] Tracy Sulkin and Adam F. Simon, "Habermas in the Lab: A Study of Deliberation in an Experimental Setting," *Political Psychology* 22 (2001), 809–82.

[34] Sulkin and Simon, "Habermas in the Lab," 820.

[35] Christopher Gibson and Michael Woolcock, "Empowerment, Deliberative Development, and Local-Level Politics in Indonesia," *Studies in Comparative International Development* 43 (2008), 151–80.

theory.[36] Specifically, they investigate the potential causality between deliberation and integration for Muslims in Great Britain. They formulate their research question in the following way: "does deliberative theory work as advertised or is the relationship between public deliberation and political integration more complex than many deliberative theorists seemingly assume?"[37] The empirical basis for the investigation are two quality newspapers, *The Times* and *The Guardian*, during the course of 2007. The units of analysis are interventions in these two newspapers by institutional actors like parliament and executive agencies, by intermediate actors like political parties and unions, by civil society actors like ethnic and religious organizations, and also by individuals. For Muslim organizations and individuals all interventions are considered, for non-Muslim actors only interventions that are related to ethnic relations. In this way, Cinalli and O'Flynn arrive at a total of 1,007 interventions. Each intervention is coded according to the level of deliberation and the level of integration. To measure the level of deliberation, Cinalli and O'Flynn use a modified version of the DQI; they focus on whether "actors couch their interventions in language that is manipulative, offensive, neutral or respectful," they "check for the presence of a supporting argument and, more specifically, whether arguments are valid or spurious," finally they "check whether the argument contains an appeal to a particular interest ... or to a general interest."[38] To measure integration, they "check whether Muslim actors engage extensively with other actors in the field – that is, whether they have forged channels that in principle allow them to work together with others, overcome points of distance, share resources, and so forth."[39]

Cinalli and O'Flynn find with regard to deliberation that Muslims use respectful language and support their arguments just as much as other actors. "However, when it comes to the requirement of appealing to the general interest, Muslims score relatively poorly. About half the time, they only see policy issues from their own particular perspective, ignoring

---

[36] Manlio Cinalli and Ian O'Flynn, "Public Deliberation, Networks Analysis, and the Political Integration of Muslims in Britain," paper presented at the Workshop on Frontiers of Deliberation, ECPR Joint Sessions, St. Gallen, April 12–17, 2011.

[37] Cinalli and O'Flynn, "Public Deliberation, Networks Analysis," p. 8.

[38] Cinalli and O'Flynn, "Public Deliberation, Networks Analysis," p. 9.

[39] Cinalli and O'Flynn, "Public Deliberation, Networks Analysis," p. 7.

or discounting the general interest in those issues."[40] Given that, overall, Muslims score relatively low on deliberation, deliberative theory would expect that they are less integrated in British society than other actors. But this expectation is not supported by the data. Cinalli and O'Flynn conclude "that Muslim actors are reasonably well integrated, despite what, for example, elements in the British popular press and right-wing demagogues of one sort or another would have us believe. They clearly want to engage and clearly are engaged with a broad range of actors across both policy and public domains."[41] Cinalli and O'Flynn interpret their unexpected finding in the following creative way:

the fact that Muslim actors score relatively poorly when it comes to appealing to the general interest does not seem to be a major impediment to their political integration in the field … [an actor's] desire to pursue its own interest need not cost in the support of others or its position in the field. This may be because there is a great deal more respect for difference in the field of ethnic relations than one might perhaps have assumed. Or it may be because the traditional British emphasis on toleration, which stretches back at least to Locke, also pervades this field.[42]

Cinalli and O'Flynn warn, however, that "there may be a tipping point. If enough actors fail to appeal to the general interest on enough occasions, the level and indeed very point of public deliberation may recede accordingly, with all that that implies for political integration."[43] This is an important caveat meaning that the effects in deliberation are not linear but proceed in thresholds; it is only if deliberation falls below a particular level that negative consequences result.

In their experiments on climate change in the French region of Poitou-Charentes, Julien Talpin and Laurence Monnoyer-Smith examined whether citizen deliberation has an impact on policy outcomes.[44] This project is part of a larger study of the EU,[45] and the idea was that the recommendations derived from these experiments should be

---

[40] Cinalli and O'Flynn, "Public Deliberation, Networks Analysis," p. 18.
[41] Cinalli and O'Flynn, "Public Deliberation, Networks Analysis," p. 20.
[42] Cinalli and O'Flynn, "Public Deliberation, Networks Analysis," pp. 19–20.
[43] Cinalli and O'Flynn, "Public Deliberation, Networks Analysis," p. 20.
[44] Julien Talpin and Laurence Monnoyer-Smith, "Talking with the Wind? Discussion on the Quality of Deliberation in the Ideal-EU Project," paper presented at the IPSA International Conference, Luxembourg, March 18–20, 2010.
[45] See: www.ideal-debate.eu.

transmitted to the Temporary Committee on Climate Change of the European Parliament. A member of this committee gave the following assurances that the recommendations resulting from the experiments would be taken seriously:

I shall circulate your final report to all Euro-parliamentarians, with of course, special emphasis on members of the Temporary Committee on Climate Change. We shall review your proposals carefully. In addition, we shall send copies to other partner Regions, so that they can pass on to you a summary of the climate change laws that will highlight your input and the provisions that incorporate your proposals.[46]

A Regional Councilor of Poitou-Charentes expressed similar promises: "Your suggestions will indeed be taken into account, not just by the European Union, but by our Regional Council. I invite you to check our website to see how and when your suggestions are taken into account."[47] The experiments involved young people aged 14 to 30, and were done both online and face-to-face. Talpin and Monnoyer-Smith report that "overall the picture presented here indicates that the deliberative quality was high both online and face-to-face. Discussions were inclusive, oriented towards the common good, informed and responsive."[48] Thus, conditions seemed very good for these citizen experiments to have a policy impact for issues of climate change since the level of citizen deliberation was high and policy-makers gave assurances that they would take account of the recommendations resulting from the experiments. But, with great disappointment, Talpin and Monnoyer-Smith report that the experiments "failed to have any impact on regional and European public policies."[49] The member of the European Parliament quoted above as looking forward to taking account of the results of the experiments, acknowledges grudgingly when interviewed that the experiments had no policy impact:

So, it was quite an experience, right? But, um, uh [embarrassed] about impact, I am not sure if anybody has thought about follow-up. It was sort of, let's say, a special experiment ... Yes, I think it had a slight effect, in the way we underscored the importance of local action and the inclusion of the

---

[46] Talpin and Monnoyer-Smith, "Talking with the Wind?," p. 23.
[47] Talpin and Monnoyer-Smith, "Talking with the Wind?," p. 22.
[48] Talpin and Monnoyer-Smith, "Talking with the Wind?," p. 21.
[49] Talpin and Monnoyer-Smith, "Talking with the Wind?," p. 22.

citizenry. In that way, yes. But on specific policy choices, um, uh [embarrassed], the fight against climate change is a complex issue.[50]

This quotation says enough about the lack of policy impact of the experiments. What went wrong? Talpin and Monnoyer-Smith see an important part of the reason being how the recommendations were transmitted to the policy-makers in the sense that "in practice, the comments were formulated in terms so general as to be useless for public policymaking purposes." As examples they mention "use bicycles, expand public transport and re-absorb $CO2$ through reforestation. What is left are laudable battle cries rather than actionable ideas that can be written into law."[51] The lack of policy impact of the experiments led to cynicism among the participants. As one participant stated in a later interview: "I mean, if it has no impact, it's useless. Like it was a cool day, but well, me, I can't help thinking and wondering about the impact. I mean, me, I've been disappointed a lot. A little too much. I think it's because I don't believe in it anymore." Or another negative reaction: "A lot of things got said that were really beautiful and I think that, because nothing happened about it, I think, that's ... um ... It's going to put off people because they were really expecting a lot from the day." Still another negative reaction: "Me? Yeah, I will do another one, but if they say it's gonna be like the Ideal-EU, you can be sure I am not going."[52] Talpin and Monnoyer-Smith conclude from such negative reactions: "While experiencing with new forms of democratic governance is fascinating and urgent given the ever growing gap between EU institutions and politicians and their constituents, citizens hardly ever participate for the sake of it. From this perspective, it is only when they are empowered that deliberative innovations can have a positive impact on the citizenry."[53] Such empowerment we encountered in the Introduction, where I described how in the Italian town of Piombino citizens deliberated over several months on the renovation of the town square and how many of their recommendations were implemented by the town authorities. The difference from the deliberation in the French region of Poitou-Charentes is that in Piombino the discussion concerned a well-defined and simple local issue, whereas in

---

[50] Talpin and Monnoyer-Smith, "Talking with the Wind?," p. 24.
[51] Talpin and Monnoyer-Smith, "Talking with the Wind?," p. 26.
[52] Talpin and Monnoyer-Smith, "Talking with the Wind?," pp. 28–9.
[53] Talpin and Monnoyer-Smith, "Talking with the Wind?," p. 29.

Poitou-Charentes the citizens had to deal with an ill-defined and complex issue at the level of the EU.

Lucio Baccaro *et al.* want to know whether participating in deliberation makes citizens more likely to support the notion that legal residents regardless of nationality be allowed to vote and stand for public office.[54] Since deliberative theory emphasizes inclusiveness in the sense that all persons affected by a decision should be involved in decision-making, Baccaro and his colleagues expected that deliberation should favor attitudes to let non-national residents vote and hold public office. In order to test this hypothesis, they organized experiments with students of the University of Geneva. In addition to control groups, they had four groups with moderators and four groups without moderators. The moderators encouraged participants to be deliberative in letting everyone speak, in justifying arguments in terms of the common good, and in respecting arguments of others. As expected, using a modified form of our DQI, Baccaro *et al.* found a higher level of deliberation in the groups with a moderator than in the groups without a moderator. But surprisingly, the groups without moderators were more willing to give political rights to non-national residents. Although this finding rejects a basic hypothesis in the deliberative literature, Baccaro *et al.* interpret it in a creative way, thus moving the deliberative discussion forward. Their argument is that one has to distinguish between different kinds of moderation. Their moderators may have structured the discussion too much from the beginning:

We found that facilitated debate appears to freeze the initial preference distribution, possibly because it encourages a kind of "stiff-backed" deliberation in which participants are encouraged from the beginning to take a stance and justify it. This is in contrast to the more relaxed, free-form deliberation, in which participants are less likely to take a stance, more likely to use banter, and more likely to introduce relevant facts and arguments in isolation from any particular proposition. In short, free-form deliberation appears to be more conducive to preference change than facilitated deliberation.[55]

This interpretation fits well with what I discussed in Chapter 2 on rationality and stories. Too much rationality, such as in an academic

---

[54] Lucio Baccaro, Conor Cradden, and Marion Deville-Naggay, "Should Foreigners Vote? Outcomes of a Deliberative Experiment in the City of Rousseau," paper presented at the Workshop on the Frontiers of Deliberation, ECPR Joint Sessions, St. Gallen, April 12–17, 2011.

[55] Baccaro *et al.*, "Should Foreigners Vote?," p. 5.

seminar, may indeed stiffen positions, while adding to some extent bantering with stories and emotions may loosen up the atmosphere, making preference changes more likely. The research of Baccaro *et al.* helps us to think more clearly about the role of moderators in deliberation. Their finding does not necessarily mean that groups without moderators will discuss issues at a higher level of deliberation. If moderators do not insist too much on rationality but also allow some bantering, they may be able to greatly contribute to good deliberation. This is an important lesson for the praxis of deliberation to which I will return in the concluding chapter.

There are also empirical data with regard to the question raised in the first section, on whether deliberation helps to clarify the dimensions of the conflict under discussion. Simon Niemeyer and John S. Dryzek studied citizen juries in Australia, and could indeed demonstrate that such effects exist.[56] Deliberation tends to lead to a meta-consensus on what a conflict is all about, making its solution more tractable. In another paper, Dryzek shows that deliberation has a positive impact on environmental quality; summarizing a rich literature of empirical studies, he states that "effective environmental governance benefits from both deliberative empowered space and deliberative public space at a distance."[57]

New data on deliberative experiments[58]

I begin with *Colombia*. Did ex-guerrillas and ex-paramilitaries look at the armed conflict in a different way after the experiments? Did the direction of possible changes depend on the level of deliberation in their discussion groups? On the ideological dimension from left to right, ex-guerrillas and ex-paramilitaries were far apart in both their family background and their current values. Ex-guerrillas were much to the left, ex-paramilitaries to the right. Thus, there was a very deep divide between the two groups. In the questionnaires filled out before and after the experiments, ex-combatants were asked for their attitudes toward their former enemies, whether they contribute to increased

---

[56] Simon Niemeyer and John S. Dryzek, "The Ends of Deliberation: Meta-consensus and Inter-subjective Rationality as Ideal Outcomes," *Swiss Political Science Review* 13 (2007), 497–526.

[57] John S. Dryzek, "The Deliberative Global Governance of Climate Change," paper presented at the Conference on Democratizing Climate Governance, Australian National University, Canberra, July 15–16, 2010, p. 7.

[58] For the research designs, see Introduction, Section (b).

violence and whether they help to make Colombia a stronger country. Our expectation was that participation in the experiments would contribute to a better understanding of the ideological position of the other side of the armed struggle and consequently to less hostile attitudes. The data, however, show exactly the opposite. The following data reveal how attitudes toward former enemies have changed from before the experiments until after the experiments:

	Before experiment	*After experiment*
(Former enemy) increases violence		
Ex-guerrillas agree	55%	69%
Ex-paramilitaries agree	75%	78%
(Former enemy) helps to make		
Colombia stronger country		
Ex-guerrillas disagree	40%	44%
Ex-paramilitaries disagree	66%	73%

Overall, the increase in negative attitudes from both sides is not very big but still noteworthy, especially since we expected a decrease in negative attitudes. The biggest increase in negative attitudes is expressed by ex-guerrillas with regard to the item that paramilitaries contribute to an increase in violence. Whereas before the experiments, 55 percent agreed with this item, after the experiment 69 percent did so. Thus, just meeting around a table did not help ex-combatants to improve attitudes toward the other side; if there was any noticeable change it went in the opposite direction. This is a not so unexpected finding, after all; it is prominently linked with social psychologist Muzafer Sherif, who could demonstrate that simply meeting without a common goal may very well worsen the relations between two groups unknown to each other beforehand.[59] The unknown is always threatening to some extent, so it is not too surprising that many ex-combatants became more hostile when they heard what the other side had to say.

Perhaps only the ex-combatants who intervened little or not at all in the discussion tended to increase their negative attitudes toward the former enemies, because being outsiders in the discussion led to frustration, which contributed to more negative attitudes toward the

---

[59] Muzafer Sherif, *Group Conflict and Co-operation: Their Social Psychology* (London: Routledge, 1967).

other side. On the other hand, one may expect that the frequent contributors to the discussion felt involved and tended to decrease their negative attitudes toward the former enemy. The data show exactly the opposite from these expectations. The ex-combatants who spoke up the most worsened the most in their attitudes toward the former enemies. The ad hoc interpretation could be that by speaking up a lot, these ex-combatants were more and more convinced that they were right and the former enemy wrong. From a deliberative perspective, one may say that the point is not to speak up but to listen. The ex-combatants who frequently spoke up may have focused on what they wanted to say and not on what the others said.

For deliberative theory, the finding is not unexpected that mere talk does not improve attitudes. The argument of the theory has always been that in order to obtain positive attitude changes, one does not need any talk but, specifically, deliberatively oriented talk. Therefore, the crucial research question is whether the level of deliberation in the experimental groups made a difference for attitude changes. For several deliberative elements, we cannot answer this question because the distribution of the data is too skewed. We remember, for example, from Chapter 1 that of the total of 1,027 speech acts only 5 were interrupted, and from Chapter 4 that only 8 speech acts expressed respect and 9 speech acts disrespect. On the other hand, we have good variation for the level of rational justification, as we have seen in Chapter 2. A comparison among the 28 experimental groups indicates that the level of justification in a group has neither a positive nor a negative influence on attitude changes toward the former enemy. When we break down the data by ex-guerrillas and ex-paramilitaries, however, interesting differences emerge for the item about making Colombia a stronger country. In the experimental groups with the highest level of rational justification,[60] before the experiment 22 percent of ex-guerrillas disagreed with the item that the former enemy helps to make Colombia a stronger country; after the experiment the disagreement with this item increased to 45 percent, indicating a stark worsening of attitudes toward the other side. For ex-paramilitaries, it was just the opposite: before the experiment 71 percent disagreed with the item, 60 percent after the experiment, indicating an improvement in the attitude toward the former enemy. For the experiments with the lowest level

---

[60] Based on the six groups with the highest level of rational justification.

of rational justification,[61] there was little attitude change toward the former enemy from before until after the experiment. Therefore, we can conclude that a high level of justification in a group had an influence on attitude changes, but in different directions for ex-guerrillas and ex-paramilitaries. How can these results be interpreted? Many ex-guerrillas, in listening to rational arguments of the ex-paramilitaries, began to realize that the former enemy was overemphasizing law and order and social hierarchies, so they could not be trusted to help to make Colombia a stronger country. By contrast, many ex-paramilitaries, coming mostly from a poor background, in listening to the rational arguments of the former enemy, began to acknowledge that the position for more social justice advocated by ex-guerrillas could help make Colombia a stronger country. Going deep into empirical data, the world looks more complex than deliberative theorists expected. In Chapter 2, we have seen the great controversy among theorists about positive and negative consequences of rational justification. We can now see that one cannot simply say that high rationality improves or worsens attitudes toward former enemies. It depends on whose attitudes we talk about and who the former enemies are. In other words, causality is context-dependent.

Equality in participation is another deliberative element where we have enough variation to study changes in attitudes (see Chapter 1). For both questionnaire items of contributing to increased violence and making Colombia a stronger country, the level of equality in the experimental groups did not have a significant effect on attitude changes toward the former enemy. There were also no significant effects on attitude changes for the frequency of references to the common good and to abstract moral principles. Here, we have to consider that such references were relatively rare, 9 percent of all speech acts with regard to the common good and 5 percent with regard to abstract moral principles (see Chapter 3). Thus, the distribution of the speech acts for these two deliberative elements was rather one-sided, so there was not much variation among the experimental groups. We have the same problem for the acknowledgment of the value of other arguments, in only 5 percent of all speech acts (see Chapter 6). This skewed distribution may explain why for this deliberative element, too, there was no significant effect on attitude changes. We have a result that is not

---

[61] Based on the seven groups with the lowest level of rational justification.

statistically significant, but still remarkable; ex-combatants who used illustrations were more likely to increase positive attitudes toward the other side and to decrease negative attitudes than those who did not use illustrations. This finding reinforces the positive effect of storytelling for deliberation, which we have already found in Chapter 2.

In sum, the level of the various deliberative elements in the 28 experimental groups had little influence on attitude changes of ex-guerrillas and ex-paramilitaries toward their former enemies. This may have much to do with the skewed distribution of the speech acts for most deliberative elements. But we should also consider that a single experimental session of not quite an hour is very short for any attitude changes to occur, especially for ex-combatants meeting their former enemies for the first time. In the future, we would need research where such sessions could be repeated over weeks and even months and years to see whether deliberation has an influence on positive attitude changes toward former enemies.

For *Bosnia-Herzegovina*, Simona Mameli used a long battery of items for the attitude changes toward the other ethnic groups. Like in Colombia, these items were put in the questionnaires filled out by the participants in the experiments. For the Serbs in Srebrenica, Mameli used the following items for their attitudes towards Bosnjaks. The response categories were strongly agree, agree, neither agree nor disagree, disagree, strongly disagree.

- The presence of Bosnjaks increases crime rates.
- I would get very angry if I saw a Bosnjak person being ill treated.
- Bosnjaks are generally good for the economy.
- Bosnjaks are the most responsible for war and crimes during the 1990's.
- Bosnjak people are generally unreliable because they tend to cheat.
- It upsets and bothers me to see Bosnjak people who are helpless and in need.
- Bosnjaks are generally rude.
- Bosnjaks think that the country is theirs and nobody else's.

For the following items the response categories were never, seldom, sometimes, quite often. Please indicate how often you have ever felt the following about the Bosnjak community:

- grateful;
- proud;

		Outgroup feelings		
		Became slightly more negative	Became slightly more positive	Became much more positive
Discourse Quality Index (DQI) score	Low	1 group		2 groups
	Medium			3 groups
	High		2 groups	1 groups

Figure 2 Change of outgroup feelings in Belgium by DQI

- uneasy;
- disgusted;
- angry;
- afraid.

Bosnjaks in Srebrenica had to respond to the same items for their attitudes towards Serbs. In Stolac, the same happened for Croats and Bosnjaks in their attitudes toward the other group. This long battery of attitude items led to complex analyses. As was to be expected, attitude changes and dependence of these changes on the level of deliberation varied greatly from item to item. As of this writing, Simona Mameli has not yet finished these analyses, so that the reader has to wait in this special respect for further publications, either by Mameli herself or the entire research group in the planned co-authored book, see Introduction.

In *Belgium* the results were very different than in Columbia. As the following table shows (see Figure 2), out of the nine experimental groups there were eight in which attitudes became more positive toward the other language group after the experiments than before, in six even strongly so, while there was only one group where attitudes became more negative and this only to a small degree. It did not matter, however, how strong the DQI score was in a group. To be sure, the one group with more negative attitudes also had a low DQI score, but only slightly so, and the other two groups with a low DQI had a much more positive attitude after the experiments than before. With only 9 groups, in Belgium we are on weaker ground than in Colombia with 28 experiments. But taking the results from both countries together, the level of deliberation does not seem to have a great influence on attitude changes toward former enemies, at least if the experiments are only one-shot events. It remains the question why participation in the experiments worsened attitudes toward the other side in Colombia but improved them in Belgium. The obvious answer is that in Belgium, without internal political violence, people are more willing to give the other side the benefit of the doubt, whereas Colombian ex-combatants have the opposite attitude, expecting the worst from the other side. There is, however, another interpretation of the data offered by Juan Ugarriza who did this part of the analysis for Colombia. He speculates that when filling out the questionnaire before the experiment ex-combatants were so cagey that many of them did not dare to characterize the other side in negative terms. Participation in the experiments and seeing the human nature of the other side may have made some ex-combatants more open to expressing their true feelings, no longer being hesitant to articulate critique of the former enemies. These are interesting speculations that cannot be proven one way or the other but that one should keep in mind.

Whereas the experiments in Colombia, Bosnia–Herzegovina, and Belgium were free-floating in the sense that no special measures were taken to encourage deliberation, in the *Europolis* project a great effort was made to create a deliberative atmosphere, as described in detail in the Introduction. Key measures were that participants received extensive documentation before leaving for Brussels and that the moderators were trained to encourage a deliberative discourse. It also contributed to the good atmosphere that participants had all their expenses paid. In light of all these measures, it is not surprising that, irrespective of the level of deliberation, major changes in attitudes and preferences occurred. As we remember, the two issues discussed were immigration from outside the EU and climate change. The influence of participation in the experiments was greater for climate change. Knowledge and enthusiasm for measures to combat climate change all increased as a consequence of the two days of discussions. The average score for how serious a problem climate change is rose from an already high 7.5 to 8.3 on a scale of 1 to 10.[62] The discussions also made the participants "greener" in their policy preferences, even when invited to consider possible trade-offs and the costs of their policy preferences. The support for the Greens

---

[62] Raphaël Kies and Patrizia Nanz (eds.), *European Citizens' Deliberation: A Promising Path of EU-Governance?* (Farnham: Ashgate, forthcoming).

increased from 8 to 18 percent.[63] With regard to immigration from
outside the EU, out of 30 items 12 showed significant changes; they
were mostly more favorable toward immigrants. For example, the percentage of respondents who considered immigrants "honest" increased
from 25 to 34 percent, while those agreeing that "immigrants have a lot
to offer our cultural life" rose from 37 to 43 percent. In a similar vein,
those who thought that "immigration increases crime in our society"
fell from 48 to 40 percent. By contrast, when Muslims were mentioned
in the item, it did not produce any change; 34 percent thought that
Muslims had a lot to offer to our culture before the experiments and
33 percent thought the same after the experiments.[64] The Europolis
data are also used for more detailed analyses. Thus, Pierangelo Isernia
and Kaat Smets look specifically at participants with no post-second-
ary schooling and investigate how their attitudes toward immigrants
changed; they found that participants with a leftist political position
became more positive toward immigrants while those with a rightist
political position did not show any change.[65]

Europolis is just one example of how the method of Deliberative
Polling has been applied around the world. John Gastil *et al.* offer
an overview of how, generally speaking, attitudes have changed in
all the Deliberative Pollings. Their main finding is that participants
became more cosmopolitan, more egalitarian, and more collectivist.[66]
An important aspect of Deliberative Polling is how enduring attitude changes are. György Lengyel *et al.* took a long perspective of an
entire year. After undertaking a project of Deliberative Polling in the
Hungarian district of Kaposvár in June 2008, they did a survey one
year afterward to see whether the attitude changes persisted.

The empirical results of the Kaposvár follow-up survey show that the
Deliberative poll had minor lasting effect on people's mind ... One year later,
in the long run most of these effects disappeared: the level of knowledge and
most of the opinion change did not differ from that of the control group ...

---

[63] Kies and Nanz, *European Citizens' Deliberation*.
[64] Kies and Nanz, *European Citizens' Deliberation*.
[65] Pierangelo Isernia and Kaat Smets, "Revealing Preferences: Does Deliberation
   Increase Ideological Awareness Among the Less Sophisticated Public?," paper
   presented at the ECPR General Conference, Reykjavik, August 25–27, 2011.
[66] John Gastil, Chiara Bacci, and Michael Dollinger, "Is Deliberation Neutral?
   Patterns of Attitude Change During Deliberative Polls," *Journal of Public
   Deliberation* 6 (2) (2010).

Deliberative poll is not for lastingly change people's mind according to our results.[67]

Focusing again on Europolis, in order to determine whether the level of deliberation in the discussion groups had an influence on attitude changes, in our research group we measured the level of deliberation in the nine groups included for the analysis. The research question was whether the groups with a high level had a different pattern of attitude changes than the groups with a low level. However, we are unable to answer this question since there was no significant variation in the level of deliberation among the experimental groups. Why no such variation for Europolis? For the Europolis experiments the moderators intervened to encourage a high level of deliberation. Since the moderators were trained to direct the discussions in a uniform way, this must have led to an equalization in the level of deliberation.

(c) Normative implications of empirical results

I now address one of the key question of this book, namely whether deliberation is a good thing. Based on the empirical research presented in the previous section, does deliberation lead to normatively desirable consequences? In answering this question, I use my normative standards as *citoyen engagé* as announced in the Introduction. A high priority for me is that political decisions are *socially just* in the sense of helping the poor and socially discriminated against. This is an elementary principle of fairness. All people should have the chance of a full life and not have to constantly worry about economic misery and social discrimination. There is some empirical evidence that deliberation helps social justice defined in this way. We have seen in the preceding section that in the Mediation Committee of the German Bundestag deliberation helps social justice, although the effects are small and do not involve all elements of deliberation. We have also seen that in a computer-based experiment decision outcomes were more socially just when participants were allowed to deliberate beforehand; I have cautioned, however, that deliberation was defined in a narrow way, meaning merely

---

[67] György Lengyel, Borbála Göncz, and Éva Vépy-Schlemmer, "Temporary and Lasting Effects of a Deliberative Event: The Kaposvár Experience," paper presented at the Workshop on Frontiers of Deliberation, ECPR Joint Sessions, St. Gallen, April 12–17, 2011.

communication without further specification. Most convincing to me is the experimental research in Indonesia where deliberative interventions clearly led to more social justice in local communities. These three studies are a narrow empirical basis to claim in any definite way that deliberation helps social justice. We are on firmer empirical ground, however, in rejecting the claim of some theorists like Mouffe that deliberation hurts the lower classes; there is no evidence in the three studies that this is the case. In a cautious way, I conclude that deliberation does no harm to social justice but rather seems to help somewhat.

Legitimacy is another high priority according to my normative standards. Thereby, I do not primarily look at the legitimacy of individual political outcomes but of a political system at large. To be sure, citizens may be displeased with particular political outcomes, and they may claim that these outcomes have come about in an illegitimate way. Although looking at legitimacy from such a micro perspective of individual decisions has a certain importance, it is, however, much more important to investigate legitimacy at the macro level of entire political systems. If it is not individual decision processes that are considered as illegitimate but entire political systems, political stability is in danger, and there is the risk of outbreak of violence. The question now is whether at this systemic level deliberation helps or hurts legitimacy, or has no influence. It is not a simple matter to establish the level of deliberation at the macro level of entire political systems. As we have seen in Chapter 9, it is not necessary and not even desirable that all deliberative elements are constantly present in all forums of a political system. There are forums, for example, where it is better when discussions take place behind closed doors, which violates the deliberative principle of public openness, but such behind-closed-doors discussions may very well have merits from a systemic perspective. In other forums, for sure, discussions must certainly be open to the public. The key point at the systemic level is that all deliberative elements be present in a sufficient amount. It is not clear, however, what "sufficient" means in this context. Research has almost exclusively focused on the micro level of specific discussions. The next big research agenda must be to investigate deliberation at the macro level. We must be able to answer whether country X or country Y better meets the criteria of deliberative democracy. On this basis, we then can check whether the hypothesis postulated by many theorists that deliberation helps legitimacy is indeed valid. Since such research has not even begun in a serious way, I must leave the question open.

Another high priority according to my normative standards is that policy outcomes have a high rationality in the sense that each outcome is internally consistent and that there are no contradictions among various outcomes. According to this definition, I speak of a low quality of policy outcomes if they are muddled and if it is not transparent which precise goals they aim to achieve. As we have seen earlier in the chapter, Dryzek and his collaborators could empirically demonstrate that deliberation helps to clarify what dimensions are involved in a particular issue and how individual positions are located on the various dimensions. To achieve such a meta-consensus on what a conflict is all about helps to find solutions that are logically consistent in clearly stating the goals that are to be achieved and by what means. It is then possible to do systematic policy research to evaluate whether the postulated goals have been achieved, and, if they have not done so, to change course. In this way, deliberation brings a strong element of rationality in how to define policy goals and in how to reach them. Such rationality helps to make decision-makers accountable since ordinary citizens can see what policy goals are pursued and how successfully they are reached. The opposite is muddling through, where it never becomes quite clear what goals are being pursued, so decision-makers are not accountable for missing their goals. It seems to me that there are good theoretical and empirical reasons why deliberation has a good potential to prevent such muddling through.

Some theorists worry that deliberation is too time-consuming and therefore impractical. Deliberation may indeed take up much time. I have seen this in an experiment that I did with the 20 students in my honors seminar in European Politics at the University of North Carolina at Chapel Hill. After having discussed for several sessions the model of deliberative democracy, I told them that we should attempt to put in practice what we had learned. I submitted to the seminar the question of whether the final exam should be take-home or in-class, and that it would be up to students to make the decision. I encouraged them to be as deliberative as possible. All students should participate, presenting their arguments fully and being willing in the sense of reciprocity to reply to arguments of others. The decision rule was unanimity. The discussion began at a high level of deliberation according to our DQI. All kinds of elaborate arguments were put forward for why it would be better to have the final exam either in-class or take-home. All students engaged in the discussion, which was very civilized with no one interrupting others and all arguments being taken seriously. After an hour, the time of the seminar was over, and the debate had hardly begun. If it continued at the same deliberative level, it could easily have continued for many more hours. For practical reasons, I had to stop the discussion, and I let the students take a vote on how to do the final exam.

Does this experiment show that deliberation is indeed impractical for arriving at any decisions in the real world? I do not think so. During the hour of high-level deliberation, students became familiar with the wide range of arguments on how to do the final exam, so their vote had a good foundation. The outcome of the vote was accepted by everyone without complaints, which reinforces the argument that deliberation is compatible with taking a vote when all the arguments have been sufficiently debated. For more complex issues than the format of a final exam, more time may have to be invested to bring to the forefront all the arguments, perhaps continuing the discussion over several sessions. A consensus may still not be achieved, but when the discussion continues long enough, it will become sufficiently clear what the conflict is all about so that the vote has a good rational basis. I conclude that deliberation is certainly time-consuming, but time spent deliberating at a high level is worthwhile for a good outcome, and, if consensus is not an absolute necessity and a vote can be taken, deliberation is practical and can be used in the real world.

Another critique of deliberation is that it has no impact. Here, we need to differentiate between impact on policy outcomes and impact on individual participants. I address first the policy impact aspect, which is mainly raised with regard to deliberation of ordinary citizens in mini-publics. The criticism has been made that such deliberations have no impact on policy outcomes. As we have seen earlier in the chapter, a prime example of such criticism is revealed in the experiments of Talpin and Monnoyer-Smith on climate change in the French region of Poitou-Charentes. Participants were promised that their recommendations would have some impact on the decision-making in the European Parliament; it turned out, however, that this was not the case. As we recall, this led to negative reactions among the participants, with many claiming that without any impact in Brussels their discussions were useless and they would not participate in further such experiments. A positive counter-example are the experiments in the Italian town of Piombino, discussed in the Introduction. There, the issue was the renovation of the main town square, and the recommendations arrived at by the group discussions of ordinary citizens indeed had a strong influence on what was ultimately done with the square.

The main difference between the two cases is that in Piombino the discussions of the citizens were an integral part of the decision process of the town, whereas in the case of Poitou-Charentes the citizen discussions were only vaguely linked to what happened in the European Parliament. It must be acknowledged, of course, that it is easier at the local level than at the level of the EU to integrate mini-publics of citizens in a decision process. I would still argue that even in the case of Poitou-Charentes a bigger effort could have been made to link the citizen discussions with what went on in the European Parliament. Representatives of the citizen discussions, for example, could have been invited to hearings of the parliamentary committee on climate change in Brussels. My normative position is that at all levels of government mini-publics of citizens should be made an integral part of decision-making. Thereby, it is advantageous if such mini-publics have a say at the beginning of a decision process, as indeed happened in Piombino. Like lobbyists of special-interest groups, citizens should have the chance to shape a decision process at its very beginning. For more on the place of mini-publics in a decision process, see my discussion of political participation in general in Chapter 1.

Second, one also needs to consider the impact of deliberation on the individual participants. Regardless of whether deliberation has any impact on policy outcomes, many theorists argue that deliberation has a value per se. They hope that participants in deliberation become *better citizens* in being better informed about political matters, more open-minded, more tolerant and respectful toward other opinions, better able to present and justify their own opinions, more oriented toward the common good, and more engaged in public life. The empirical data presented in Chapter 6 on the force of the better argument confirm the expectation of many theorists that deliberation makes better citizens as just described. We should note that the assumed characteristics of good citizens are also the characteristics needed for good deliberation. This opens the possibility for a beneficial positive feedback process where deliberation increases deliberative characteristics of the participants, which helps to further increase the level of deliberation.

I have argued above that mini-publics of citizens should be made part of regular political decision-making and in this way have a direct policy impact. This does not mean, however, that there should not also be mini-publics outside the regular decision processes. The research reported in Chapter 9 shows that deliberation is facilitated if the discussion is free-floating and no decision has to be made at the end. One can think of the discussions in the salons in Paris of the eighteenth century or the literary circles in Königsberg involving not only philosophers like Immanuel Kant but also businessmen, public officials, and military officers.[68] Such discussion groups of the eighteenth century influenced Jürgen Habermas when he developed his deliberative ideas. In my view, deliberating with others on the big issues of the world is something that students should learn early on in school. Deliberation should not be judged only on whether it has positive direct policy implications but also on whether it contributes to a fuller life. Therefore, it is appropriate to organize free-standing mini-publics not linked to concrete decision processes. To spend a weekend away from the daily routine talking with others about the big issues of the world may be a fulfilling experience. To make such conversations part of the daily routine in circles of family and friends is even better. In this way, deliberation can have the greatest policy impact in the long run in contributing to a more reflective public opinion. As we will see in the final chapter, Richard Posner harshly criticizes intellectuals like myself for trying to foist their values on the larger population. He argues that ordinary people have "as little interest in complex issues as they have aptitude for them."[69] For me, this is too pessimistic a view. As I try to show in the concluding chapter on the praxis of deliberation, schools can play a key role in shaping a deliberative culture. And such a culture becomes more and more necessary as in a globalized world political issues become increasingly complex. If ordinary citizens want to have a say, they must be able and willing to think about complex issues. Such reflective thinking can certainly be done individually, but, to beneficial effect, also with others. If we give up on the willingness and aptitude of ordinary citizens to think about complex issues, as Posner does, we might just as well give up on the notion of a vibrant democracy. Citizens may still vote in elections but, without appropriate understanding of the complexities of the world, they are easily manipulated by the powerful and wealthy, so that elections no longer have much to do with real democracy where ordinary citizens have a say.

[68] Manfred Kuehn, *Kant: A Biography* (Cambridge University Press, 2001).
[69] Richard Posner, *Law, Pragmatism, and Democracy* (Cambridge, MA: Harvard University Press, 2003), p. 107.

11 | *The praxis of deliberation*

In the Introduction, I stated that this is a book that should have relevance for political praxis. I now take up this challenge in this final chapter. Having presented in the earlier chapters the normative implications that I draw from empirical research on deliberation, I now hope to have a solid basis for reflections on the praxis of deliberation in the real world of politics. Claudia Landwehr notes that reflections on the praxis of deliberation need a solid philosophical and empirical basis: "As deliberative democracy becomes more influential not only in theory, but also in democratic praxis, there is an increasing expectation to justify its empirical premises, make more explicit its suggestions regarding institutionalization, and clarify its role in the democratic process."[1] Michael A. Neblo *et al.* "suggest that the deliberative approach represents opportunities for practical reform quite congruent with the aspirations of normative political theorists and average citizens alike."[2] There are, however, still skeptics about the practical viability of deliberative democracy. A particularly harsh critic is Richard Posner, for whom deliberative democracy is "purely aspirational and unrealistic … with ordinary people having as little interest in complex policy issues as they have aptitude for them."[3] This book should have demonstrated that not only politicians but also ordinary citizens are able and willing to deliberate political issues, to some extent even in crisis countries such as Colombia and Bosnia–Herzegovina.[4] I agree with Giovan Francesco Lanzara that as human beings we have a natural cognitive aptitude for deliberation.

[1] Claudia Landwehr, "Discourse and Coordination: Modes of Interaction and Their Roles in Political Decision-Making," *Journal of Political Philosophy* 18 (2010), 101.
[2] Michael A. Neblo, Kevin M. Esterling, Ryan P. Kennedy, David M.J. Lazer, and Anand E. Sokhey, "Who Wants to Deliberate: And Why?" *American Political Science Review* 104 (2010), 582.
[3] Richard Posner, *Law, Pragmatism, and Democracy* (Cambridge, MA: Harvard University Press, 2003), p. 107.
[4] See also my comments at the end of Chapter 10.

I share his opinion that the cognitive aptitude for deliberation is much more evenly distributed than one usually assumes. Ordinary citizens have this aptitude, perhaps even more than professional politicians. Lanzara further argues that this aptitude must be constantly practiced so that it does not erode.[5] I will show in this final chapter different ways that deliberation can be practiced throughout life.

In the previous chapters, I have shown what I mean by deliberation, for example that storytelling and some aspects of self-interest should also be part of the definition of deliberation; I have also argued that deliberation does not necessarily mean that all phases of a decision process should be open to the public or that consensus must always be reached. With this definition, I consider deliberation a "good thing" for democracy. I would even go as far as John S. Dryzek when he writes that "democracy cannot do without deliberation ... deliberation that is authentic, inclusive, and consequential is central to democracy and ought to be incorporated into any definition of democratization."[6] In the same vein, Charles Girard postulates: "La démocratie doit être délibérative."[7] The question then is how we can encourage more deliberation both at the elite level and at the level of ordinary citizens. For Jürgen Habermas, deliberation is certainly "a demanding form of communication,"[8] but to strive for deliberation in political praxis is not "utopian exuberance."[9] Andrew Knops uses the metaphor "don't abandon ship!" when he argues that "we should and can retain deliberative ideals in practice."[10] To stress the importance and feasibility of

---

[5] Giovan Francesco Lanzara, "La deliberazione come indagine publicca," in Luigi Pellizzoni (ed.), *La deliberazione publicca* (Rome: Meltemi editore, 2005), p. 60: "giusticare decisioni che hanno solo una motivazione politica, la competizione per il potere"; "La capacità di deliberare sia una dote cognitiva quasi naturale degli esseri umani e che sia più uniformemente distribuita di quanto non si creda ... Come tutte le capacità essa viene sviluppata e alimentata attraverso l'esercizio in contesti concreti. Chi non è abituato a deliberare, non sviluppa la competenza a deliberare."

[6] John S. Dryzek, "Democratization as Deliberative Capacity Building," *Comparative Political Studies* 42 (2009), 1380, 1399.

[7] Charles Girard, "La démocratie doit-elle être délibérative?" *Archives de Philosophie* 74 (2011), 239: "Democracy must be deliberative."

[8] Jürgen Habermas, *Ach, Europa* (Frankfurt a.M.: Suhrkamp, 2008), p. 149: "anspruchsvolle Formen der Kommunikation."

[9] Habermas, *Ach, Europa*, p. 148: "utopische Überschwenglichkeit."

[10] Andrew Knops, "Don't Abandon Ship! Why We Should, and Can Retain Deliberative Ideals in Practice," paper presented at the Conference on Deliberation at the University of Bern, October 4, 2008.

deliberation does not mean, of course, that democracy should consist only of deliberation. It is also an essential element of democracy that preferences are aggregated, in particular in elections and parliamentary votes. It is also proper in a democracy that sometimes bargaining takes place. Finally, street protests, strikes, and the like belong in a democracy. Among the various elements of a democracy, deliberation is often underdeveloped, as we have seen in earlier chapters. Therefore, we should take special measures to increase the level of deliberation. I consider it as particularly important that we have more deliberation among ordinary citizens so that we truly have a democracy based on the demos. Therefore, we have to be careful that mini-publics are not manipulated by political elites for their own purposes, as I have extensively discussed in Chapter 1.

In the Introduction, I presented a successful example of how ordinary citizens can deliberate a public issue. In the Italian town of Piombino, small groups of ordinary citizens discussed the renovation of the main town square and made recommendations to the town authorities. Since these citizens' deliberations took place at the very beginning of the decision process, they had a strong influence on how the town square was renovated. The Piombino project was part of a large experiment in Tuscany to institutionalize deliberative democracy, as I have described in the Introduction.[11] Piombino was an easy case for deliberation, being a well-defined issue in a small town. Citizens' discussions can also be successfully organized on complex issues in wider areas. A good example is Québec, where on February 8, 2007 Prime Minister Jean Charest announced the establishment of the Consultation Commission on Accommodation Practices Related to Cultural Differences. The background for this announcement was that Québec had been troubled in recent years by controversies about immigration, religion, language, and, most generally, about its identity within Canada. The commission was co-chaired by sociologist Gérald Bouchard and philosopher Charles Taylor. An example of a recent controversy was the continued presence of the crucifix above the Speaker's chair in the Québec parliament building. The task of the commission was to find ways to overcome such controversies. The commission set

---

[11] Antonio Floridia and Rodolfo Lewanski, "Institutionalizing Deliberative Democracy," paper presented at the Workshop on Effects of Participatory Innovations, ECPR Joint Sessions, St. Gallen, April 12–17, 2011.

the goal to solve this task in deliberative ways, as the following pas-
sage of its final report shows:

> Among the ethical reference points that should guide any negotiation, let us
> mention openness to other, reciprocity, mutual respect, the ability to listen,
> good faith, the ability to reach compromises, and the willingness to rely on
> discussion to solve stalemates ... Through the deliberative dimension the
> interveners engage in dialogue, and the reflective dimension allows them to
> engage in self-criticism and mend their ways when necessary.[12]

Deliberative goals could hardly be expressed in a clearer way than the
commission does. To organize discussions in a deliberative way is a
challenging and time-consuming affair, so it is not surprising that the
commission was allocated a large budget of five million Canadian dollars. Ordinary citizens were involved in different ways; four province-
wide forums were held and 22 forums in the various regions of Québec.
Furthermore, there were hearings in 16 regions, over 900 briefs were
submitted, and the commission's website received over 400,000 visits.
On this broad deliberative basis, the commission arrived at a long
list of recommendations. For the controversy about the crucifix in the
parliament building, for example, it was proposed that it be removed
from the plenary chamber but kept in a special room dedicated to the
history of the Québec parliament. In its final report, the commission
states with satisfaction that it

> cannot overemphasize what our consultations have revealed, beyond well-
> known hitches, openness to the other. The vast majority of the briefs sub-
> mitted and the testimony heard confirm this point. Both in the regions and
> in Montréal, we observed a wealth of good faith and willingness. This is the
> foundation on which we must rely to pursue the edification of an integrated
> Québec that respects its diversity.[13]

With this complex task of cultural accommodation, recommendations could not be as easily implemented in Québec as the recommendations in Piombino for the renovation of the town square. The
transfer of the crucifix from the plenary parliamentary chamber to a

---

[12] Gérald Bouchard and Charles Taylor (commission co-chairs), *Building the
Future: A Time for Reconciliation*, abridged report of the Commission on
Accommodation Practices Related to Cultural Differences, Bibliothèque et
Archives Nationales du Québec, 2008, pp. 52, 55.
[13] Bouchard and Taylor, *Building the Future*, p. 5.

separate room for the history of parliament, for example, was rejected in the political process with the justification of a 350-year history of this Catholic symbol above the chair of the Speaker. Other recommendations, however, were fully or partly implemented. It is comforting for supporters of deliberative democracy that in Québec a serious effort was made to address hot cultural controversies in a deliberative way. But the case also shows that deliberation has its limits when it comes to hard facts of political power, for example with regard to the crucifix.

A third example of a deliberative event stems from Belgium, where Didier Caluwaerts of our research group was directly involved as one of the chief organizers and was responsible for the methodological part of the event. Given the Belgian crisis over the inability of Flemish and Walloon politicians to form a stable cabinet, the idea was to let a random sample of 1,000 ordinary citizens discuss the future of Belgium. Given the target number of 1,000 participants, the project was called *G1000* and took place on November 11, 2011 in Brussels. To advertise the event all the modern technologies were used, in particular email, Facebook, Twitter, and a website.[14] The point was made that the political authorities were not involved, not even with financial support. It should be a purely grass-roots event. Ordinary citizens were encouraged to make a financial contribution; thereby no contribution could be more than 5 percent of the total revenues. Participants at the event did not get any stipend. Ordinary citizens could also sign up to offer their time for the event. The project G1000 was quickly noted and applauded in the international community; thus, in the electronic journal *Social Europe Journal* René Cuperus wrote on June 22, 2011 that such projects "may well be the future for democracy."[15] Of the 1,000 persons who had signed up for the event, 704 actually showed up. A further approximately 200 people participated in discussions in their local communities and about 500 online. The discussions covered three topics: social security, welfare in times of financial crisis, and immigration. These topics emerged from the grass roots with the help of an online selection process with initially about 5,000 suggested ideas to be discussed. An international observer team was pleased by how the event was organized.

---

[14] See www.g1000.org.
[15] See www.social-europe.eu/2011/06/the-party-paradox.

A fourth well-known example of a citizens' conference is the Australian Citizens' Parliament that met in 2009.[16] This forum involved 150 randomly selected citizens, who discussed issues both face-to-face and online. The question submitted to the participants was on how the Australian political system can be strengthened to serve citizens better. The recommendations arrived at were delivered to the prime minister and members of parliament. The minutes of the discussions were audio-recorded and transcribed and are the basis of a book entitled *The Australian Citizens' Parliament and the Future of Deliberative Democracy* (published by Penn State University Press).[17]

In earlier parts of the book I have presented several other citizens' conferences or mini-publics. Such events now take place around the world. It is particularly noteworthy that the Chinese Communist Party makes a great effort to organize citizen discussions, labeling these events deliberative democracy. Baogang He and Mark E. Warren speak of authoritarian deliberation and point out that party officials still decide whether or not to introduce deliberative meetings and determine the agenda, as well as the extent to which the people's opinions will be taken into account.[18] He and Warren summarize what is going on in China in this respect as follows:

Deliberative venues have become widespread, though they are widely variable in level, scale, design, and frequency. They exhibit a variety of forms such as elite debates in different levels of People's Congress, lay citizen discussions via the internet, formal discussions in the public sphere and informal debates in non-governmental domains. They can be, and often are, held monthly, bimonthly, or even quarterly in streets, villages, townships and cities.[19]

He and Warren link this deliberative turn

to deep roots within Chinese political culture … Centuries ago Confucian scholars established public forums in which they deliberated national affairs.

---

[16] See www.newdemocracy.com.au.

[17] Lyn Carson, John Gastil, Ron Lubenski, and Janette Hartz-Karp, *The Australian Citizens' Parliament and the Future of Deliberative Democracy* (College Park: Penn State University Press, forthcoming).

[18] Baogang He and Mark E. Warren, "Authoritarian Deliberation: The Deliberative Turn in Chinese Political Development," *Perspectives on Politics* 9 (2011), 269–89.

[19] He and Warren, "Authoritarian Deliberation," 276–7.

Though elitist, the Confucian tradition took seriously elite duties to deliberate conflicts, as well as certain duties to procedures of discussion. These traditions are alive today, expressed in the high value intellectuals and many leaders place on policy-making through combinations of reasoned deliberation, scientific evidence, and experimentation-based policy cycles.[20]

It is not only Confucian tradition that has led to a deliberative turn but certainly also the hard-nosed interests of Communist Party leaders. According to the analysis of He and Warren, "deliberative mechanisms can co-opt dissent and maintain social order … generate information about society and policy … provide forums for and exchange with business in a marketizing economy … protect officials from charges of corruption in increasing credible transparency … enable leaders to deflect responsibility … generate legitimacy."[21] He and Warren are cautious in making predictions on where the deliberative turn will lead China: "The concept of authoritarian deliberation frames two possible trajectories of political development in China: the increasing use of deliberative practices stabilizes and strengthens authoritarian rule, or deliberative practices serve as a leading edge to democratization."[22] I find it fascinating that the discussion about deliberation has now expanded from developed democracies to authoritarian regimes like China. This opens avenues for important research to follow up these developments in places like China. As He and Warren correctly point out, deliberative practices in such regimes have unpredictable consequences.

Given the strong interest in deliberation all over the world, it may be helpful for practitioners of deliberation if I make some recommendations about how to organize and moderate discussions. (A good supplement to this list are the notes for facilitators used for Australian Citizens' Parliament, www.newdemocracy.com.au, appendix 6).[23]

1. Early on in the discussion, all participants should be called upon to speak up. If someone remains silent at the beginning of a discussion, he or she easily takes up the role of a mute participant.

---

[20] He and Warren, "Authoritarian Deliberation," 276.
[21] He and Warren, "Authoritarian Deliberation," 281.
[22] He and Warren, "Authoritarian Deliberation," in abstract on p. 269.
[23] See also Lyn Carson, "Designing a Public Conversation Using the World Café Method," *Social Alternatives* 30 (2011), 10–14.

2. When participants speak up for the first time, they should be encouraged to delay saying where they stand and instead to explore pertinent problems of the issue under discussion. Moderators should assist participants to take a stand relatively late in the discussion.

3. The sitting arrangement should be such that all participants can face each other. In this way, facial expressions and gestures get their due impact.

4. Participants should be told to also include the interests of absentees, in particular children and future generations, and the disadvantaged at a global scale, also of non-humans and the environment.

5. If arguments are made without or with unclear justifications, moderators should ask for clarifications. Formulations like the following are appropriate in such situations: "I am curious why you make this argument; could you please elaborate a little so that we all understand better what is behind your thinking." The demand for more clarification should not be put in a threatening way.

6. The moderator should also allow stories to be told. Even if stories are off-topic, they may help to loosen up the atmosphere in the discussion group. If such off-topic stories go on too long, moderators should attempt to lead the conversation back to the topic under discussion. If stories are used to support an argument, moderators should encourage the storytellers to put the stories in a broader context, using formulations as the following: "Having heard how your story has influenced your thinking on our topic, what lessons can we learn from your story for other people?"

7. If participants support an argument with personal or group interests, moderators should welcome such justifications. However, they should relate these special interests to the public interest, with formulations like the following: "We have now heard how this measure will help you or your group, which we understand. Could you now please reflect on how the measure will impact other people, perhaps also in other countries and future generations?"

8. Moderators should say at the beginning in a firm voice that racist or sexist remarks will not be tolerated and that the discussion should take place in a civilized and respectful way. If these rules are violated, moderators should immediately intervene. In severe cases, violators must be excluded from the discussion.

9. Mini-publics that are part of the formal political process must come to some conclusion. It is an important task of moderators to

help participants to reach a decision at the end of their discussion. Therefore, moderators should emphasize that there is no time pressure and that participants should be open to change their preferences based on arguments heard from others. Although it may be desirable to reach consensus, a majority vote is also fine, as long as the arguments of the minorities have properly been heard and considered.

10. The selection of the participants should not be imposed from above but should also involve ordinary citizens. This is the case even when mini-publics are drawn in a random way since random selection must be based on a particular population, and here ordinary citizens should also have a say. An issue may be, for example, whether a random sample should consider only citizens or all residents, perhaps even illegal residents. Many issues today have a global dimension, which presents a particular challenge for the selection of mini-publics. With modern technology, online discussions allow the involvement of ordinary citizens from around the world.

These rules for moderators need to be somewhat adapted when mini-publics have their discussions *online*. For political praxis, I see greater prospects for online than for face-to-face mini-publics because the former are easier and cheaper to organize. However, we have to be aware that online discussions are more open to abuse. To reduce the risks of abuse, participants should register with their full names and get access only with a password. It is also beneficial if the number of participants is relatively small, perhaps not more than 20, so that real discussion with everyone participating can emerge.

It is, however, also possible to have fruitful online deliberation if great care is taken in the organization of such events. A sophisticated proposal is made by Mark Klein, a computer expert at the MIT Center for Collective Intelligence.[24] He sees the problems in current online discussions that the messages are widely scattered and repetitive. He presents a technique to arrive at *argument maps* with tree structures that begin with questions to be answered and continue with possible answers for these questions and arguments that support or negate

---

[24] Mark Klein, "Enabling Large-Scale Deliberation Using Attention-Mediation Metrics," *Social Science Research Network*, posted May 10, 2011, online: http://papers.ssrn.com/sol3/papers.cfm?abstract_id=1837707.

these answers. The truly innovative part of this computer program is that similar questions, answers, and arguments are put right next to each other and, most importantly, only once. Moderators help ensure that new posts are correctly structured; their role is not to evaluate the merits of a post, but simply to ensure that the content is structured in a way that maximizes its utility to the scholarly community. What is really fascinating with this program is that participants get feedback about how they can make best use of their skills and perspectives to contribute to the current deliberation. Klein concludes that "the key contribution of this work is to explore how automated algorithms can help users allocate their effort, in a large-scale argumentation context, to where they can do the most good."[25] Technically, it is hard to understand how the program works in detail, but, as Klein shows with an empirical application at the University of Naples, for the users it is not too complicated.[26] It is a wonderful example of the interdisciplinary character of deliberative research.

Although such computer programs make good online deliberation increasingly feasible, face-to-face deliberation still has its value. Ideally, face-to-face and online discussion are combined. A good example is a citizen discussion in the Parisian agglomeration on the possible replacement of an old waste-treatment facility with a modern methanization unit.[27] There were nine face-to-face meetings of ordinary citizens with experts in attendance. Before and after these meetings, on a participatory website, experts were available to answer questions. This website was also open to persons who did not participate in the face-to-face meetings. To further stimulate online discussions, the web portal displayed the public meetings.

Attendance is always a problem for mini-publics, whether they are face-to-face or online. We have seen this problem in earlier chapters, for example in Chapter 9 for a German mini-public that discussed embryonic stem cells over three weekends. Although 20 participants were randomly selected, only 17 showed up for the first session and

---

[25] Klein, "Enabling Large-Scale Deliberation," 13.
[26] The attention allocation metrics were included only to a small extent in this empirical test.
[27] Laurence Monnoyer-Smith and Stéphanie Wojcik, "Technology and the Quality of Public Deliberation: A Comparison Between On and Off-line Participation," paper presented at the 61st Conference of the International Communication Association, Boston, May 26–30, 2011.

five more dropped out over the next two sessions. Such problems with attendance cannot be avoided, but it helps if participants are given incentives, for example, a snack or a stipend.

Participants in mini-publics may have one of their members taking the role of moderator. It may be better, however, to have professional moderators, who are trained in the many aspects of deliberation. Mini-publics may also be joined by experts in the field under discussion, for example, geographers and biologists when the issue of climate change is discussed. Bernard Reber suggests increasing the quality of deliberation by giving a greater role to ethicists, an idea that I support.[28] His focus is on complex technological developments with great uncertainties, such as genetically modified plants. Discussions on such issues with the participation of ordinary citizens and scientific experts have already taken place, but with little involvement of ethicists.[29] Reber's idea is not at all that ethicists would take the lead in these discussions, imposing their views of the good life. Ethicists would rather have an auxiliary role in pointing out ethical dilemmas and how such dilemmas could be solved. Thus, Reber has not a monistic but a pluralistic view of ethics. From this position, he considers a consensus at the end of such deliberative experimentations not as an absolute necessity. The main point for Reber is that people learn to live with ethical disagreements in appreciating the ethical positions of others, and for this learning process professional ethicists could be of great help.

For the organization of discussions in mini-publics Mauro Barisione raises another issue with his concept of *deliberative frame*.[30] By this concept he means "the context of meanings within which a deliberation is constructed."[31] The task of research would be to *deconstruct* such frames. According to Barisione, deliberative frames influence the outcome of a discussion, consciously or unconsciously: "those with the power to structure the deliberation introduce a bias in favour of a pre-established outcome, and do this over and beyond the cognitive

---

[28] Bernard Reber, "La délibération des meilleurs des mondes, entre précaution et pluralisme, monographie inédite en vue de l'obtention d'une habilitation à diriger des recherches," Université Paris IV, Sorbonne, 2010.

[29] For an exception, see an Australian Citizens' Parliament that was attended by ethicists. See www.newdemocracy.com.au

[30] Mauro Barisione, "Framing Deliberative Politics," paper presented at the International Conference on Democracy as Idea and Practice, University of Oslo, January 14–15, 2010.

[31] Barisione, "Framing Deliberative Politics," p. 7.

horizon and testifying limits of the participants, who would be incap-
able of grasping the element of communicative distortion."[32] Barisione
uses as an illustration the Deliberative Polling *Tomorrow's Europe*,
which was carried out at the European level in 2007 to show how
deliberative framing works. One striking result was that after the
discussions the support for raising the retirement age was markedly
higher than before the discussions. Barisione acknowledges that this
change may be due to the force of the better argument encountered
during the debate. But he also sees the possibility that the change was
caused by how this Deliberative Polling event was framed. In investigating at which location the discussions took place, how the questions
for the discussions were formulated, which experts were invited to
attend, and what background material was submitted to the participants, Barisione characterizes the frame as "establishing a discourse in
terms of efficiency, productivity, economic growth and public finance.
In this sense, the language and wording of arguments reinforce an
overall economic framing of the issue under discussion."[33] There could
have been other deliberative frames, for example a frame of social justice, and the issue of retirement age could very well have been addressed
in a different way. Barisione considers it as particularly problematic if
there is a "monopolistic frame" and he postulates frame reflection,
reframing, and counter-framing during deliberation itself: "if inspired
by an authentically pluralistic approach, public deliberation itself
becomes, by its very nature, an efficient moderator of the framing
effect, to the extent that it generates a procedure that contrasts truly
different perspectives, rather than presenting an array of arguments
and counterarguments framed throughout a unique political, social
or cultural perspective."[34] In this way, Barisione suggests a welcome
research agenda to get an empirical handle on the issue of deliberative
framing. According to this agenda, researchers should investigate the
organizational setting of experiments with mini-publics, the identity of
the promoting organizations and sponsors, the location of the deliberative events, the selection of experts, and the background material distributed to the participants. Barisione's paper suggests that care
must be taken when organizing experiments with mini-publics and

[32] Barisione, "Framing Deliberative Politics," p. 9.
[33] Barisione, "Framing Deliberative Politics," p. 19.
[34] Barisione, "Framing Deliberative Politics," p. 24.

that it is essential that such events are accompanied by serious and systematic research.

For the practical organization of discussions in mini-publics, one has also to consider the empirical findings of Heather Walmsley, who worked on a deliberative public consultation in British Columbia on biobanking, which is the collecting and storing of human data for research purposes.[35] She had altogether 23 participants who gathered first in an informational plenary session, then discussed biobanking in three groups, and finally continued discussion again in plenary session. In her "ethnographic observations," she found "that deliberation was more frustrating and agreement more elusive for participants in the large group than it was in small groups."[36] The large-group discussion "ended in confusion, with few agreements."[37] The interpretation of Walmsley is that in the small groups good deliberation led to group solidarity, and when the recommendations of the three small groups were brought together in the plenary meeting, they clashed with each other. Organizers of such events must be careful when linking discussions in small groups and plenary sessions. It might have been better in the first plenary session to have a substantive discussion so that some solidarity could have developed across the three small groups. In this way, the final plenary session might have been more deliberative.

Even if all problems of mini-publics could be resolved, there remains the vexing problem of how such mini-publics can be linked to the larger public. In other words, the question is of how democratic *deliberation* in mini-publics can be related to *deliberative* democracy at large. Espen D.H. Olsen and Hans-Jörg Trenz have addressed this question in a systematic way for Europolis,[38] but their arguments have wider applications.[39] In order to produce political legitimacy at the societal level, what happens in mini-publics "needs to create public resonances within the wider audience of citizens who 'reflect' about the validity

---

[35] Heather Walmsley, "Biobanking, Public Consultation, and the Discursive Logics of Deliberation: Five Lessons from British Colombia," *Public Understanding of Science* 19 (2010), 452–68.

[36] Walmsley, "Biobanking," 454.

[37] Walmsley, "Biobanking," 457.

[38] For the research design of Europolis, see Introduction.

[39] Espen D.H. Olsen and Hans-Jörg Trenz, "From Citizens' Deliberation to Popular Will Formation: Generating Democratic Legitimacy Through Transnational Deliberative Polling," paper presented at the Workshop on Frontiers of Deliberation, ECPR Joint Sessions, St. Gallen, April 12–17, 2011.

of the propositions made in the democratic experiment."[40] Olsen and Trenz are concerned that "the claims for the scientific authority of the experiment make it possible to conceive the representative judgment of the microcosm as a substitute of the judgment as a whole. We could then perfectly imagine deliberative polling as a tool to arrive at public judgment while the whole body of citizens no longer need to bother to deliberate at all."[41] Olsen and Trenz warn that "scientific authority alone is not sufficient to generalize the validity of the results of the experiment and defend them as publicly legitimate."[42] Ideally, the results of the discussions in the mini-publics should be widely reported in the media, stimulating further discussions in the citizenship at large. As Olsen and Trenz show for Europolis, this ideal is very difficult to reach because the echo in the media is quite meager. They conclude on the pessimistic note "that there is no straightforward process from group deliberation to public deliberation."[43]

An ambitious goal is the introduction of a "deliberation day" before national elections, where all the important issues could be debated in a great number of mini-publics. I have discussed this idea, launched by Bruce Ackerman and James S. Fishkin, in Chapter 5. I am supportive of this and similar projects, and I see a great future of democratic renewal if mini-publics of randomly chosen ordinary citizens are systematically made part of formal political decision processes. In this way, the voices of citizens are truly heard when important political issues are decided. To be sure, only a small number of citizens will actually take part in these endeavors, but the more randomly they are chosen and the more they actually show up, the more they have legitimacy to speak for all citizens, and they will do so not superficially, but in a reflective way. Lawrence R. Jacobs *et al.* agree with the emphasis on mini-publics when they write that a "constructive path forward is to develop approaches for incorporating deliberation into representative government ... Deliberation has important and increasingly

---

[40] Olsen and Trenz, "From Citizens' Deliberation to Popular Will Formation," p. 16.

[41] Olsen and Trenz, "From Citizens' Deliberation to Popular Will Formation," p. 16.

[42] Olsen and Trenz, "From Citizens' Deliberation to Popular Will Formation," p. 20.

[43] Olsen and Trenz, "From Citizens' Deliberation to Popular Will Formation," p. 21.

valuable roles in putting issues on the government agenda, developing broad proposals for lawmakers to consider, and creating incentives for policymakers to respond to the broad public."[44] They also warn against "phony deliberation" that is ultimately ignored.[45]

Another ambitious plan is to involve ordinary citizens at the global level, as proposed by Robert E. Goodin and Steven R. Ratner with "Global Citizens' Juries."[46] As they put it in the very title of their paper, their goal is "Democratizing International Law." This should happen at the level of *jus cogens*, which expresses "core norms of international order and ethics."[47] They "do not propose supplanting the existing machinery for determining *jus cogens*. Rather, [they] merely propose adding a deliberative democratic component alongside all the rest."[48] The argument for their proposal is that "letting ordinary people from different nations talk it through directly among themselves is more democratic than discussions purely through their elected officials or diplomats."[49] Global Citizens' Juries should be composed of around 20 people drawn from around the world, and there should be about 20 such juries.

In the composition of the Global Citizens' Juries, diversity matters more than representativeness. The whole point is to discover what is common among all people of the world. For that, it is important to get many different perspectives represented; it is not particularly important to get them represented in exactly the same proportion as in the population of the world as a whole. It is a consensus among positions, not a vote of the people, that would justify deeming that something should be regarded as a "preemptory norm of general international law."[50]

Global Citizens' Juries would be helped in their deliberations by briefing papers "prepared by a panel of experts, balanced so as to represent

---

[44] Lawrence R. Jacobs, Fay Lomax Cook, and Michael X. Delli Carpini, *Talking Together: Public Deliberation and Political Participation in America* (University of Chicago Press, 2009), pp. 164, 166.

[45] Jacobs *et al.*, *Talking Together*, p. 165.

[46] Robert E. Goodin and Steven R. Ratner, " Democratizing International Law," paper presented at the Workshop on Frontiers of Deliberation, ECPR Joint Sessions, St. Gallen, April 12–17, 2011.

[47] Goodin and Ratner, "Democratizing International Law," p. 3.

[48] Goodin and Ratner, "Democratizing International Law," p. 5.

[49] Goodin and Ratner, "Democratizing International Law," p. 6.

[50] Goodin and Ratner, "Democratizing International Law," p. 7.

all the major perspectives on the issue."[51] The hope would be that the deliberatively democratic designs of these juries would "evoke considered, informed opinions from people."[52] These opinions would then be forwarded to the UN General Assembly or its Human Rights Council, as well as to other international organizations like the Council of Europe or the African Union.

The Obama Administration created an Open Government Initiative in the White House whose goal is "more than simply informing the American people about how decisions are made. It means recognizing that government does not have all the answers and that public officials need to draw on what citizens know ... the way to solve the problems of our time as one nation is by inviting the American people in the policies that affect them." As the head of this initiative puts it, "now we can use technology to achieve an entirely new vision of non-hierarchical and collaborative democracy, where the state shares power and decision making authority with the public."[53]

I now move from the level of ordinary citizens to the level of parliaments, which are the forums where, ideally, the broad political issues of the people should be addressed in a true deliberative sense. Yet, as Landwehr correctly states, "it is comparatively easy to set up an artificial deliberative forum like a citizen conference and much more of a challenge to consider how the parliament with its specific history, traditions, informal rules of conduct, high workload, role as an arena of competitive politics, can be rendered more deliberative."[54] Previous chapters have indeed shown that parliamentarians tend to be less willing to change their political positions than ordinary citizens are. Parliamentarians are often stuck with previous public statements, and when they change them, they are criticized as being unprincipled and wishy-washy. There are several proposals on how to supplement parliaments with other institutions more amenable to deliberation. John S. Dryzek and Simon Niemeyer suggest the establishment of a "Chamber of Discourses."[55] They show different ways of how such a

---

[51] Goodin and Ratner, "Democratizing International Law," p. 8

[52] Goodin and Ratner, "Democratizing International Law," p. 9.

[53] Beth Simone Noveck, "Peer to Policy," paper presented at the Conference on Epistemic Democracy in Practice, Yale University, October 20–22, 2011, pp. 1, 4.

[54] Personal communication, March 10, 2010.

[55] John S. Dryzek and Simon Niemeyer, "Discursive Representation," *American Political Science Review* 102 (2008), 481–93.

chamber could be put in practice, more formally or informally. Their hope is that a Chamber of Discourses "can help render policy making more rational, respect individual autonomy by more fully representing diverse aspects of the self, assist in realizing the promise of deliberative democracy, and make democratic theory more applicable to a world where the consequences of decisions are felt across national borders."[56] Michael E. Morrell proposes still another institution to aid further deliberation, a "Federal Deliberation Commission" (FDC).[57] Its goal would be "to enhance attentive deliberation in the broader public sphere," and in order to reach this goal, this institution should be "as independent as possible from the ruling party or government at any particular time."[58] The plan of Morrell "would be to staff the FDC with full-time deliberators and structure deliberations so that all deliberators would have to present all sides of an issue."[59] An important aspect of Morrell's plan would be that the media

broadcast the deliberations to the public on television and over the internet, thus encouraging people to engage in internal-reflective deliberation. The FDC should also support face-to-face deliberative forums of groups of citizens following the public deliberation. The publicly broadcast deliberations might also spark more discussions of the issues among families, friends, and colleagues, and would almost certainly affect the public discourse on the issues.[60]

Alex Zakaras makes a proposal that he calls "modest" but that seems quite radical.[61] For the US, he wants to replace, at both the federal and state levels, the Senate with a "Citizens' Assembly." Its members would be chosen by lot, and "all adults would be eligible for selection, but could decline if they did not wish to participate."[62] These Citizens' Assemblies "would have reduced responsibilities: they would not initiate new legislation; rather they would review legislation approved by the elective chamber, deliberate about its merits, and then vote to

---

[56] Dryzek and Niemeyer, "Discursive Representation," 492.
[57] Michael E. Morrell, *Empathy and Democracy: Feeling, Thinking, and Deliberation* (University Park: Pennsylvania State University Press, 2010).
[58] Morrell, *Empathy and Democracy*, p. 190.
[59] Morrell, *Empathy and Democracy*, p. 190.
[60] Morrell, *Empathy and Democracy*, p. 191.
[61] Alex Zakaras, "Lot and Democratic Representation: A Modest Proposal," *Constellations* 17 (2010), 455–71.
[62] Zakaras, "Lot and Democratic Representation," 457.

approve or veto it. They could not alter the legislation; vetoed bills would be sent back to the elective house for redrafting."[63]

Creating new institutions such as a Chamber of Discourses, a Federal Deliberation Commission, Global Citizens' Juries, or Citizens' Chambers is all worthwhile but needs a lot of organizational work to be implemented. Of more immediate practical relevance is the idea of organizing discussions among stakeholders for a particular political issue. Stephen Elstub investigated such a discussion among stakeholders with the Stanage Forum, the purpose of which was to produce an effective management plan for the North Lees Estate, a national park in the UK.[64] The invited stakeholders were recreationists, environmentalists, and locals. Such partisan groups are different from mini-publics because they are not randomly chosen but represent the various interests involved in an issue. Such partisan discussion groups are nothing new and are used under many circumstances; it would be worthwhile to make them more deliberative by applying to them the techniques developed for mini-publics. Another institutional idea is by Jan Sieckmann, who wants to give a greater role to the courts because courts have a higher level of deliberation than parliaments. "Parliaments are influenced by factors that show rather little interest in standards of rational argumentation ... courts may in this respect be in a better position to comply with requirements of democracy, [they are] independent from the political process, bound to impartiality and designed to comply with constitutional principles."[65]

All the institutional proposals discussed so far, from mini-publics to the courts, ultimately depend for their success on the development of a more deliberative culture, and here I see a key role for schools from kindergarten to universities. To be sure, culture depends on many other factors like family life, the media, and the arts. However, schools can be influenced directly. In Chapter 1, I have outlined how schools can better contribute to the development of a deliberative culture. I add here a very recent example of a particularly creative way of

---

[63] Zakaras, "Lot and Democratic Representation," 457.

[64] Stephen Elstub, "Linking Micro Deliberative Democracy and Decision Making: Trade-offs Between Theory and Practices in a Partisan Citizen Forum," *Representation* 46 (2010), 309–24.

[65] Jan Sieckmann, "Legislative Argumentation and Democratic Legitimation," *Legisprudence: International Journal for the Study of Legislation* 4 (2010), 89.

how to integrate deliberation into a school curriculum. At the Jacobs University, Bremen, in Germany, students were first taught about deliberation in class and then participated in a Deliberative Day to discuss the issue of public service.[66]

I want to finish the book by giving voice to some of my students. In an honors seminar in the fall of 2010 at the University of North Carolina at Chapel Hill, I asked students to reflect on what they learned or did not learn about deliberation in all their school years and how schools could be improved in this respect. Many students wrote that their school years were not deliberative at all. William May gives a particularly bleak picture of how in primary school there was no deliberative culture:

> My primary school experience very much followed the factory model of American education: everywhere we went we walked in single file lines, the time we spent at certain tasks and in locations was determined by the ringing of a bell, and we all took the same orders from the teacher – orders we were expected to obey. In this way the teacher was always right, the authority, the sovereign. Students were charged with finding the answers the teacher wanted because the teacher had the right answer, and very rarely did we come up with our own answers to questions. Problems were solved in the same way – if there was a dispute between yourself and another person, or between two groups, you went to the teacher to arbitrate and ultimately decide who gets to do what.

Rachel Myrick gives a specific example of how emphasis on competition left no room for deliberation:

> Later in my schooling, I found such discussions and debates were often more competitive in nature then cooperative. This was largely because teachers began grading the content of our discussion, and students, worried about their individual grade, would monopolize the conversation. In my English class, when we had discussions about literature, all of our conversation turned into vicious arguments as students fervently tried to prove each other wrong. Similarly, in my History of the Americas class, we were put into pairs and assigned to represent the viewpoint of either John Adams or Thomas Jefferson on a particular topic. We had five minutes to debate our opponent, and the winning team received a better grade. In this environment, all

---

[66] Franziska Deutsch and Matthijs Bogaards, "The Deliberative Referendum: Learning Democracy by Doing," paper presented at the ECPR General Conference, Reykjavik, August 25–27, 2011.

of our focus was on viciously attacking the opponent so we could receive higher marks.

However, students also reported experiences of teachers making a real effort to develop a deliberative culture among their students. Connor Crews reports such an experience from an American history class:

In my eighth grade American history class, we were required to create a "class constitution" which governed classroom behavior and expectations for work produced by students. This, by its collaborative nature, required a great deal of deliberation. We came into the process of creating the constitution with very few guidelines from my teacher. The only directions were to address how students should behave in class and be penalized for misuse of class time, if at all. As I recall, we had to reach some sort of a supermajority for the constitution to be passed. Because this was a project which would have an impact on how the class was conducted, all students had a vested interest in ensuring that the outcome was to their liking. Thus, arguments were largely justified in terms of the common good.

Rachel Myrick, who reported above her non-deliberative school experiences, had fond memories of Ms. Reid who was very creative in developing a deliberative culture in her classes:

The most effective example I have seen of a deliberative culture was my fifth grade classroom, led by my teacher, Ms. Reid, who had designed her own educational program and curricula. One integral component of the class was the "Socratic Seminar," in which we would discuss a controversial topic related to something we studied in class. This environment was my first exposure to the seminar method, which arguably many students don't see until high school or college. Being exposed to this deliberative discussion, in which all ideas are respected and arguments must be logical and consistent, helps students develop sound arguments and respect diverse opinions. This concept seems quite sophisticated for ten-year-olds. However, instead of jumping right into the seminar style, Ms. Reid gradually introduced us to the idea. We read articles about effective communication and went over the basic rules. In our first discussions, we began by passing a ball. Whoever had the ball was able to speak. If you wanted to say something, you would raise your hand until the ball was passed to you. We had a seminar multiple times a week, and after the first few weeks, we stopped passing the ball and raising our hands. The conversation began to flow naturally.

Keith Grose remembers that even problems of mathematics could be solved in a deliberative way:

I witnessed the engaging power of deliberative teaching when I entered the North Carolina School of Science and Mathematics. The mathematics department had a novel way of teaching topics such as geometry and calculus. Rather than sitting in class learning the theorems and methods in a lecture format, the students were split into groups and given lab assignments to learn how these theorems and methods work firsthand. For example, when we were studying geometry, rather than being told about relative triangles by our teachers, we were given the assignment of determining the height of the clock tower on campus with only a small triangle and roll of measuring tape. Then each group had to brainstorm on how best to accomplish this task. Usually at least one group would realize how to use the correct method, in this case relative triangles, to accomplish the task. Afterwards all of the groups would return to the classroom and present their various methods and the class would decide on the best method and why it worked.

These examples of how schools can have an impact on how children are socialized in a deliberative way is a good ending for the book. The examples show that schools are an excellent vehicle to have more deliberation. Teachers must be trained and supervised to instill deliberative skills in their students and to encourage them to use these skills outside class as well. For me, this is the best hope to make deliberative democracy viable.

Appendix: Newest version of Discourse Quality Index (DQI)

The DQI was initially developed to measure the discourse quality of speech acts in parliamentary debates.[1] To be applied to experiments with ordinary citizens, as in the current book, the DQI had to be somewhat modified and also to be adapted to the local context of the experiments. As with the initial DQI, the units of analysis to be coded are the individual speech acts. If a speech act is briefly interrupted (just a few seconds) and the speaker continues afterwards, this counts as a single speech act. The interruption also counts as a speech act.

Nature of speech act

1. Interruption: speaker interrupts another speaker with a few utterances of not more than a few seconds.
2. Regular speech act: all other speeches, including briefly interrupted speech acts.

Participation (length of time)

Code in minutes and seconds the length of the speech act.

Participation (constraints)

1. The speaker indicates verbally or by body language that he or she is constrained by the behavior of other participants (interruptions, private conversations, body language such as making faces, yawning, etc.).
2. The speaker can speak in an unconstrained way.

---

[1] Jürg Steiner, André Bächtiger, Markus Spörndli, and Marco R. Steenbergen, *Deliberative Politics in Action: Analysing Parliamentary Discourse* (Cambridge University Press, 2004).

Respect (foul language)

1. The speaker uses foul language to attack other participants on a personal level. Include also mild foul language, not only statements such as "you are a liar" but also statements such as "you seem a little confused." Code the names of the participants attacked in this way and give the exact quotation of the foul language.
2. The speaker uses foul language to attack the arguments of other participants but abstains from personal attacks. Here again include also mild foul language, not only statements such as "this argument is stupid" but also statements such as "this argument is a little weak." Code the names of the participants whose arguments are attacked in this way and give the exact quotation of the foul language.
3. No foul language.

Respect (respectful language)

1. The speaker uses respectful language toward other participants and/or their arguments. Include also moderately respectful language, not only statements such as "your argument is truly brilliant" but also statements such as "your argument is not bad." Code the names of these other participants and give the exact quotations of the respectful language.
2. No respectful language used.

Respect (listening)

1. The speaker ignores arguments and questions addressed to him or her by other participants. Code the names of these other participants.
2. The speaker does not ignore arguments and questions addressed to him or her by other participants but distorts these arguments and questions. Code the names of these other participants.
3. The speaker does not ignore arguments and questions addressed to him or her by other participants and engages these arguments and questions in a correct and undistorted way. Code the names of these other participants.
4. As yet no arguments and questions addressed to speaker.

Level of justification of arguments

1. The speaker does not present any arguments (asks, for example, merely for additional information).
2. The speaker only says that X should or should not be done, that it is a wonderful or a terrible idea, etc. But no reason is given for why X should or should not be done.
3. The speaker justifies only with illustrations why X should or should not be done.
4. The speaker gives a reason Y why X should or should not be done. But no linkage is made why Y will contribute to X.
5. The speaker gives a reason Y why X should or should not be done, and a linkage is made why Y will contribute to X.
6. The speaker gives at least two reasons why X should be done and for at least two reasons a linkage is made with X.

Content of justifications of arguments (own group)

1. The speaker refers to benefits and costs for own group. Give exact quotation of how the group is referred to. Also give exact quotation if a postulated improvement of one's own group is justified by reference to its past discrimination in the larger society.
2. The speaker does not refer to benefits and costs for own group.

Content of justification of arguments (other groups)

1. The speaker refers to benefits and costs for other groups represented in the experiment. Give exact quotations of how these groups are referred to.
2. The speaker does not refer to benefits and costs for other groups represented in the experiment.

Content of justification of arguments (common good)

1. The speaker refers to benefits and costs for all groups represented in the experiment. Give exact quotations of how the groups are referred to.
2. The speaker does not refer to benefits and costs for all groups represented in the experiment.

Content of justification of arguments (abstract principles)

1. The speaker refers to abstract principles, for example social justice, quality of life, peace. Give exact quotations of how these principles are formulated.
2. The speaker does not refer to any abstract principles.

Force of better argument

1. The speaker indicates a change of position. Gives as reason for change arguments heard during the experiment.
2. The speaker indicates a change of position. Does not refer to arguments heard during the experiment.
3. The speaker does not indicate a change in position. Does acknowledge the value of other positions heard during the experiment.
4. The speaker does not indicate a change of position. Does not acknowledge the value of other positions heard during the experiment.

Stories

1. no story
2. story unrelated to argument
3. story related to argument, sole justification
4. story related to argument, reinforces rational justification.

Index